Mathematics in Finance

June 12, 2011

Contents

Chapter 0

Introduction

0.1 The Different Asset Classes

....

0.2   The Correct Price for Futures and Forwards

A *future contract* can be seen as a standardized *forward* agreement. Futures are for instance only offered with certain maturities and contract sizes, whereas forwards are more or less customized. However, from a mathematical point of view, futures and forwards can be considered to be identical and therefore we will only concentrate on the first in our considerations throughout this chapter. A *future contract*, or simply *future*, is the following agreement:

> Two parties enter into a contract whereby one party agrees to give the other one an underlying asset (for example the share of a a stock) at some agreed time T in the future in exchange for an amount K agreed on now.

Usually K is chosen such that no cash flow, i.e. no exchange of money is necessary at the time of the agreement. Let us assume the underlying asset was a stock then we can introduce the following notation :

S_0: Price of a share of the underlying stock at time 0 (present time).

S_T: Price of a share of the stock at maturity T. This value is not known at time 0 and hence considered to be a *random variable*.

$S_T - K$: Value of the future contract at time T seen from the point of view of the buyer.

The crucial problem and the repeating theme of these notes will be questions of the following kind:

> What is the value or fair price of such a future at time 0? How should K be chosen so that no exchange of money is necessary at time 0?

Game theoretical approach: pricing by expectation

One way to look at this problem, is to consider the future contract to be a game having the following rule: at time T player 1 (long position) receives from player 2 (short position) the amount of $S_T - K$ in case this amount is positive. Otherwise he has to pay player 2 the amount of $K - S_T$. What is a "fair price" V for player 1 to participate in this game? Since the amount V is due at time 0 but the possible payoff occurs at time T we also have to consider the time value of money or simply interest. If r is the annual rate of return, compounded continuously, the value of the cash outflow V paid by player 1 at time 0 will be worth $e^{rT} \cdot V$ at time T.

Game theoretically this game is said to be fair if the *expected amount of exchanged money* is 0.

Theorem 0.2.1 *(Kolmogorov's strong law of large numbers).*

Suppose $X_1, X_2, X_3, \ldots$ are i.i.d random variables, i.e. they are all independently sampled from the same distribution, which has mean (= expectation) μ. Let S_n be the arithmetical average of $X_1, X_2, \ldots, X_n$, i.e.

$$S_n = \frac{1}{n} \sum_{i=1}^{n} X_i.$$

Then, with probability 1, S_n tends to μ as n gets larger, i.e. $\lim_{n \to \infty} S_n = \mu$ a.s.

Thus, if the expected amount of exchanged money is 0, and if our two players play their game over and over again, the average amount of money exchanged per game would converge to 0.

Since the exchanged money has the value $-V e^{rT} + S_T - K$ at time T, we need:

$$\mathbb{E}(-V \cdot e^{rT} + (S_T - K)) = 0,$$

or

(1) $$V = e^{-rT}(\mathbb{E}(S_T) - K).$$

Here $\mathbb{E}(S_T)$ denotes the expected value of the random variable S_T.

Conclusion: In order to participate in the game player 1 should pay player 2 the amount of $e^{-rT}(\mathbb{E}(S_T) - K)$ at time 0, if this amount is positive. Otherwise player 2 should pay player 1 the amount of $e^{-rT}(K - \mathbb{E}(S_T))$. Moreover, in order to make an exchange of money unnecessary at time 0, we have to choose $K = \mathbb{E}(S_T)$.

This approach seems quite reasonable. Nevertheless, there are the following two objections. The second one is fatal.

1) V depends on $\mathbb{E}(S_T)$. Or, if we choose K so that $V = 0$ then K depends on $\mathbb{E}(S_T)$. But, usually $\mathbb{E}(S_T)$ is not known to investors. Thus, the two players can only agree to play the game if they agree on $\mathbb{E}(S_T)$, at least for player 1 $\mathbb{E}(S_T)$ should seem to be higher than for player 2.

2) Choosing $K = \mathbb{E}(S_T)$ can lead to arbitrage possibilities as the following example shows.

Example: Assume $\mathbb{E}(S_T) = S_0$, and choose the "game theoretically correct" value $K = S_0$. Thus, no exchange of money is necessary at time 0. Now an investor could proceed as follows:

At time 0 she sells short n shares of the stock, and invests the received amount (namely nS_0) into riskless bonds. In order to cover her short position at the same time she enters into a future contract in order to buy n shares of the stock for the price at $S_0 = \mathbb{E}(S_T)$.

At time T her bond account is worth $ne^{rT}S_0$. So she can buy the n shares of the stock for nS_0, close the short position and end up with a profit of $nS_0(e^{rT} - 1)$. In other words, although there was no initial investment necessary at time 0, this strategy will lead to a guaranteed profit of $nS_0(e^{rT} - 1)$. This example represents a typical *arbitrage opportunity*.

Pricing by arbitrage

The following principle is the basic axiom for valuation of financial products. Roughly it says : "There is no free lunch".

In order to formulate it precisely, we make the following assumption: Investors can buy units of assets in any denomination, i.e. θ units where θ is any real number.

Suppose that an investor can take a position (choose a certain portfolio) which has no net costs (the sum of the prices is less than or equal to zero). Secondly, it guarantees no losses in the future but some chance of making a profit. In this (fortunate) situation we say that the investor has an *"arbitrage opportunity"*. The principle now states that in an efficient market, there are no arbitrage opportunities.

This is the idealized version of the real world. In reality the statement has to be relativized. In an efficient market there are no arbitrage opportunities for a longer period of time. If an arbitrage situation opens up, investors will immediately jump on that opportunity and the market forces, namely supply and demand, will regulate the price in a way so that this "loop whole" closes after a short time period. One might say there are no major arbitrage opportunities because everybody is looking for them.

We now use this principle to find the correct value of K.

Proposition 0.2.2 . *There is exactly one arbitrage free choice for the forward price of a future. It is given by*

$$K = e^{rT} S_0.$$

Proof. We will show that any other choice leads to arbitrage.

Case 1: $K < e^{rT} S_0$.

At time $t = 0$: Sell short n units of the asset, lend the received amount of nS_0 at an interest rate of r and enter into a contract to buy forward n units of the asset for the price of K.

At time $t = T$: Buy n units, and close the short position. Net gain: $ne^{rT} S_0 - nK > 0$.

Case 2: $K > S_0 e^{rT}$.

At time $t = 0$: Borrow the amount of nS_0, buy n units of the asset, and enter into a contract to sell n units for the price of K at time T.

At time $t = T$: Sell the n units and pay off the loan. Net gain: $nK - nS_0 e^{rT} > 0$. □

Note that the arbitrage free choice for the forward price K is exactly the value of a riskless bank account at time T in which one invested at time 0 the amount of S_0. This observation is a special case of a more general principle which we will encounter again and again:

We want to price a claim which pays the amount of $F(S_T)$, where S_T is the price of an asset at some future time T. In the case of a future we have $F(S_T) = S_T - K$. We want to find a fair price of this claim and to do that we proceed in the following way. We first need to find a *risk neutral probability* $\mathbb{Q}$ for the random variable S_T. This is an "artificial probability" distribution which might not (and usually does not) coincide with the "real distribution" for the random variable S_T. This risk neutral probability distribution $\mathbb{Q}$ has the property that under $\mathbb{Q}$ the expected value of S_T equals to $S_0 e^{rT}$, i.e. the value of a bond account in which one invested the amount S_0 at time 0. Then we obtain a fair price of our claim by evaluating $e^{-rT} \mathbb{E}_\mathbb{Q}(F(S_T))$, which represents the discounted expected value of the payoff $F(S_T)$ with respect to $\mathbb{Q}$. This means that the formula (1) we obtained in the case of $F(S_T) = K - S_T$ using the game theoretic approach becomes correct if we use the risk neutral probability distribution of the stock price instead of the real distribution.

In the case of futures the payoff function is linear in S_T, and it can easily be seen that this implies that in this case $\mathbb{E}_\mathbb{Q}(F(S_T))$ does not depend of which risk neutral probability was chosen. For other claims, for example puts and calls, the computations are not that easy and different riskneutral probabilities may lead to different prices. So was an arbitrage free pricing of general (nonlinear) claims achieved by Black and Scholes in 1973 assuming that the distribution of the underlying assets are lognormal (see Chapter 2). On the other hand the pricing formula for futures in proposition 0.2.2 was known and used since centuries.

Let us finally discuss a question a reader might have who is the first time confronted with the problem of pricing contingent claims. Such a reader might have the following objection to the pricing formula of futures: How can it be that the price of a future does not depend at all on the expected development of the price of the underlying asset?

We could for example imagine the following situation which seems to contradict at first sight the result of Proposition 0.2.2. The world demand for cotton is more or less constant while the supply depends heavily on the wheather conditions, in particular on the amount of rain in spring. Since cotton is mainly grown in only two regions, the Indian Subcontinent and in the southeast of the United States drought in one of these regions during spring time can dramatically reduce the number of cotton balls harvested in the fall of that year, and thus increase the price of cotton. Thus, assuming there was a drought in spring, it is safe to assume a shortage in fall and an increase of prices. Given this scenario, why should a cotton farmer enter into a contract to sell cotton in fall, if the exercise price is only based on the price of cotton in spring and the interest rate, but does not incorporate the expected raise of prices in fall? Wouldn't it be much more profitable for the farmer to wait until fall and sell then?

The answer is simple: Since there is an expected shortage in fall based on data which are already known in spring to all parties involved the price of cotton went already up in spring. In other words all expected developments of the price are already contained in the present price. Of course the situation is not always so easily foreseeable as the effect of a drought on the cotton price. More generally, present prices of assets mirror the expectations of the investors, which might differ, and one could see the price as the result of a complicated averaging procedure of the investors' expectations.

Chapter 1

Discrete Models

1.1 The Arrow-Debreu Model

In the following model, we only consider two times, T_0, the present time, and T_1, some time in the future. We consider N securities, $S_1, S_2, S_3, \ldots, S_N$ which are perfectly divisible and which can be hold long or short. At time T_0 an investor takes a position by choosing a vector $\theta = (\theta_1, \theta_2, \ldots \theta_N) \in \mathbb{R}^N$, where θ_i represents the number of units of security S_i. θ is called a *portfolio*. At T_0 the price of a unit of S_i is denoted by q_i, $q = (q_1, \ldots, q_N) \in \mathbb{R}^N$ is called the *price vector*. The value of the portfolio θ at time T_0 is then given by:

$$\theta \cdot q = \theta_1 q_1 + \theta_2 q_2 + \ldots + \theta_N q_N = \sum_{i=1}^{N} \theta_i q_i.$$

The future bears some uncertainty, but we assume that only finitely many possible situations (with regard to the securities) can occur and we call these different situations *states*. We assume there are M such states.

For a security S_i, $i = 1, 2, \ldots, N$, and a state j, with $j = 1, 2, \ldots, M$, D_{ij} denotes the occurring cash flow for one unit of security i if state j occurs. By "occurring cash flow of one unit of security S_i" we mean its price at time T_1 and possible dividend payments. We put

$$D = \begin{bmatrix} D_{11} & D_{12} & \cdots & D_{1M} \\ D_{21} & D_{22} & \cdots & D_{2M} \\ \vdots & \vdots & & \vdots \\ D_{N1} & D_{N2} & \cdots & D_{NM} \end{bmatrix} \quad (N \text{ by } M \text{ matrix}).$$

The pair (q, D) is referred to as the *price-dividend pair*.

Remark:

1) For $i = 1, 2, \ldots, N$

$$D_{(i, \cdot)} = i\text{-th row of } D = (D_{(i,1)}, D_{(i,2)}, \ldots, D_{(i,M)})$$

is the vector consisting of all possible cash flows for holding one unit of security S_i.

2) For $j = 1, \ldots, M$

$$D_{(\cdot, j)} = j\text{-th column of } D = \begin{bmatrix} D_{1j} \\ D_{2j} \\ \vdots \\ D_{Nj} \end{bmatrix}$$

is the vector consisting of the cash flows for each security if state j occurs.

3) The transpose of D is defined by

$$D^t = \begin{bmatrix} D_{11} & D_{21} & \cdots & D_{N1} \\ D_{12} & D_{22} & \cdots & D_{N2} \\ \vdots & \vdots & & \vdots \\ D_{1M} & D_{2M} & \cdots & D_{NM} \end{bmatrix}.$$

If $\theta \in \mathbb{R}^N$ is a portfolio

$$D^t \circ \theta = \begin{bmatrix} D_{11} & D_{21} & \cdots & D_{N1} \\ D_{12} & D_{22} & \cdots & D_{N2} \\ \vdots & \vdots & & \vdots \\ D_{1M} & D_{2M} & \cdots & D_{NM} \end{bmatrix} \circ \begin{bmatrix} \theta_1 \\ \theta_2 \\ \vdots \\ \theta_N \end{bmatrix} = \begin{bmatrix} D_{(\cdot,1)} \cdot \theta \\ D_{(\cdot,2)} \cdot \theta \\ \vdots \\ D_{(\cdot,M)} \cdot \theta \end{bmatrix}.$$

Consider the j-th coordinate of this vector: $D_{(\cdot,j)} \cdot \theta = \sum_{i=1}^{N} D_{ij}\theta_i$ represents the total cash flow for the portfolio θ, assuming state j occurs. Thus $D^t \circ \theta$ represents the vector of all possible cash flows of the portfolio θ.

Now we can define what we mean by an arbitrage opportunity within this model as follows.

Definition: A portfolio $\theta \in \mathbb{R}^N$ is called an *arbitrage* if one of the following two conditions hold

Either: $\theta \cdot q < 0$ and $\theta \cdot D_{(\cdot,j)} \geq 0$ for all $j = 1, 2, \ldots, M$.

Or: $\theta \cdot q = 0$ and

$$\left\{ \begin{array}{l} \theta \cdot D_{(\cdot,j)} \geq 0 \text{ for all } j = 1, \ldots, M \text{ and} \\ \theta \cdot D_{(\cdot,j_0)} > 0 \text{ for at least one } j_0 = 1, \ldots, M \end{array} \right\}.$$

In words, an arbitrage is a portfolio which either has a negative value at time T_0 (investor receives money at T_0) but represents no liability at time T_1. Or it is a portfolio which has the value zero at time T_0, represents no liability in the future, and, more over, has a positive chance to create some positive cashflow.

Before we state the next observation we want to introduce the following notations. By $\mathbb{R}_+^M$ we denote the *closed positive cone in* $\mathbb{R}^M$, i.e.

$$\mathbb{R}_+^M = \{x = (x_1, x_2, \ldots x_M) \in \mathbb{R}^M | x_i \geq 0 \text{ for } i = 1, 2, \ldots M\}.$$

The *open positive cone in* $\mathbb{R}^M$ is denoted by $\mathbb{R}_{++}^M$, i.e.

$$\mathbb{R}_{++}^M = \{x = (x_1, x_2, \ldots x_M) \in \mathbb{R}^M | x_i > 0 \text{ for } i = 1, 2, \ldots M\}.$$

Proposition 1.1.1 .   *A portfolio* $\theta \in \mathbb{R}^N$ *is an arbitrage if and only if*

$$\begin{bmatrix} -q_1 & -q_2 & \cdots & -q_N \\ D_{11} & D_{21} & \cdots & D_{N1} \\ D_{12} & D_{22} & \cdots & D_{N2} \\ \vdots & \vdots & & \vdots \\ D_{1M} & D_{2M} & \cdots & D_{NM} \end{bmatrix} \circ \theta = \begin{bmatrix} -q \cdot \theta \\ D^t \circ \theta \end{bmatrix} \in \mathbb{R}_+^{M+1} \setminus \{0\}.$$

Principle of "no arbitrage":

We say the price-dividend pair (q, D) does not admit an arbitrage opportunity, or equivalently is arbitrage-free, if no portfolio $\theta \in \mathbb{R}^N$ represents an arbitrage, i.e. if for all $\theta \in \mathbb{R}^N$ for which $\theta \cdot q \leq 0$ the following holds:

if $\theta \cdot q < 0$ then $\theta \cdot D_{(\cdot, j_0)} < 0$ for at least one $j_0 = 1, 2, \ldots, M$,

if $\theta \cdot q = 0$ then $\theta \cdot D_{(\cdot, j)} = 0$ for all $j = 1, \ldots, M$ or $\theta \cdot D_{(\cdot, j_0)} < 0$ for at least one $j_0 = 1, 2, \ldots, M$.

The following proposition is a useful consequence. It says that portfolios which generate at time T_1 the same cashflow, no matter which state occurs, must have at time T_0 the same price.

Proposition 1.1.2 .   *Assume that (q, D) is arbitrage-free. Consider two portfolios $\theta^{(1)}$ and $\theta^{(2)}$ for which*

$$\theta^{(1)} \cdot D_{(\cdot, j)} = \theta^{(2)} \cdot D_{(\cdot, j)} \text{ for all } j = 1, 2, \ldots, M$$

Then it follows that $\theta^{(1)} \cdot q = \theta^{(2)} \cdot q$.

Proof.   Assume for example that $\theta^{(1)} \cdot q < \theta^{(2)} \cdot q$. Then it is not hard to see that $\theta^{(1)} - \theta^{(2)}$ is an arbitrage possibility. $\square$

We now come to the first important result of the Arrow-Debreu model. The first time reader might not yet see a connection between the theorem below and option pricing. This connection will be discussed in the next section.

Theorem 1.1.3 .   *A dividend pair (q, D) does not admit an arbitrage if and only if there is a vector $\psi \in \mathbb{R}^M_{++}$ such that $q = D \circ \psi$.*

Before we can start with the proof of Theorem 1.1.3 we need the following result from the theory of linear programming often called the *Theorem of the Alternative*. It can be deduced from the Theorem of Farkas. Both Theorems will be proved in Appendix A where we also recall some basic notions and results of Linear Algebra.

Theorem 1.1.4 . *For an m by n matrix A one and only one of the following statements is true.*

1) *There is an $x \in \mathbb{R}^m_{++}$ for which $A^t \circ x = 0$.*

2) *There is a $y \in \mathbb{R}^n$ for which $A \circ y \in \mathbb{R}^m_+ \setminus \{0\}$.*

Remark. Although a more detailed discussion of this Theorem will be given in Section A.2 we want to give a geometrical interpretation here.

Let $L \subset \mathbb{R}^m$ be a subspace and let $L^\perp = \{x \in \mathbb{R}^m | x \cdot y = 0 \text{ for all } y \in L\}$ its orthogonal complement. L can be seen as the range $\mathcal{R}(A)$ of some m by n matrix A, and in that case $L^\perp$ is the Nullspace $\mathcal{N}(A^t)$ of A^t (see section A.1). Now Theorem 1.1.4 states as follows:

Either L contains a non zero vector whose coordinates are non negative, or its orthogonal complement $L^\perp$ contains a vector having only strictly positive entries.

In dimension two this fact can be easily visualized by the following picture.

Proof of Theorem 1.1.3. We first show "(1) $\Leftarrow$ (2)". Assume $\psi \in \mathbb{R}^M_{++}$ and $q = D \circ \psi$.

Let $\theta \in \mathbb{R}^N$, we have to show that it is not an arbitrage. First we observe that

(1.1) $$\theta \cdot q = \theta \cdot (D\psi) = (D^t\theta) \cdot \psi$$

where the last equality can be seen as follows:

$$\theta \cdot (D\psi) = \sum_{i=1}^{N} \theta_i \cdot \left(\sum_{j=1}^{M} D_{ij}\psi_j\right)$$
$$= \sum_{j=1}^{M} \psi_j \left(\sum_{i=1}^{N} D_{ij}\theta_i\right)$$
$$= \sum_{j=1}^{M} \psi_j(D^t\theta)_j = \psi \cdot (D^t\theta).$$

We have to show:

① if $q \cdot \theta < 0$ then for at least one j_0, $D_{(\cdot,j_0)} \cdot \theta < 0$

② if $q \cdot \theta = 0$ then either $D_{(\cdot,j)} \cdot \theta = 0$ for all $j = 1, \ldots, M$ or $D_{(\cdot,j_0)} \cdot \theta < 0$ for at least one $j_0 = 1, \ldots, M$.

Note that by (1.1)

$$\theta \cdot q = (D^t\theta) \cdot \psi = \sum_{j=1}^{M} \psi_j \cdot (D^t\theta)_j = \sum_{j=1}^{M} \psi_j(D_{(\cdot,j)} \cdot \theta).$$

If $q \cdot \theta < 0$ then at least one of the above summands must be negative, since all coordinates of ψ are strictly positive we deduce that $(D_{(\cdot,j_0)} \cdot \theta) < 0$ for at least one $j_0 \in \{1, 2, \ldots M\}$.

If $q \cdot \theta = 0$ then either all of above summands are zero or some of them are negative and some of them are positive, and the claim follows as before.

Proof of "(1) $\Rightarrow$(2)". Assume there is no arbitrage and define the matrix

$$A = \begin{bmatrix} -q_1 & -q_2 & \cdots & -q_N \\ D_{11} & D_{21} & \cdots & D_{N1} \\ D_{12} & D_{22} & \cdots & D_{N2} \\ \vdots & \vdots & & \vdots \\ D_{1M} & D_{2M} & \cdots & D_{NM} \end{bmatrix} = \begin{bmatrix} -q \\ D_{(\cdot,1)} \\ D_{(\cdot,2)} \\ \vdots \\ D_{(\cdot,M)} \end{bmatrix} = \begin{bmatrix} -q \\ D^t \end{bmatrix}.$$

Now the condition that (q, D) is arbitrage free implies according to Proposition 1.1.1 that A does not satisfy the second alternative in Theorem 1.1.4 (with $m = M + 1$ and $n = N$) and we conclude that there is a vector $x \in \mathbb{R}^{M+1}_{++}$ so that

$$
A^t x = \begin{bmatrix} -q_1 & D_{11} & \cdots & D_{1M} \\ -q_2 & D_{21} & \cdots & D_{2M} \\ \vdots & \vdots & & \vdots \\ -q_N & D_{N1} & \cdots & D_{MM} \end{bmatrix} \circ x = -x_1 \begin{bmatrix} q_1 \\ q_2 \\ \vdots \\ q_N \end{bmatrix} + D \circ \begin{bmatrix} x_2 \\ x_3 \\ \vdots \\ x_{M+1} \end{bmatrix} = 0.
$$

Putting now

$$
\psi = (\frac{x_2}{x_1}, \ldots, \frac{x_{M+1}}{x_1})
$$

we conclude that ψ has strictly positive coordinates and that

$$
D \circ \psi = \frac{1}{x_1} D \circ \begin{bmatrix} x_2 \\ x_3 \\ \vdots \\ x_{M+1} \end{bmatrix} = q,
$$

which finishes the proof. □

Definition: Assume the dividend pair (q, D) does not admit an arbitrage, and thus there is a $\psi \in \mathbb{R}^M_{++}$ for which $q = D \circ \psi$. Such a vector ψ is called a *state-price vector*.

1.2   The State-Price Vector

A. Risk neutral probabilities

Remark: Assume we have assigned to each state j a probability p_j, i.e. $p_j > 0$ for $j = 1, 2, \ldots, M$, with $\sum_{j=1}^{M} p_j = 1$. For $i = 1, \ldots, M$, the vector $D_{(i,\cdot)}$ can be seen as a random variable on the set of all states:

$$D_{(i,\cdot)}: \{1, \ldots, M\} \ni j \mapsto D_{(i,j)}.$$

The expected value, or mean, of $D_{(i,\cdot)}$ with respect to the probability $\mathbb{P} = (p_1, \ldots, p_M)$ is then

$$\mathbb{E}_{\mathbb{P}}(D_{(i,\cdot)}) = \sum_{j=1}^{M} p_j D_{(i,j)}.$$

Assume now that the considered price-dividend pair (q, D) is arbitrage free. By Theorem 1.1.3 there exists a state-price vector $\psi \in \mathbb{R}_{++}^{M}$, i.e.

$$(1.2) \qquad\qquad\qquad\qquad\qquad q = D \circ \psi$$

Define $\widehat{\psi}_j = \psi_j / \sum_{\ell=1}^{M} \psi_\ell > 0$, for $j = 1, \ldots, M$. Since it follows that $\sum_{j=1}^{M} \widehat{\psi}_j = 1$, $\widehat{\psi} = (\widehat{\psi}_1, \ldots, \widehat{\psi}_M)$ can be seen as a probability on the set of all states. By (1.2) it follows that

$$(1.3) \qquad\qquad\qquad\qquad\qquad \frac{q}{\sum_{\ell=1}^{M} \psi_\ell} = D\widehat{\psi}.$$

We also assume that one of the securities, say S_1, is a riskless bond which guarantees a payment of \$1 in all possible states, i.e. $D_{(1,j)} = 1$ for $j = 1, 2, \ldots, M$.

On the one hand the price of the bond is

$$q_1 = \text{first coordinate of } (D \circ \psi) = D_{(1,\cdot)} \cdot \psi = \sum_{i=1}^{M} \psi_i.$$

On the other hand if R is the interest paid over the period $[T_0, T_1]$ on that bond then

$$q_1(1 + R) = 1, \text{ thus } q_1 = \frac{1}{1 + R}.$$

Thus, we conclude

(1.4)
$$\frac{1}{1+R} = q_1 = \sum_{\ell=1}^{M} \psi_\ell.$$

Using (1.2) we rewrite q_i for $i \geq 2$ as:

(1.5)
$$q_i = i\text{-th coordinate of } (D \circ \psi)$$

$$= \sum_{j=1}^{M} D_{ij} \psi_j$$

$$= \sum_{j=1}^{M} D_{ij} \widehat{\psi}_j \cdot \sum_{l=1}^{M} \psi_l$$

$$= \frac{1}{1+R} \cdot \sum_{j=1}^{M} D_{ij} \widehat{\psi}_j$$

$$= \frac{1}{1+R} \mathbb{E}_{\widehat{\psi}}(D_{(i,\cdot)}).$$

Thus $\mathbb{E}_{\widehat{\psi}}(D_{(i,\cdot)}) = (1+R)q_i$. Conversely, assume that $\mathbb{P} = (p_1, p_2, \ldots p_m) \in \mathbb{R}_{++}^{M}$ is a probability on the states, with the property that

$$\mathbb{E}_{\mathbb{P}}(D_{(i,\cdot)}) = (1+R)q_i, \text{ for all } i = 1, 2, \ldots, N.$$

If we let $\psi = \frac{1}{1+R}\mathbb{P}$ we deduce as in (1.4) and (1.5) that $D \circ \psi = q$, i.e. that ψ is a state-price vector. This observation proves the following Theorem.

Theorem 1.2.1 .   *Let (q, D) be a price-dividend pair and assume that security S_1 is a riskless bond whose interests over the time period between T_0 and T_1 are R.*
Then $\psi \in \mathbb{R}_{++}^{M}$ is a state-price vector, i.e. ψ has strictly positive components and satisfies $q = D \circ \psi$, if and only if $\widehat{\psi} = \psi/\sum_{\ell=1}^{M} \psi_\ell$ is a probability on the states which satisfies

$$q_i = \frac{1}{1+R}\mathbb{E}_{\widehat{\psi}}(D_{(i,\cdot)}) \text{ for all } i = 1, 2, \ldots N.$$

Note that 1.2.1 means that with respect to $\widehat{\psi}$ the expected yield of each security is the same, namely $1 + R$. Therefore, we call such a probability *risk neutral probability* .

B. State prices seen as prices of derivatives

Assume that in addition to the given securities $S_1, \ldots, S_N$ we introduce for each state $j = 1, 2, \ldots, M$ the following security S_{N+j}

$$S_{N+j} \text{ pays} \begin{cases} \$1 & \text{if state } j \text{ occurs} \\ \$0 & \text{if not,} \end{cases}$$

thus S_{N+j} can be seen as a "bet on state j". We call these securities "*state contingent securities*". The new dividend matrix will be

(1.6)
$$\widetilde{D} = \begin{bmatrix} D_{11} & D_{12} & \ldots & D_{1M} \\ D_{21} & D_{22} & \ldots & D_{2M} \\ \vdots & \vdots & & \vdots \\ D_{N1} & D_{N2} & \ldots & D_{NM} \\ 1 & 0 & \ldots & 0 \\ 0 & 1 & \ldots & 0 \\ \vdots & \vdots & & \vdots \\ 0 & & \ldots & 1 \end{bmatrix}.$$

Question: What is a fair price for S_{N+j}, $j = 1, 2 \ldots M$?

Proposition 1.2.2 .   *Assume the price-dividend pair (q, D) is arbitrage free.*
Let $i \in \{1, \ldots, N\}$ and consider the following two portfolios $\theta^{(1)}, \theta^{(2)}$ in $\mathbb{R}^{N+M}$:

$$\theta^{(1)} = (0, \ldots, \quad \underset{\substack{\uparrow \\ ith\ coordinate}}{1} \quad \ldots, 0, 0, \ldots, 0)$$

$$\theta^{(2)} = (\underbrace{0, 0, \ldots \ldots, 0}_{N}, D_{i1}, D_{i2}, \ldots, D_{iM}).$$

Thus $\theta^{(1)}$ consists of one unit of security S_i and $\theta^{(2)}$ consists of D_{i1} units of S_{N+1}, D_{i2}
units of S_{N+2} etc.
Then $\theta^{(1)}$ and $\theta^{(2)}$ have the same arbitrage free price at T_0.

Proof.   Note that

$$\tilde{D}^t \circ \theta^{(1)} = \begin{bmatrix} D_{i1} \\ D_{i2} \\ \vdots \\ D_{iM} \end{bmatrix} \quad \text{and } \tilde{D}^t \circ \theta^{(2)} = \begin{bmatrix} D_{i1} \\ D_{i2} \\ \vdots \\ D_{iM} \end{bmatrix}$$

Thus, assuming no arbitrage, they must have the same prices by Proposition 1.1.2.   □

Now let us assume that $q_{N+1}, q_{N+2}, \ldots, q_{N+M}$ are prices for the state contingent securities
$S_{N+1}, \ldots, S_{N+M}$ for which the augmented dividend pair $(\tilde{q}, \tilde{D})$ with $\tilde{q} = (q_1, \ldots q_N, q_{N+1}, \ldots, q_{N+M})$
and $\tilde{D}$ as defined in (1.6) is arbitrage free.

We first note that q_{N+j} must be strictly positive for $j = 1, \ldots, M$ (S_{N+j} represents no
liability at time T_1 and might generate a positive cashflow).

Secondly, we deduce for $i = 1, \ldots, N$, with $\theta^{(1)}$ and $\theta^{(2)}$ as defined in Proposition 1.2.2

that

$$q_i = \text{price of } (\theta^{(1)}) = \text{price of } (\theta^{(2)})$$

$$= \sum_{j=1}^{M} D_{ij} q_{N+j}$$

$$= i\text{th row of } D \circ \begin{bmatrix} q_{N+1} \\ \vdots \\ q_{N+M} \end{bmatrix}.$$

This implies that $(q_{N+1}, q_{N+2}, \ldots, q_{N+M})$ must be a state price vector for (q, D).

Conversely, if $(q_{N+1}, q_{N+2}, \ldots, q_{N+M})$ is a state price vector for (q, D), then

$$\tilde{D} \circ \begin{bmatrix} q_{N+1} \\ \vdots \\ q_{N+M} \end{bmatrix} = \begin{bmatrix} q_1 \\ \cdots \\ q_N \\ q_{N+1} \\ \vdots \\ q_{N+M} \end{bmatrix},$$

which means $(q_{N+1}, q_{N+2}, \ldots, q_{N+M})$ is a also a state price vector for $(\tilde{q}, \tilde{D})$.

We therefore proved the following result.

Theorem 1.2.3 .   *Let (q, D) be an arbitrage free price-dividend pair.*
Then a vector $(q_{N+1}, q_{N+2}, \ldots, q_{N+M})$ is a state price vector for (q, D), if and only if the
new dividend pair $(\tilde{q}, \tilde{D})$ with

$$\tilde{q} = (q_1, q_2, \ldots, q_N, q_{N+1}, \ldots, q_{N+M})$$

and

$$
\tilde{D} = \begin{bmatrix}
D_{11} & D_{12} & \cdots & D_{1M} \\
D_{21} & D_{22} & \cdots & D_{2M} \\
\vdots & \vdots & & \vdots \\
D_{N1} & D_{N2} & \cdots & D_{NM} \\
1 & 0 & \cdots & 0 \\
0 & 1 & \cdots & 0 \\
\vdots & \vdots & & \vdots \\
0 & & \cdots & 1
\end{bmatrix}.
$$

is arbitrage free.
In other words, state price vectors are fair prices for the state contingent securities.

In our model we can now think of a general derivative being a vector $f = (f_1, \ldots, f_M)$,
interpreting f_j as the amount the investor receives if state j occurs.

For example in the case of a call on security S_i, $i = 1, \ldots, N$ with exercise price K, we
have

$$f_j = (D_{i,j} - K)^+,$$

(assuming no dividend was paid during the considered time period).

Since f can be thought of a portfolio containing f_j units of the j-th state contingent derivative for each $j = 1, \ldots M$ the price of a our derivative f is given by

(1.7) $$\text{price}(f) = f \cdot \psi,$$

where ψ is a state-price vector.

Using Theorem 1.2.1 we can rewrite 1.7 as

(1.8) $$\text{price}(f) = \frac{1}{1+R}\mathbb{E}_{\widehat{\psi}}(f),$$

where $\widehat{\psi}$ is a risk neutral propbability on the states and we consider f to be a random variable $f : \{1, \ldots, M\} \to \mathbb{R}$ on the states.

Remark: Unless D is invertible the equation

$$q = D \circ \psi$$

does not need to have a unique solution ψ and the state prices are usually not determined by the equation above, i.e. there could be several "fair prices" for the state contingent securities.

Definition. A price dividend pair (q, D) is called *a complete market* /, if D is invertible.

Note that if (q, D) is complete it follows that (q, D) is arbitrage free if and only if

$$D^{-1}q \in \mathbb{R}^M_{++}$$

and in that case $\psi = D^{-1}q$ is the state price vector .

Let us recapitulate the main result we obtained in this and the previous section. The following conclusion is a special version, of what is called in the literature "the fundamental theorem of asset pricing":

Conclusion: We are given a price-dividend pair (q, D). Then the following are equivalent.

1) (q, D) is arbitrage-free

2) There exists a state-price vector for (q, D), i.e. a vector having strictly positive components, satisfying $q = D \circ \psi$. ψ can be interpreted in the following two ways:

2.1) Writing $\widehat{\psi} = \psi/\sum_{j=1}^{M}\psi_j$, $\widehat{\psi}$ is a riskneutral probability on the states, i.e. a probability under which all securities have the same expected yield.

2.2) ψ can be seen as a fair price for the state-contingent securities, i.e. a price which makes the augmented price-dividend pair $((q,\psi), \widetilde{D})$ arbitrage-free, where $\widetilde{D}$ is the $N + M$ by M matrix which one obtains by writing D above the identity matrix.

Using above notations the price for any derivative $f = (f_1, \ldots f_M)$ equals to:

$$\text{price}(f) = f \cdot \psi = \frac{1}{1 + R}\mathbb{E}_{\widehat{\psi}}(f).$$

This means that the price of a derivative is the discounted expected value of f, where the expected value is taken with respect to the risk neutral probability $\widehat{\psi}$.

1.3   The Up-Down and Log-Binomial Model

We discuss in this section the simplest of all models for the price of a stock. We will consider only two securities : a riskless bond with interest rate R (over the investment horizon of one time period) and a stock which can only move to two possible states. Despite its simplicity and seeming to be rather unrealistic it leads eventually to the famous Black-Scholes formula of option pricing, as shown by Cox, Ross and Rubinstein (see Section 1.5).

We are given a riskless zero-bond, it will repay the amount of \$1 at the end of the time period. If R denotes its interest paid over that period, the price of this bond at the beginning of the time period must be

$$(1.9) \qquad\qquad q_1 = \frac{1}{1+R}.$$

Secondly we are given a stock having the price $q_2 = S_0$. At the end of the time period the value of the stock (plus possible dividend payments) can either be DS_0 or US_0 with $D < U$ (D for "down" and U for "up").

$$
\begin{array}{ccc}
\text{Bond:} & q_1 & \to & 1 \\
& & & US_0 \\
& & \nearrow & \\
\text{Stock:} & S_0 & & \\
& & \searrow & \\
& & & DS_0
\end{array}
$$

Thus our price vector is $q = \left(\frac{1}{1+R}, S_0\right)$ and our cash flow matrix is

$$
D = \begin{bmatrix} 1 & 1 \\ S_0 D & S_0 U \end{bmatrix}.
$$

Since $D \neq U$ (otherwise the stock would be a riskless bond), D is invertible and we arrive to a unique state price vector $\psi = (\psi_D, \psi_U)$. Solving the linear system

$$
\begin{bmatrix} 1 & 1 \\ S_0 D & S_0 U \end{bmatrix} \circ \begin{bmatrix} \psi_D \\ \psi_U \end{bmatrix} = \begin{bmatrix} \frac{1}{1+R} \\ S_0 \end{bmatrix}
$$

we get

$$(1.10) \qquad \psi_D = \frac{1}{1+R} \frac{U-(1+R)}{U-D}$$

$$\psi_U = \frac{1}{1+R} \frac{(1+R)-D}{U-D}$$

Remark: In order for ψ to have strictly positive coordinates we need that $D < 1+R < U$. Within our model these inequalities are then equivalent to the absence of arbitrage.

From (1.10) we are able to compute the risk neutral probability $\mathbb{Q} = (Q_D, Q_U)$ and get

$$(1.11) \qquad Q_D = \frac{U-(1+R)}{U-D}$$

$$Q_U = \frac{(1+R)-D}{U-D}.$$

Consider now a security which pays $f(S_0 D)$ in case "down" and $f(S_0 U)$ if "up" occurs. Then its fair price is

$$(1.12) \qquad \text{price}(f) = \psi_D \cdot f(S_0 D) + \psi_U f(S_0 U)$$

$$= \frac{1}{1+R}[Q_D f(S_0 D) + Q_U f(S_0 U)]$$

$$= \frac{1}{1+R}\mathbb{E}_{\mathbb{Q}}(f)$$

Example: If we consider a call option with exercise price K, we have

$$f(S) = (S-K)^+ = \begin{cases} (DS_0 - K)^+ & \text{if } S = DS_0 \\ (US_0 - K)^+ & \text{if } S = US_0. \end{cases}$$

(S being the value of the stock at the end of the time period.) Then the fair price of the call is

$$C = \frac{1}{1+R}[Q_D(DS_0 - K)^+ + Q_U(US_0 - K)^+].$$

Now we turn to a "multi-period" model. We assume the time period $[0, T]$ being divided in $n \in \mathbb{N}$ time intervals of length $t = T/n$. We also assume that the securities can only be traded at the times

$$t_0 = 0, \quad t_1 = \frac{T}{n}, \quad t_2 = 2\frac{T}{n}, \dots, t_n = T.$$

At each trading time t_j the stock price can either change by the factor U or by the factor D. Assuming the stock price at $t = 0$ was S_0, at time t_1 it is either DS_0 or US_0, at time t_2 it is $D^2 S_0$, $DU S_0$ or $U^2 S_0$, more generally at time t_j the stock price can be $S_j^{(i)} = U^i D^{j-i} S_0$, where $i \in \{0, 1, \ldots, j\}$ is indicating the number of up-movements.

This is best pictured by a tree diagram

Thus the possible states of the stock at time t_j are given by $(S_j^{(i)})_{i=0,1,\ldots,j}$, where i is the number of "ups" (thus $j - i$ = number of "downs"). We also assume that R is the interest paid for \$1 invested in the riskless bond over a time period of length $\frac{T}{n}$.

Now we consider a security which pays $f(S_n^{(i)})$ at time $t_n = T$ if the stock price is $S_n^{(i)} = S_0 U^i D^{n-i}$.

For given $j = 0, 1, 2, \ldots, n$ and $i = 0, 1, \ldots, j$ we want to find the fair value of that security at time t_j assuming the stock price is $S_j^{(i)}$. Let us denote that value by $f_j^{(i)}$.

Eventually we want to find f_0^0, the price of that security at time 0.

The value of our security at the end of the time period is of course given by its payoff:

$$(1.13) \qquad\qquad\qquad f_n^{(i)} = f(S_n^{(i)}) \qquad i = 0, 1, \ldots, n.$$

How do we find $f_{n-1}^{(i)}$ for $i = 0, 1, \ldots, n-1$? If the state at time t_{n-1} was $S_{n-1}^{(i)}$, there are two possible states at time t_n, namely $S_n^{(i)} = S_{n-1}^{(i)} D$ or $S_n^{(i+1)} = S_{n-1}^{(i)} U$, thus we are exactly in the "up-down" model, discussed before (with $S_0 = S_{n-1}^{(i)}$). We therefore conclude that

$$
\begin{aligned}
f_{n-1}^{(i)} &= \frac{1}{1+R}[Q_D f(S_{n-1}^{(i)} D) + Q_U f(S_{n-1}^{(i)} U)] \\
&= \frac{1}{1+R}[Q_D f(S_n^{(i)}) + Q_U f(S_n^{(i+1)})] \\
&= \frac{1}{1+R}[Q_D f_n^{(i)} + Q_U f_n^{(i+1)}].
\end{aligned}
$$

More generally, if we assume that for $1 \le j \le n$ we know the values $f_j^{(i)}$, $i = 0, 1, \ldots, j$, we derive the values for $f_{j-1}^{(i)}$ using the "up-down"-model.

(1.14) $$ f_{j-1}^{(i)} = \frac{1}{1+R}[Q_D f_j^{(i)} + Q_U f_j^{(i+1)}]. $$

Thus f_0^0 can be obtained by first computing all $f_{n-1}^{(i)}$'s $i \le n-1$, then all $f_{n-2}^{(i)}$'s $i \le n-2$ etc., i.e. by "rolling back the tree".

Using (1.14) and reversed induction we now can prove a formula for $f_j^{(i)}$.

Theorem 1.3.1 . *Suppose a security pays $f(S_n^{(i)})$ at time t_n if $S_n^{(i)}$ occurs. Then its arbitrage free price at time t_j, $0 \le j \le n$, assuming $S_j^{(i)}$ occurs at time t_j, is*

$$
f_j^{(i)} = \frac{1}{(1+R)^{n-j}} \sum_{k=0}^{n-j} \binom{n-j}{k} Q_U^k Q_D^{n-j-k} f(S_n^{(i+k)}),
$$

in particular if $j = 0$ we have

$$
f_0^0 = \frac{1}{(1+R)^n} \sum_{k=0}^{n} \binom{n}{k} Q_U^k Q_D^{n-k} f(S_n^{(k)})
$$

where $\binom{\ell}{m} = \frac{\ell!}{m!(l-m)!}$.

Proof. For $j = n$ we get $f_n^{(i)} = f(S_n^{(i)})$, the rest will follow from "reverse induction". We assume the formula to be true for some $0 < j \le n$, and will show it for $j - 1$.

Thus, let $0 \le i \le j - 1$. From (1.14) we obtain

$$
\begin{aligned}
f_{j-1}^{(i)} &= \frac{1}{1+R}[Q_D f_j^{(i)} + Q_U f_j^{(i+1)}] \\
&= \frac{1}{(1+R)^{n-j+1}} \left[Q_D \sum_{k=0}^{n-j} \binom{n-j}{k} Q_U^k Q_D^{n-j-k} f(S_n^{(i+k)}) \right. \\
&\quad \left. + Q_U \sum_{k=0}^{n-j} \binom{n-j}{k} Q_U^k Q_D^{n-j-k} f(S_n^{(i+1+k)}) \right]
\end{aligned}
$$

[Induction hypothesis]

$$
\begin{aligned}
&= \frac{1}{(1+R)^{n-(j-1)}} \left[\sum_{k=0}^{n-(j-1)} \binom{n-(j-1)-1}{k} Q_U^k Q_D^{n-(j-1)-k} f(S_n^{(i+k)}) \right. \\
&\quad \left. + \sum_{k=1}^{n-(j-1)} \binom{n-(j-1)-1}{k-1} Q_U^k Q_D^{n-(j-1)-k} f(S_n^{(i+k)}) \right]
\end{aligned}
$$

$$
\left[
\begin{array}{l}
\text{for first sum set } \binom{n-(j-1)-1}{n-(j-1)} = 0 \\
\text{for second sum replace } k \text{ by } k+1
\end{array}
\right]
$$

$$
= \frac{1}{(1+R)^{n-(j-1)}} \sum_{k=0}^{n-(j-1)} \left[\binom{n-(j-1)-1}{k} + \binom{n-(j-1)-1}{k-1} \right] Q_U^k Q_D^{n-(j-1)-k} f(S_n^{(i+k)})
$$

$\left[\text{use } \binom{m}{-1} := 0 \right]$

$$
\stackrel{(*)}{=} \frac{1}{(1+R)^{n-(j-1)}} \sum_{k=0}^{n-(j-1)} \binom{n-(j-1)}{k} Q_U^k Q_D^{n-(j-1)-k} f(S_n^{(i+k)})
$$

which is exactly the claim, once we convinced ourselves of $(*)$:

For $(*)$ note:

$$
\begin{aligned}
&\frac{(n-(j-1)-1)!}{k!(n-(j-1)-1-k)!} + \frac{(n-(j-1)-1)!}{(k-1)![n-(j-1)-1-(k-1)]!} \\
&\quad = \frac{(n-(j-1)-1)![(n-(j-1)-k)+k]}{k!(n-(j-1)-k)!} \\
&\quad = \frac{[n-(j-1)]!}{k![n-(j-1)-k]!} = \binom{n-(j-1)}{k}. \qquad \square
\end{aligned}
$$

1.4 Path Dependent Options and Hedging in the Log-Binomial Model

In the previous section we computed the value of an European style option assuming the price of the underlying stock follows a simple path. From one trading time to the next it either changes by the factor U or by the factor D. Now we want to discuss this model further, in particular we want to interpret the pricing formula obtained in Theorem 1.3.1 in a more probabilistic way and extend it to more general options. Secondly, we want to discuss the "Hedging Problem": Given an option, is it possible to find a *trading strategy* (to be defined later) which replicates the option?

We will need some notions and results from probability theory, notions like σ-algebras, random variables, measurability of random variables, expected values and conditional expected values. In this section we will need these notions only for finite probability spaces. To keep this exposition as compact as possible we moved the introduction of these concepts to Appendix B.1. There we discuss binomial and log-binomial processes in detail and introduce the necessary probabilistic concepts by means of these processes.

As before we are given a bond whose value at the last trading time is $ 1. If R are the interests this bond pays for the period between two consecutive trading times, the bond has at time $i = 0, 1, \ldots, n$ the value

$$\frac{1}{(1+R)^{n-i}}.$$

The possible outcomes are all sequences of length n whose entries are either U or D.

$$\Omega = \{U, D\}^n = \{(\omega_1, \omega_2, \ldots \omega_n) | \omega_i = U \text{ or } \omega_i = D, \text{ for } i = 1, 2 \ldots n\}.$$

The i-th *change of the stock price*, $i = 1, 2 \ldots n$, is the random variable

$$X_i : \Omega \to \mathbb{R}, \quad \omega \mapsto \omega_i, \text{ and}$$

$$H_i : \Omega \to \mathbb{R}, \quad \omega \mapsto \#\{j \leq i | \omega_j = U\}$$

$$T_i : \Omega \to \mathbb{R}, \quad \omega \mapsto \#\{j \leq i | \omega_j = D\}$$

the number of "up"- respectively "down"-moves up to time i. The stock price at time i is then given by

$$S_i = S_0 \prod_{j=1}^{i} X_i = S_0 U^{H_i} D^{T_i}.$$

For $i = 0, 1, \ldots, n$ we let $\mathcal{F}_i$ be the set of all events which are realized by the time i. More precisely, it is the σ-algebra consisting of all possible unions of events of the form $A(\nu) = \{(\omega_1, \ldots \omega_n) | \omega_1 = \nu_1 \ldots \omega_i = \nu_i\}$, with $\nu = (\nu_1, \ldots, \nu_i) \in \{H, T\}^i$ (see B.1). We observed in B.1 that a random variable X on Ω is $\mathcal{F}_i$-measurable if and only if for $\omega \in \Omega$ the value $X(\omega)$ only depends on the first i outcomes $\omega_1, \ldots, \omega_i$. We write in this case also $X(\omega_1, \omega_2, \ldots \omega_i)$.

We make a very weak assumption on the probability $\mathbb{P}$ on Ω which measures the likelihood of the different possible outcomes. We only assume that for each $\omega \in \Omega$ $\mathbb{P}(\{\omega\}) > 0$, i.e. all outcomes of Ω must be possible.

As we already observed in Section 1.3 the "real" probability $\mathbb{P}$ is actually irrelevant for the pricing of options. More important is the *risk neutral probability* $\mathbb{Q}$. Following (1.11) in Section 1.3 we define $\mathbb{Q}$ to be the probability on Ω for which $X_1, X_2, \ldots$ are independent and

$$(1.15) \qquad \mathbb{Q}(X_i = D) = Q_D = \frac{U - (1 + R)}{U - D} \text{ and } \mathbb{Q}(X_i = U) = Q_U = \frac{(1 + R) - D}{U - D}.$$

This determines $\mathbb{Q}$ since we conclude $\mathbb{Q}(\{\omega\}) = \mathbb{Q}(\bigcap_{i=1}^{n} \{X_i = \omega_i\}) = \prod_{i=1}^{n} \mathbb{Q}(\{X_i = \omega_i\})$ for each $\omega \in \Omega$.

Recall that the conditional expectation of a random variable X with respect to the σ-algebra $\mathcal{F}_i$, is the unique existing random variable $Y = \mathbb{E}_{\mathbb{Q}}(X | \mathcal{F}_i)$, which is $\mathcal{F}_i$-measurable and has the property that for all $A \in \mathcal{F}_i$ it follows that $\mathbb{E}_{\mathbb{Q}}(1_A Y) = \mathbb{E}_{\mathbb{Q}}(1_A X)$. In our case we can represent $\mathbb{E}_{\mathbb{Q}}(X | \mathcal{F}_i)$ as (see B.1)

$$(1.16) \qquad \mathbb{E}_{\mathbb{Q}}(X | \mathcal{F}_i) = \sum_{(\omega_1, \ldots \omega_i) \in \{U, D\}^i} 1_{A(\omega_1, \ldots \omega_i)} \frac{\mathbb{E}_{\mathbb{Q}}(1_{A_{(\omega_1, \ldots \omega_i)}} X)}{\mathbb{Q}(A_{(\omega_1, \ldots \omega_i)})}.$$

This means that for $\omega \in \Omega$

$$\mathbb{E}_{\mathbb{Q}}(X | \mathcal{F}_i)(\omega) = \mathbb{E}_{\mathbb{Q}}(X | \mathcal{F}_i)(\omega_1, \ldots, \omega_i) = \frac{\mathbb{E}_{\mathbb{Q}}(1_{A_{(\omega_1, \ldots, \omega_i)}} X)}{\mathbb{Q}(A_{(\omega_1, \ldots, \omega_i)})}.$$

The next Proposition explains why $\mathbb{Q}$ is called risk neutral.

Proposition 1.4.1 .   *The discounted stock process*

$$\left(\frac{1}{(1+R)^i} S_i : i = 0, 1, \ldots, n \right)$$

is a martingale with respect to the filtration $(\mathcal{F}_i)_{i=0,\ldots,n}$, *i.e.*

$$\mathbb{E}_{\mathbb{Q}} \left(\frac{1}{(1+R)^j} S_j | \mathcal{F}_i \right) = \frac{1}{(1+R)^i} S_i$$

Note that 1.4.1 means that under the probability $\mathbb{Q}$ the stock price changes in average at the same rate as the price of the bond.

Proof.   Since for $0 \le i < j \le n$ we have $S_j = S_i \prod_{k=i+1}^{j} X_k$ and since S_i is $\mathcal{F}_i$-measurable while $\prod_{k=i+1}^{j} X_k$ is independent of $\mathcal{F}_i$ it follows that

$$\mathbb{E}_{\mathbb{Q}}(S_j | \mathcal{F}_i) = S_i \mathbb{E}_{\mathbb{Q}}(\prod_{k=i+1}^{j} X_k | \mathcal{F}_i) \ \text{ (By B.1.6 (2))}$$

$$= S_i \mathbb{E}_{\mathbb{Q}}(\prod_{k=i+1}^{j} X_k) \ \text{ (By B.1.7 (4))}$$

$$= S_i \prod_{k=i+1}^{j} \mathbb{E}_{\mathbb{Q}}(X_k)$$

$$= S_i [U Q_U + D Q_D]^{j-i}$$

$$= S_i (1+R)^{j-i} \ \text{ (By (1.15))}.$$

This implies the claim. $\square$

A general derivative will now be simply a map $F : \Omega \to \mathbb{R}$. We interpret $F(\omega_1, \ldots \omega_n)$ to be the pay off (or the liability) at the time n assuming $(\omega_1, \ldots \omega_n)$ happened. Note that an European style derivative is of the form $f(S_n(\cdot))$. Since the value $S_n(\omega)$ only depends on how many U's and how many D's are contained in ω but not in which order they appear $f(S_n(\cdot))$

has the same property. For a general option F this is not necessarily true. Therefore these more general options are often also called *path dependent*.

Nevertheless, the problem for finding arbitrage free prices for these kind of derivatives can be done like in case of European style derivatives. For $i \in \{0, 1, \ldots n\}$ we want to know the value of the derivative at time i. We denote that value by F_i. F_i should (only) depend on the present and the past, thus $F_i = F_i(\omega_1, \ldots \omega_i)$.

At the time n it follows of course $F_n(\omega_1, \ldots, \omega_n) = F(\omega_1, \ldots, \omega_n)$. Pricing now the derivative at time $n - 1$ brings us back to the simple up-down model. Assuming $\omega_1, \ldots \omega_{n-1}$ happened up to time $n - 1$ the two possible future values of the derivative are $F(\omega_1, \ldots \omega_{n-1}, U)$ and $F(\omega_1, \ldots \omega_{n-1}, D)$. Using now the formula (1.12) of Section 1.3 with $\tilde{S}_0 = S_{n-1}(\omega_1 \ldots \omega_{n-1})$, $\tilde{f}(U\tilde{S}_0) = F(\omega_1, \ldots \omega_{n-1}, U)$ and $\tilde{f}(D\tilde{S}_0) = F(\omega_1, \ldots \omega_{n-1}, D)$ we obtain

$$(1.17) \qquad F_{n-1}(\omega_1, \ldots, \ldots \omega_{n-1})$$
$$= \frac{1}{1+R}[Q_D F(\omega_1, \ldots \omega_{n-1}, D) + Q_U F(\omega_1, \ldots \omega_{n-1}, U)]$$
$$= \frac{1}{1+R}\mathbb{E}_{\mathbb{Q}}(F|\mathcal{F}_{n-1})(\omega_1, \ldots \omega_{n-1})$$

For the last equality note that by (1.16)

$$\mathbb{E}_{\mathbb{Q}}(F|\mathcal{F}_{n-1})(\omega_1, \ldots \omega_{n-1})$$
$$= \frac{\mathbb{E}_{\mathbb{Q}}(F 1_{A(\omega_1, \ldots \omega_{n-1})})}{\mathbb{Q}(A(\omega_1, \ldots \omega_{n-1}))}$$
$$= \frac{\mathbb{Q}(A(\omega_1, \ldots \omega_{n-1}, D))F(\omega_1, \ldots \omega_{n-1}, D) + \mathbb{Q}(A(\omega_1, \ldots \omega_{n-1}, U))F(\omega_1, \ldots \omega_{n-1}, U)}{\mathbb{Q}(A(\omega_1, \ldots \omega_{n-1}))}$$
$$= Q_D F(\omega_1, \ldots \omega_{n-1}, D) + Q_U F(\omega_1, \ldots \omega_{n-1}, U)$$

More generally using the same argument we can prove the following recursive formula for F_i, $i = 1, \ldots n$.

$$(1.18) \qquad F_{i-1}(\omega_1, \ldots, \ldots \omega_{i-1}) = \frac{1}{1+R}[Q_D F_i(\omega_1, \ldots \omega_{i-1}, D) + Q_U F_i(\omega_1, \ldots \omega_{i-1}, U)]$$
$$= \frac{1}{1+R}\mathbb{E}_{\mathbb{Q}}(F_i|\mathcal{F}_{i-1})(\omega_1, \ldots \omega_{i-1})$$

Using (1.18) we can prove by reversed induction the following pricing formula (see Exercise.....).

Theorem 1.4.2 . *For a general derivative $F : \Omega \to \mathbb{R}$ in the log-binomial model the arbitrage free value at time $i \in \{0, 1, \ldots\}$ is given by*

$$F_i = \frac{1}{(1+R)^{n-i}} \mathbb{E}_{\mathbb{Q}}(F|\mathcal{F}_i).$$

In particular

$$F_0 = \mathbb{E}_{\mathbb{Q}}(F).$$

Remark. For the case of an European style option $f(S_n)$ it is easy to regain the formula obtained in Theorem 1.3.1 from the result in 1.4.2. Indeed, using the fact that for $j \in \{0, \ldots, n\}$

$$\mathbb{P}(H_n = j) = \binom{n}{j} Q_U^j Q_D^{n-j} \quad \text{(Binomial formula)}$$

we obtain

$$\mathbb{E}_{\mathbb{Q}}(f(S)) = \sum_{j=0}^{n} \mathbb{P}(H_n = j) f(S_0 U^j D^{n-j}) = \sum_{j=0}^{n} \binom{n}{j} f(S_0 U^j D^{n-j}) Q_U^j Q_D^{n-j},$$

which after dividing both sides by $(1+R)^n$ leads to the pricing formula obtained in Theorem 1.3.1. A similar computation can be done for the times $i = 1, 2, \ldots n - 1$.

We now turn to the question whether or not and how an investor can replicate a given derivative F in the log-binomial model using bonds and stocks. First we have to determine exactly what an allowable investment strategy is.

Defintion. An *investment strategy* is a sequence $(\theta^{(0)}, \theta^{(1)}, \ldots, \theta^{(n)})$ so that for $i = 0, 1, 2, \ldots n$ $\theta^{(i)} = (\theta_B^{(i)}, \theta_S^{(i)})$ with $\theta_B^{(i)}$ and $\theta_S^{(i)}$ being $\mathcal{F}_i$-measurable mappings on Ω into $\mathbb{R}$.

Interpretation. At each trading time i the investor can choose a portfolio consisting out of $\theta_B^{(i)}$ units of the bonds and $\theta_S^{(i)}$ units of the stock. This choice can only depend on present and past events since the investor can of course not "look into the future". This means mathematically that $\theta_B^{(i)}$ and $\theta_S^{(i)}$ have to be $\mathcal{F}_i$-measurable and, thus, can only depend on $\omega_1, \ldots, \omega_i$.

Note that the value of a strategy $(\theta^{(0)}, \theta^{(1)}, \ldots, \theta^{(n)})$ at time i, i.e. the value of the portfolio at time i, is given by

$$(1.19) \qquad V_i(\theta^{(i)}) = S_i \theta_S^{(i)} + \frac{\theta_B^{(i)}}{(1+R)^{n-i}}$$

We call a strategy $(\theta^{(0)}, \theta^{(1)}, \ldots, \theta^{(n)})$ *self financing* if at all times $i = 1, 2, \ldots n$ the value of the portfolio $\theta^{(i-1)}$ is equal to the value of $\theta^{(i)}$, for $i = 1, \ldots, n$, i.e.

$$(1.20) \qquad \theta_S^{(i)} S_i + \frac{\theta_B^{(i)}}{(1+R)^{n-i}} = \theta_S^{(i-1)} S_i + \frac{\theta_B^{(i-1)}}{(1+R)^{n-i}}.$$

This means that the investor neither consums part of his portfolio, nor does he add capital to it.

Theorem 1.4.3 .   *The log-normal model is* complete. *This means the following. For any derivative F there is a self financing strategy $(\theta^{(i)})_{i=0}^n$ so that*

$$V_i(\theta^{(i-1)}) = F_i = \frac{1}{(1+R)^{n-i}} \mathbb{E}_\mathbb{Q}(F \mathcal{F}_i), \quad \text{for } i = 1, 2, \ldots, n.$$

Moreover, if $\omega_1, \ldots \omega_i \in \{U, D\}$, and if $i = 0, 1 \ldots, n-1$, then $\theta_B^{(i)}$ and $\theta_S^{(i)}$ are given by:

$$(1.21) \qquad \theta_B^{(i)}(\omega_1, \ldots \omega_i) = (1+R)^{n-i-1} \frac{U F_{i+1}(\omega_1, \ldots \omega_i, D) - D F_{i+1}(\omega_1, \ldots \omega_i, U)}{U - D}$$

$$(1.22) \qquad \theta(i)_S(\omega_1, \ldots \omega_i) = \frac{F_{i+1}(\omega_1, \ldots \omega_i, U) - F_{i+1}(\omega_1, \ldots \omega_i, D)}{S_i(\omega_1, \ldots \omega_i)(U - D)}$$

Remark.   Before we start the proof of Theorem 1.4.3 we first want to explain how one obtains that (1.21) and (1.22) are the only possible choices. Indeed, for $i = 0, 1 \ldots i$, and given past outcomes $(\omega_1, \ldots, \omega_i)$ we need to choose $\theta^{(i)} = (\theta_B^{(i)}, \theta_S^{(i)})$ so that no matter whether the next move of the stock is D or U, the portfolio $\theta^{(i)}$ will have the value F_{i+1}. This leads to the following two equations

$$V_{i+1}(\theta^{(i)})(\omega_1, \ldots, \omega_{i-1}, D) = \theta_S^{(i)} S_i D + \frac{\theta_B^{(i)}}{(1+R)^{n-(i+1)}} = F_{i+1}(\omega_1, \ldots, \omega_i, D)$$

and

$$V_{i+1}(\theta^{(i)})(\omega_1, \ldots, \omega_{i-1}, U) = \theta_S^{(i)} S_i U + \frac{\theta_B^{(i)}}{(1+R)^{n-(i+1)}} = F_{i+1}(\omega_1, \ldots, \omega_i, U).$$

Solving now these two equations leads to (1.21) and (1.22).

Proof of Theorem 1.4.3. We first will observe that the value of $\theta^{(i)}$ as given in (1.21) and (1.22) equals to F_i.

Let $(\omega_1, \ldots, \omega_i) \in \{U, D\}^i$ (if $i = 0$, then $(\omega_1, \ldots, \omega_i) = \emptyset$). In the following computation we suppress the dependance in $(\omega_1, \ldots, \omega_i)$ and write for example $F_{i+1}(U)$ instead of $F_{i+1}(\omega_1, \ldots, \omega_i, U)$.

$$\begin{aligned}
V_i(\theta^{(i)}) &= \theta_S^{(i)} S_i + \frac{\theta_B^{(i)}}{(1+R)^{n-i}} \\
&= \frac{F_{i+1}(U) - F_{i+1}(D)}{U - D} + \frac{1}{1+R} \frac{U F_{i+1}(D) - D F_{i+1}(U)}{U - D} \\
&= \frac{1}{1+R} \left[F_{i+1}(U) \frac{1+R-D}{U-D} + F_{i+1}(D) \frac{U-(1+R)}{U-D} \right] \\
&= \frac{1}{1+R} [F_{i+1}(U) Q_U + F_{i+1}(D) Q_D] \qquad [\text{By } (1.15)] \\
&= F_i \qquad [\text{By } (1.18)],
\end{aligned}$$

which proves our first claim.

Secondly, we have to show that $(\theta^{(i)})_{i=1}^{n-1}$ is self financing. For that we have to show that for $i = 0, 1 \ldots n-1$ the value of $\theta^{(i)}$ is F_{i+1} after the $i + 1$st move of the stock no matter whether the $i + 1$st move is D or U. Indeed, if it is D then we obtain

$$
\begin{aligned}
V_{i+1}(\theta^{(i)})(D) &= \theta_S^{(i)} S_i D + \frac{\theta_B^{(i)}}{(1+R)^{n-(i+1)}} \\
&= D \frac{F_{i+1}(U) - F_{i+1}(D)}{U - D} + \frac{U F_{i+1}(D) - D F_{i+1}(U)}{U - D} \\
&= F_{i+1}(D).
\end{aligned}
$$

If the $i + 1$st move is U we proceed in a similar way. $\square$

1.5 The Approach of Cox, Ross and Rubinstein to the Log-Normal Model

1.6 The Factors

1.7 Introduction to the Theory of Bonds

1.8 Numerical Considerations

Chapter 2

Introduction to Stochastic Calculus, the Brownian Motion

The theory of stochastic processes, and in particular Stochastic Calculus, turned out to become one of the most important tools of modern theory of security pricing. Black and Scholes. Therefore we will give in this chapter an introduction to this theory.

The reader who is at this point not interested in a rather detailed exposition of Stochastic Calculus might only want to go through the first section of this chapter. In this first section we will introduce the Brownian Motion, and develop in a rather heuristic approach the key result, the formula of Ito.

The following sections present a more rigorous and selfcontained exposition of the basics on stochastic processes. After proving some important properties of the Browninian Motion in Section (2.2) we will define stochastic integrals with respect to the Brownian Motion (Section 2.3). Finally we will present in Section (2.4) the "Fundamental Theorem of Stochastic Integration", the Theorem of Ito.

For the reader whose background in probability theory got a little rusty we included a presentation of the basics in Appendix B.2. We also wrote a more detailed introduction to the notion of conditional expectations in B.3 and presented several notions of convergence for random variables in Appendix B.4.

2.1   Introduction of the Brownian Motion

We introduce a model for describing stock prices using *stochastic processes* indexed over a continous time interval.

Let $S_t, t \geq 0$, be the price of a certain stock (or any other financial security) at time t. We think of S_t as being a random variable defined on some probability space $(\Omega, \mathcal{F}, \mathbb{P})$. We want to write the change ΔS_t from S_t to $S_{t+\Delta t}$, with $\Delta t > 0$ being small, in the following way:

(2.1) $$\frac{\Delta S_t}{S_t} = \frac{S_{t+\Delta t} - S_t}{S_t} = \Delta t \cdot \mu + \text{``white noise''}$$

where μ is the "drift" and the term "white noise" causes the typical "wiggling" of the stock price. We will develop this concept more rigorously later. Let us first explain the "white noise" by an analogy.

Consider a very small oil drop (about $\frac{1}{1000}$mm radius) in a gas or a liquid. Observing it under a microscope, one would notice that it seems to move randomly on zig-zag shaped paths, even if no force is acting and if the flow of the medium is zero. The reason of that movement is caused by the molecules of the medium kicking and banging against the oil drop from all sides.

Over a long period of time, the oil drop gets approximately on average the same momentum in each direction. Nevertheless, in a short period of time there could be more momentum in a single direction.

The stock price is exposed to similar forces. On one hand its movement depends on deterministic forces, like general perception of the market, expectations of profit etc. (comparable to the flow of the medium in which the oil drop is situated). On the other hand it might simply happen that during a short period of time there are more buyers than sellers or vice versa, pushing the stock price up or down respectively.

Going back to the oil drop, let us develop a model for its random movement. Let X_t be the, say, x-coordinate of the oil drop at time t.

In the time interval $[t, t + \Delta t]$ the drop gets kicked by say n molecules, each of them causing a small displacement denoted by d_i, $i = 1, \ldots, n$.

Then the total displacement after Δt in $x - direction$ is

$$\Delta X_t = \sum_{i=1}^{n} d_i$$

$d_1, d_2, \ldots, d_n$ can be seen as independent random variables with expectation $\mathbb{E}(d_i) = 0$, and variance $\mathbb{V}\mathrm{ar}(d_i) = \sigma_i^2$. Since we assume the d_i's to be independant the variance of the total diplacement is $\Delta \sigma^2 = \sum_{i=1}^{n} \sigma_i^2$.

Since n is very big and the d_i's have mean zero and are independent the distribution of ΔX_t is approximately normal distributed with mean zero and variance $\sum \sigma_i^2$ (Central Limit Theorem B.2.16 in Appendix B.2). Assuming homogeneity in time, $\Delta \sigma^2$ should be proportional to Δt. Thus, it follows that

$$\sum_{i=1}^{n} \sigma_i^2 = \Delta t \sigma^2,$$

for some positive number σ^2.

Secondly, the displacement ΔX_t during the period $[s, t]$, caused by collisions of the oil drop with the gas molecules during that period, is independent from the movement prior to time s.

We can therefore conclude the following two properties of X_t:

1) For any $s < t$, the difference $X_t - X_s$ is normal distributed with mean being zero, and variance being proporitional to $t - s$, i.e. $X_t - X_s$ is $N(0, \sigma^2(t - s))$ distributed.

2) For any $s < t$, the difference $X_t - X_s$ is independent to X_r, $r \leq s$.

This two properties together with continuity in t characterizes the stochastic process known as *Brownian Motion*, named after the Scottish botanist Robert Brown, who studied the movements of pollen grains.

We will now switch to a more rigerous introduction of stochastic processes and the Brownian Motion.

We consider a probability space $(\Omega, \mathcal{F}, \mathbb{P})$, which we assume to be fixed throughout this section. First we introduce the notion of stochastic processes.

Definition. A *stochastic process* over a *continuous time* is a family of random variables (X_t), $X_t \colon \Omega \to \mathbb{R}$, indexed over $t \in [0, \infty)$ or $t \in [0, T]$, for which the map

$$\Omega \times [0, \infty) \ni (\omega, t) \mapsto X_t(\omega)$$

is measurable with respect to the product σ-algebra $\mathcal{F} \otimes \mathcal{B}_{\mathbb{R}_0^+}$. This is the smallest σ algebra on $\Omega \times \mathbb{R}$ which contains all sets of the form $A \times B$ with $A \in \mathcal{F}$ and $B \in \mathcal{B}_{\mathbb{R}_0^+}$. If $(X_t)_{t \geq 0}$ is a stochastic process and we fix $\omega \in \Omega$, the map

$$X_{(\cdot)}(\omega) \colon \ t \mapsto X_t(\omega)$$

is called a *path of* (X_t).

$(X_t)_{t \geq 0}$ is called a continuous stochastic process if almost all paths are continuous, i.e. if $\mathbb{P}(\{\omega \in \Omega \colon \ t \mapsto X_t(\omega) \text{ is continuous})\} = 1$.

We call a stochastic process *integrable*, respectively *square integrable*, if for all $t \geq 0$, $\mathbb{E}_{\mathbb{P}}(|X_t|) < \infty$, respectively $\mathbb{E}_{\mathbb{P}}(X_t^2) < \infty$.

Definition. A *filtration* of the probability space $(\Omega, \mathcal{F}, \mathbb{P})$ is a family of σ- algebras $(\mathcal{F}_t)_{t \geq 0}$ for which

$$\mathcal{F}_s \subset \mathcal{F}_t \subset \mathcal{F}, \ \text{if } s \leq t.$$

In this case we call $(\Omega, \mathcal{F}, (\mathcal{F}_t), \mathbb{P})$ a filtered probability space. A stochastic process (X_t) is called *adapted* to a filtration $(\mathcal{F}_t)_{t \geq 0}$ if X_t is $\mathcal{F}_t$-measurable for each $t \geq 0$.

In the sections 1.3, 1.4 and B.1 we considered processes indexed over finitely many times which had furthermore the property that they only could assume finitely many possible values. We are now in a more general situation. X_t can now assume infinitely many possible values and secondly the time is now an element of a whole interval. This more general situation will cause several technical problems we have to overcome. Nevertheless, the more general situation has the same interpretations.

At time t_0 the stock price will be assumed to be a random variable X_{t_0}, where (X_t) is a stochastic process defined on $(\Omega, \mathcal{F}, \mathbb{P})$. We will assume that (X_t) is adapted to some filtration $(\mathcal{F}_t)_{t\geq 0}$ and for time t_0 the σ-algebra $\mathcal{F}_{t_0}$ stands for the set of events for which we know whether or not they occured by the time t_0.

Also $\mathbb{E}_{\mathbb{P}}(X_t|\mathcal{F}_s)$, for $s < t$, will be intepreted as the "expected value of X_t, given all the facts known up to time s". Since X_t might and will assume infinitely many values we will not be able to compute $\mathbb{E}_{\mathbb{P}}(X_t|\mathcal{F}_s)$ in an intuitve way, as we did in Section B.1. We have to use the definition of conditional expectations as given in B.3. $\mathbb{E}_{\mathbb{P}}(X_t|\mathcal{F}_s)$ is defined to be the (up to almost sure equality) uniquely existing $\mathcal{F}_s$-measurable random variable Y so that for all $A \in \mathcal{F}_s$ it follows that $\mathbb{E}_{\mathbb{P}}(1_A Y) = \mathbb{E}_{\mathbb{P}}(1_A X_t)$.

There are stochastic processes which are of special interest: the ones which "stay stable in average", the ones which "increase in average", and the ones which "decrease in average".

Definition. An adapted and integrable stochastic process (X_t) on $(\Omega, \mathcal{F}, (\mathcal{F}_t), \mathbb{P})$ is called a

1) *Martingale* (relative to $(\mathcal{F}_t)$) if $\mathbb{E}_{\mathbb{P}}(X_t|\mathcal{F}_s) = X_s$ a.s., for all $s < t$.

2) *Super-martingale* (relative to $(\mathcal{F}_t)$) if $\mathbb{E}_{\mathbb{P}}(X_t|\mathcal{F}_s) \leq X_s$, a.s., for all $s < t$.

3) *Sub-martingale* (relative to $(\mathcal{F}_t)$) if $\mathbb{E}_{\mathbb{P}}(X_t|\mathcal{F}_s) \geq X_s$, a.s. for all $s < t$.

Inspired by the analysis of the movement of the oil drop at the beginning of this section we now can give a precise definition of a Brownian Motion.

Definition. A stochastic process $(B_t)_{t\geq 0}$ on an probability space $(\Omega, \mathcal{F}, \mathbb{P})$ adapted to a filtration $(\mathcal{F}_t)_{t\geq 0}$ is called a Brownian motion (relatively to $(\mathcal{F}_t)$) if it has the following four properties.

1) $B_0 = 0$.

2) $B_t - B_s$ is $N(0, t - s)$ distributed for any choice of $0 \leq s < t$. For the definition of the normal distribution see Appendix B.2.

3) $B_t - B_s$ is independent of $\mathcal{F}_s$ for any choice of $0 \leq s < t$. Recall that this means that for any measurable $A \subset \mathbb{R}$ and any $F \in \mathcal{F}_s$.

$$\mathbb{P}(F \cap \{B_t - B_s \in A\}) = \mathbb{P}(F)\mathbb{P}(\{B_t - B_s \in A\}) = \mathbb{P}(F)\frac{1}{\sqrt{2\pi(t-s)}}\int_A e^{-\frac{x^2}{2(t-s)}}\,dx.$$

4) The paths of B_t are continuous.

We could for example take $\mathcal{F}_t$ to be the σ-algebra generated by all B_s, $0 \leq s \leq t$. But we might want to assume that $\mathcal{F}_t$ depends also on other events, (i.e. results of other random variables.

Taking now a Brownian motion as a model for the stock price will not be very realistic, simply because of the fact that B_t can assume negative values. The widely used model for stocks is therefore an "exponential version of the Brownian motion".

Defintion.   Assume that B_t is a Brownian motion on the filtered probability space $(\Omega, \mathcal{F}, (\mathcal{F}_t), \mathbb{P})$. Let $\mu \in \mathbb{R}$, $\nu > 0$, and $S_0 > 0$

The process S_t defined by:

$$(2.2) \qquad\qquad S_t = S_0 e^{\mu t - \frac{1}{2}\nu^2 t + \nu B_t},$$

is called a *log-binomial process* or *geometrical Brownian motion*, with *drift* being μ and *volatility* being ν.

Remark. It seems at first sight unnatural to separate the the term μt from the term $\frac{1}{2}\nu^2 t$ instead of simply gather it to a term at. The reason for this separation is the fact that the process $S_0 e^{-\frac{1}{2}\nu^2 t + \nu B_t}$ is a martingale as we will see in the next section. Therefore the factor $e^{\mu t}$ determines by how fast the process increases in average.

Secondly we will see in Section 2.4 that the process S_t as defined above satisfies the following "stochastic differential equation"

$$dS_t = \mu S_t dt + \nu S_t dB_t,$$

meaning that the infinitesimal percental change of S_t, or $\frac{dS_t}{S_t}$, at time t has a deterministic part proportional to to dt, namely μdt, and a random part which is proportional to the infinitesimal changes of B_t, namely νdB_t. This will be explained in more detail during the next sections.

The log-normal model for stock prices can now be similar derived as our analysis of the movement of the oil drop. The action of the participants of the stock market have a similar effect on the stock price as the molecules have on the oil drop. But instead of assuming that this actions cause additive changes, we assume that they cause multiplicative changes.

Remark: There are some serious problems assuming log-normality of a stock price S_t.

1) The number of investors (about 1000 during a day for the stock of a large company) is much smaller than the number of molecules hitting an oil drop (about 10^{10}).

2) The molecules acting on the oil drop have comparable momenta, which implies that above mentioned variances σ_i^2 are comparable. The difference between the financial power of the different investors is much higher.

3) The impulses of the molecules hitting an oil drop can be assumed to be independent. It is not that clear, and only a rough approximation to assume that investors make their decisions independently.

Because of (1), (2) and (3) the use of the Central Limit Theorem is much more problematic in the case of a stock than in the case of the oil drop.

A very serious flaw of the log-normal model is also the fact that it assumes that stock prices move continuously. It is clear that for example a bold statement of the president of the Federal Bank can cause quite abrupt moves of the stock prices.

Therefore the log-normal model can and should only be used as a rough approximation to the real situation. History shows that in "calm times" it works quite well, but can become false in crash situations.

We now turn to the following central question concerning approximation of general functions by linear functions: assume $f(x)$ is a differentiable function. We are fixing a value a and want to estimate the difference $f(x) - f(a)$. A basic result in Calculus provides as that $f(x) - f(a)$ can be written as

$$(2.3) \qquad f(x) = f(a) + f'(a)(x - a) + o(x - a),$$

where the *rest term* $o(x-a)$ has *a smaller order than* $|x - a|$ meaning that $\lim_{x \to a} \frac{o(x-a)}{|x-a|} = 0$. this means that $x \to f(a) + f'(a)(x - a)$ is *the best linear approximation* of $f(x)$ at a. Better approximation includes the second derivative of f:

$$(2.4) \qquad f(x) = f(a) + f'(a)(x - a) + f''(a)(x - a) + o((x - a)^2),$$

where $\lim_{x \to a} \frac{o((x-a)^2)}{(x-a)^2} = 0$.

Now we want to replace the variable x by the random variable B_t. Given $t \geq 0$ and $\Delta t > 0$ we could write as in (2.3)

$$(2.5) \qquad f(B_{t+\Delta t}) = f(B_t) + f'(B_t)\Delta B_t + o(\Delta B_t),$$

where $\Delta B_t = B_{t+\Delta t} - B_t$. We are interested in an approximation in which the rest term has a smaller order that Δ_t. Since ΔB_t is a random variable whose variance is Δ_t, it follows that $\mathbb{E}(|\Delta B_t|)$ is of the order $\sqrt{\Delta_t}$ (see Exercise....). We therefore have to pass to the quadratic approximation which leads to

$$(2.6) \qquad f(B_{t+\Delta t}) = f(B_t) + f'(B_t)\Delta B_t + \frac{1}{2}f''(B_t)\Delta^2 B_t + o(\Delta^2 B_t).$$

An important property of the Brownian Motion (see Section 2.2) states now that the random variable $\Delta^2 B_t$ is *assymptotically deterministic* meaning that $\lim_{\Delta_t} \Delta^2 B_t / \Delta_t = 1$ almost surely. Therefore we deduce the following approximation formula:

$$(2.7) \qquad f(B_{t+\Delta t}) = f(B_t) + f'(B_t)\Delta B_t + \frac{1}{2}f''(B_t)\Delta_t^2 + o(\Delta^2 B_t).$$

Usually Equation 2.7 is written as an equation using the notations of differentials:

$$(2.8) \qquad df(B_t) = f'(B_t)dB_t + \frac{1}{2}f''(B_t)dt.$$

If $f(x,t)$ is a function in two variables, is once differentiable in t and twice differentiable in x, a similar approach leads to the following differential equation.

$$(2.9) \qquad df(t, B_t) = \frac{\partial f}{\partial t}(t, B_t)dt + \frac{\partial f}{\partial x}(t, B_t)dB_t + \frac{1}{2}\frac{\partial^2 f}{\partial x^2}(t, B_t)dt,$$

meaning that small changes of t cause that $f(t, B_t)$ changes approximately proportional to the change of t (with factor $\frac{\partial f}{\partial t}(t, B_t) + \frac{1}{2}\frac{\partial^2 f}{\partial x^2}(t, B_t)$) and proportional to the change of B_t (with the factor $\frac{\partial f}{\partial x}(t, B_t)$).

This differential formula can also be rewritten as integral formula similar as one can write $f(a) - f(b)$ as the integral of f' from a to b.

$$(2.10) \qquad f(T, B_T) - f(0,0) = \int_0^T \frac{\partial f}{\partial t}(t, B_t)dt + \int_0^T \frac{\partial f}{\partial x}(t, B_t)dB_t + \int_0^T \frac{1}{2}\frac{\partial^2 f}{\partial x^2}(t, B_t)dt.$$

Here the first and the third integral are interpreted as the random variables which assign to each $\omega \in \Omega$ the integral of the functions $t \mapsto \frac{\partial f}{\partial t}(t, B_t(\omega))$ and $t \mapsto \frac{1}{2}\frac{\partial^2 f}{\partial x^2}(t, B_t(\omega))$ respectively. The second integral is a *stochastic integral* and its introduction will need further explanation in the following sections.

Applying formula (2.9) to the lognormal process $S_t = S_0 e^{\mu t - \frac{v^2}{2}t + vB_t}$ we derive that

$$(2.11) \qquad dS_t = (\mu - \frac{nu^2}{2})S_0 e^{\mu t - \frac{v^2}{2}t + vB_t}dt + \frac{v^2}{2}S_0 e^{\mu t - \frac{v^2}{2}t + vB_t}dB_t + \frac{1}{2}v^2 e^{\mu t - \frac{v^2}{2}t + vB_t}dt$$

$$= \mu S_t dt + v S_t dB_t,$$

This formula explains now the heuristically introduced formula 2.1 for processes describing the value of a stock.

Using the chainrule we deduce for a function $f(t, x)$ that

$$(2.12) \qquad df(t, S_t) = \frac{\partial f}{\partial t}(t, S_t)dt + \frac{\partial f}{\partial x}(t, S_t)[\mu S_t dt + v S_t dB_t] + \frac{1}{2}v^2 S_t^2 \frac{\partial^2 f}{\partial x^2}(t, S_t)dt$$

$$= \left[\frac{\partial f}{\partial t}(t, S_t) + \mu S_t \frac{\partial f}{\partial x}(t, S_t) + \frac{1}{2}v^2 S_t^2 \frac{\partial f}{\partial t}(t, S_t)\right]dt + \frac{\partial^2 f}{\partial x^2}(t, S_t)dB_t.$$

2.2   Some Properties of the Brownian Motion

In this section we will present and prove some properties of the Brownian Motion. We assume throughout this section that (B_t) is a Brownian Motion on the filtered probability space $(\Omega, \mathcal{F}, (\mathcal{F}_t), \mathbb{P})$. Since in this section the considered probablity will always be $\mathbb{P}$ we will denote the expected value with respect to $\mathbb{P}$ by $\mathbb{E}$ instead of $\mathbb{E}_{\mathbb{P}}$.

Proposition 2.2.1 . (B_t) *is a square integrable process and:*

1) *If $s < t$, then $\mathbb{E}(B_t|\mathcal{F}_s) = B_s$, i.e. B_t is a martingale,*

2) *if $s < t$, then $\mathbb{E}((B_t - B_s)^2) = t - s$*

3) *$\mathbb{E}(B_t B_s) = \min(s, t)$.*

Proof.   The fact that B_t is normal distributed implies that (B_t) is square integrable. If $s < t$ it follows that

$$E(B_t|\mathcal{F}_s) = \mathbb{E}(B_s + B_t - B_s|\mathcal{F}_s) = B_s + \mathbb{E}(B_t - B_s|\mathcal{F}_s)$$

Since $B_t - B_s$ has mean zero and is independent to $\mathcal{F}_s$ it follows from Proposition B.3.3 (3) in Appendix B.3 that

$$\mathbb{E}(B_t - B_s|\mathcal{F}_s) = \mathbb{E}(B_t - B_s) = 0,$$

which implies the first claim.

The second claim simply follows from the fact that $B_t - B_s$ has mean zero and variance $(t - s)$.

Using similar arguments as for the proof of claim (1) we derive for $s < t$ that

$$\mathbb{E}(B_t B_s) = \mathbb{E}(B_s^2 + (B_t - B_s)B_s) = \mathbb{E}(B_s^2) + \mathbb{E}((B_t - B_s)B_s) = s + \underbrace{\mathbb{E}(B_t - B_s)}_{0}\underbrace{\mathbb{E}(B_s)}_{0} = s.$$

which implies the third claim.   □

The next Proposition will be necessary to analyse the "quadratic variation" of the paths of the Brownian motion.

Proposition 2.2.2 . *For $s < t$ it follows that*

$$\mathbb{E}([(B_t - B_s)^2 - (t - s)]^2) = 2(t - s)^2.$$

Proof. $B_t - B_s$ is $N(0, t - s)$ distributed whose density is given by

$$\rho(x) = \frac{1}{\sqrt{2\pi(t - s)}} e^{-x^2/2(t-s)}.$$

Letting $g(x) = (x^2 - (t-s))^2$. and $h = t-s$, we deduce from Proposition B.2.9 in Appendix B.2 and from basic integration techniques that

$$\mathbb{E}([(B_t - B_s)^2 - (t - s)]^2) = \int_{-\infty}^{\infty} g(x)\rho(x)dx$$

$$= \frac{1}{\sqrt{2\pi h}} \int_{-\infty}^{\infty} (x^2 - h)^2 e^{-x^2/2h} dx$$

$$= \frac{1}{\sqrt{2\pi h}} \int_{-\infty}^{\infty} (x^4 - 2x^2 h + h^2) e^{-x^2/2h} dx$$

$$= \frac{1}{\sqrt{2\pi h}} \int_{-\infty}^{\infty} x^4 e^{-x^2/2h} dx - h^2.$$

since

$$\frac{1}{\sqrt{2\pi h}} \int_{-\infty}^{\infty} x^2 e^{-x^2/2h} dx = h \text{ and } \frac{1}{\sqrt{2\pi h}} \int_{-\infty}^{\infty} e^{-x^2/2h} dx = 1.$$

We continue above computation by

$$\mathbb{E}([(B_t - B_s)^2 - (t-s)]^2) = \frac{1}{\sqrt{2\pi h}} \int_{-\infty}^{\infty} x^3 \underbrace{\underset{v}{\underbrace{xe^{-x^2/2h}}}}_{u'} dx - h^2$$

$$= \frac{1}{\sqrt{2\pi h}} \int_{-\infty}^{\infty} 3x^2 h e^{-x^2/2h} dx - h^2$$

$$= 3h^2 - h^2 = 2h^2 = 2(t-s)^2,$$

which finishes the proof.   □

Proposition 2.2.3 .

1) *The process $(B_t^2 - t)_{t \geq 0}$ is a martingale.*

2) *The log-normal process $(e^{\nu B_t - \frac{1}{2}\nu^2 t})_{t \geq 0}$ is a martingale.*

Proof. We will only prove the second claim and leave the first part to the reader.

For $s < t$ it follows from the independance of $B_t - B_s$ to $\mathcal{F}_s$ that

$$\mathbb{E}(e^{\nu B_t - \frac{1}{2}\nu^2 t} | \mathcal{F}_s) = \mathbb{E}(e^{\nu B_s - \frac{1}{2}\nu^2 s} \cdot e^{\nu(B_t - B_s) - \frac{1}{2}\nu^2(t-s)} | \mathcal{F}_s)$$

$$= e^{\nu B_s - \frac{1}{2}\nu^2 s} \cdot \mathbb{E}(e^{\nu(B_t - B_s) - \frac{1}{2}\nu^2(t-s)})$$

We are left to show that $\mathbb{E}(e^{\nu(B_t - B_s) - \frac{1}{2}\nu^2(t-s)}) = 1$. Put $h = t - s$ and note that

$$\mathbb{E}(e^{\nu(B_t - B_s) - \frac{1}{2}\nu^2 h}) = \frac{1}{\sqrt{2\pi h}} \int_{-\infty}^{\infty} e^{\nu x - \frac{1}{2}\nu^2 h} e^{-x^2/2h} dx$$

$$= \frac{1}{\sqrt{2\pi h}} \int_{-\infty}^{\infty} e^{-\frac{x^2 - 2x\nu h + \nu^2 h^2}{2h}} dx = \frac{1}{\sqrt{2\pi h}} \int_{-\infty}^{\infty} e^{-\frac{(x-\nu h)^2}{2h}} dx = 1,$$

where the last equality follows from the fact that $\frac{1}{\sqrt{2\pi h}} e^{-\frac{(x-\nu h)^2}{2h}}$ is the density of the normal distribution with mean νh and variance h.

This implies the claim.   □

We finally want to treat an extremely important property of the Brownian motion,i.e. of the "quadratic variation" of its paths.

We need the following notation.

Definition: Given an interval $[s,t]$ and a function $f\colon [s,t] \to \mathbb{R}$. For a partition $P = \{t_0, t_1, \ldots, t_n\}$, with $s = t_0 < t_1 < \cdots < t_n = t$ we put

$$\mathrm{qv}(f, P, [s,t]) = \sum_{i=1}^{n} (f(t_i) - f(t_{i-1}))^2.$$

Define also $\|P\| = \max_{i=1,\ldots,n} |t_i - t_{i-1}|$ we say f is of finite quadratic variation on $[s,t]$ if

$$\mathrm{qv}(f, [s,t]) = \lim_{\|P\| \to 0} \mathrm{qv}(f, P, [s,t])$$

exists.

By "$\lim_{\|P\| \to 0} \mathrm{qv}(f, P, [s,t]) = a$" we mean the following: For any $\varepsilon > 0$ there is a $\delta > 0$ so that whenever P is a partition of $[s,t]$ for which $\|P\| \le \delta$ then $|\mathrm{qv}(f, P, [s,t]) - a| < \varepsilon$.

Proposition 2.2.4 . *If $f\colon [s,t] \to \mathbb{R}$ is differentiable, with $\sup\limits_{s \le x \le t} |f'(x)| = C < \infty$ then* $\mathrm{qv}(f, [s,t]) = 0$.

Proof. Let $P = \{t_0, t_1, \ldots, t_n\}$ be a partition of $[s,t]$

$$\sum_{i=1}^{n} |f(t_i) - f(t_{i-1})|^2 = \sum_{i=1}^{n} (t_i - t_{i-1})^2 \left[\frac{f(t_i) - f(t_{i-1})}{t_i - t_{i-1}} \right]^2$$

$$= \sum_{i=1}^{n} (t_i - t_{i-1})^2 |f'(t_i^*)|^2$$

[Mean Value Theorem , $t_i^* \in [t_{i-1}, t_i]$ appropriately chosen]

$$\le C^2 \sum_{i=1}^{n} (t_i - t_{i-1})^2$$

$$\le C^2 \max_{i=1,\ldots,n} |t_i - t_{i-1}| \cdot \underbrace{\sum_{i=1}^{n} |t_i - t_{i-1}|}_{=t-s}$$

$$= C^2 (t - s)\|P\| \to 0, \text{ if } \|P\| \to 0. \qquad \square$$

For an $\omega \in \Omega$ we will now study the quadratic variation of the paths $B_{(\cdot)}(\omega) : [s, t] \to \mathbb{R}$. Formally $A_{[s,t]}(\omega) = \mathrm{qv}(B_{(\cdot)}(\omega), [s, t])$ is, if it happens to exist, an $\mathcal{F}_t$-measurable random variable. A very astonishing fact now says that $A_{[s,t]}$ is actually deterministic for almost all $\omega \in \Omega$. In fact it is true that $A_{[s,t]} = t - s$ a.s.. Thus, although the paths of B_t are "very random", their quadratic variations are completely deterministic. Actually, assuming we could observe and measure the quadratic variation of a realization of a path of a Brownian Motion (which causes technical problems), we could use this path as a watch: when the quadratic variation reaches t, the time is t.

Since the proof of this fact needs some technical tools which go beyond the scope of this book, we will prove a slightly weaker version, which will be good enough for our purposes.

For that we consider a partition of $[s, t]$, $P = (t_0, t_1, \ldots, t_n)$, $t_0 = s < t_1 < \ldots < t_n < t$, and let $A_{[s,t],P}(\omega) = \mathrm{qv}(B_{(\cdot)}(\omega), P, [s, t])$. Then we let $\|P\|$ tend to zero and prove that the random variable $A_{[s,t],P}(\cdot)$ converges in L_2 to $t - s$, i.e. (see section B.4 for more detail) we will show that

$$\lim_{\|P\| \to 0} \mathbb{E}\big((A_{[s,t],P} - (t - s))^2\big) = 0.$$

Remark : For better understanding we prefer to state arguments on the quadratic variation in sequential form. Note that for a process X_t saying that

$$L_2 - \lim_{\|P\| \to 0} \mathrm{qv}(X_{(\cdot)}(\cdot), P, [s, t]) = Y,$$

is equivalent to saying that for any sequence (P_n) of partitions of $[s, t]$, $P_n = (t_0^{(n)}, t_1^{(n)}, \ldots, t_{k_n}^{(n)})$, with $\lim_{n \to 0} \|P_n\| = 0$, it follows that

$$\mathbb{E}\left(\left[\sum_{i=1}^{k_n}(X_{t_i^{(n)}} - X_{t_{i-1}^{(n)}})^2 - Y\right]^2\right) \to 0.$$

Note also that for $\|P_n\| \to 0$ the number k_n has to increase to infinity. In order to avoid too many indices we will always assume that $k_n = n$.

Theorem 2.2.5 . *Let $P_n = (t_0^{(n)}, t_1^{(n)}, \ldots, t_n^{(n)})$ be a sequence of partition of the interval $[s,t]$ with $\lim_{n\to\infty} \|P_n\| = 0$. Then*

$$\sum_{i=1}^{n} (B_{t_i^{(n)}} - B_{t_{i-1}^{(n)}})^2 \to t - s \text{ in } L_2.$$

Proof. Note that

$$\mathbb{E}\left(\left[\sum_{i=1}^{n}(B_{t_i^{(n)}} - B_{t_{i-1}^{(n)}})^2 - (t - s)\right]^2\right)$$

$$= \mathbb{E}\left(\left[\sum_{i=1}^{n}[(B_{t_i^{(n)}} - B_{t_{i-1}^{(n)}})^2 - (t_i^{(n)} - t_{i-1}^{(n)})]\right]^2\right)$$

$$= \sum_{i,j=1}^{n} \mathbb{E}\left([(B_{t_i^{(n)}} - B_{t_{i-1}^{(n)}})^2 - (t_i^{(n)} - t_{i-1}^{(n)})][(B_{t_j^{(n)}} - B_{t_{j-1}^{(n)}})^2 - (t_j^{(n)} - t_{j-1}^{(n)})]\right).$$

$$\left[\left(\sum_{i=1}^{n} a_i\right)^2 = \sum_{i,j=1}^{n} a_i a_j\right]$$

If $i \neq j$ we deduce that

$$\mathbb{E}([(B_{t_i^{(n)}} - B_{t_{i-1}^{(n)}})^2 - (t_i^{(n)} - t_{i-1}^{(n)})][(B_{t_j^{(n)}} - B_{t_{j-1}^{(n)}})^2 - (t_j^{(n)} - t_{j-1}^{(n)})])$$

$$= \mathbb{E}((B_{t_i^{(n)}} - B_{t_{i-1}^{(n)}})^2 - (t_i^{(n)} - t_{i-1}^{(n)})) \cdot \mathbb{E}((B_{t_j^{(n)}} - B_{t_{j-1}^{(n)}})^2 - (t_j^{(n)} - t_{j-1}^{(n)})) = 0.$$

[Independence and Proposition 2.2.1]

If $i = j$ it follows from Proposition 2.2.2 that

$$\mathbb{E}([(B_{t_i^{(n)}} - B_{t_{i-1}^{(n)}})^2 - (t_i^{(n)} - t_{i-1}^{(n)})]^2) = 2(t_i^{(n)} - t_{i-1}^{(n)})^2.$$

Thus

$$\mathbb{E}\left(\left[\sum_{i=1}^{n}(B_{t_i^{(n)}} - B_{t_{i-1}^{(n)}})^2 - (t_i^{(n)} - t_{i-1}^{(n)})\right]^2\right) = 2\sum_{i=1}^{n}(t_i^{(n)} - t_{i-1}^{(n)})^2$$

$$\leq 2 \max_{i=1,\ldots,n} |t_i^{(n)} - t_{i-1}^{(n)}| \cdot \sum_{i=1}^{n} |t_i^{(n)} - t_{i-1}^{(n)}|$$

$$= 2\|P_n\| \cdot (t - s) \xrightarrow[n\to\infty]{} 0. \qquad \square$$

We finally note that the cubic variation vanishes for almost all paths of the Brownian Motion. The proof is similar to the proof of Theorem 2.2.5 and is therefore left to the reader.

Proposition 2.2.6 .   Let $P_n = (t_0^{(n)}, t_1^{(n)}, \ldots, t_n^{(n)})$ be a sequence of partition of the interval $[s, t]$ with $\lim_{n \to \infty} \|P_n\| = 0$. Then

$$\sum_{i=1}^{n} |B_{t_i^{(n)}} - B_{t_{i-1}^{(n)}}|^3 \to 0 \ in \ L_2.$$

2.3 Stochastic Integrals with Respect to the Brownian Motion

We have to deal with the following problem. Let (X_t) be an adapted process on the filtered space $(\Omega, \mathcal{F}, (\mathcal{F}_t), \mathbb{P})$ describing the price of a stock. An investor buys and sells during a certain time period $[s, t]$ shares of this stock. How do we compute the gains and losses of the investor?

First, we have to define what an investment strategy is. Throughout this section we are given a filtered probability space $(\Omega, \mathcal{F}, (\mathcal{F}_t), \mathbb{P})$, and as in the previous section we denote expected values with respect to $\mathbb{P}$ by $\mathbb{E}(\cdot)$.

Defintion. An *elementary process* is a process $(H_t)_{t \geq 0}$ of the following form.

There are times $t_0, t_1, \ldots, t_n$, with $0 < t_1 < \ldots < t_n = t$, and random variables $h_0, h_1, \ldots h_{n-1}$ so that h_i is $\mathcal{F}_{t_i}$-measurable and for $t \geq 0$

$$H_t = \sum_{i=0}^{n-1} h_i 1_{[t_i, t_{i+1})}(t),$$

i.e. for $\omega \in \Omega$ and $i \in \{0, 1, 2, \ldots n - 1\}$ chosen such that $t_i \leq u < t_{i+1}$, it follows that $H_u(\omega) = h_i(\omega)$.

The interpretation of this definition is obvious. At the times $t_0, t_1, \ldots, t_{n-1}$ the investor changes his or her portfolio and holds during the time period $[t_i, t_{i-1})$ h_i units of the stock. The condition that h_i has to be $\mathcal{F}_{t_i}$-measurable is forced by the fact that the decision on how many shares to hold at time t_i can only be based on the history prior to t_i.

Now, assuming that $H_u = \sum_{i=0}^{n-1} h_i 1_{[t_i, t_{i+1})}(u)$ is an elementary process, we want to compute the gain, respectively losses, this strategy generates during a time period $[s, t]$. The gains occuring during the time period $[0, t_1]$ are $h_0(X_{t_1} - X_{t_0})$, the gains during the time period $[t_1, t_2]$ are $h_1(X_{t_2} - X_{t_1})$, etc.

More generally, the gains occuring during a time period $[s, t]$ can be computed as follows.

1) If there is an $i \in \{0, 1, \ldots n-1\}$ so that $t_i \leq s < t \leq t_{i+1}$ the gains are

$$h_i(X_t - X_s).$$

2) If there are $i < j$ in $\{0, 1, \ldots n\}$ so that $t_i \leq s < t_{i+1} \leq t_j \leq t < t_{j+1}$ (let $t_{n+1} = \infty$) then the occuring gains during $[s, t]$ are:

$$h_i(X_{t_{i+1}} - X_s) + \sum_{\ell=i+1}^{j-1} h_\ell(X_{t_{\ell+1}} - X_{t_\ell}) + h_j(X_t - X_{t_j}).$$

These two formulae can be combined using the notation $p \vee q = \max\{p, q\}$ and $p \wedge q = \min\{p, q\}$ to the formula

$$\sum_{i=0}^{n-1} h_i(X_{(t_{i+1} \vee s) \wedge t} - X_{(t_i \vee s) \wedge t}).$$

This is exactly the formula which was introduced in Stochastic Calculus as the *stochastic integral of H with respect to X.*

Defintion. Let (X_t) be an adapted process on the filtered space $(\Omega, \mathcal{F}, (\mathcal{F}_t), \mathbb{P})$ and $H_{(\cdot)} = \sum_{i=0}^{n-1} h_i 1_{[t_i, t_{i+1})}(\cdot)$ be an elementary adapted process. Then we define for $s < t$ *the stochastic integral of H with respect to x over the interval $[s, t]$* to be

(2.13) $$\int_s^t H_u dX_u = \sum_{i=0}^{n-1} h_i(X_{(t_{i+1} \vee s) \wedge t} - X_{(t_i \vee s) \wedge t}).$$

We observe the following two properties of stochastic integrals.

Proposition 2.3.1 . *Let (X_t) be an adapted process on the filtered space $(\Omega, \mathcal{F}, (\mathcal{F}_t), \mathbb{P})$.*

1) *If $s < t$, $\alpha, \beta \in \mathbb{R}$, and H and G are two elementary adapted processes then*

$$\int_s^t \alpha H_u + \beta G_u dX_u = \alpha \int_s^t H_u dX_u + \beta \int_s^t G_u dX_u.$$

Moreover, this equality holds true for $\mathcal{F}_s$-measurable random variables α, β.

2) *If $s < r < t$ and H is an elementary adapted process then*

$$\int_s^t H_u dX_u = \int_s^r H_u dX_u + \int_r^t H_u dX_u.$$

The proof of 2.3.1 is simple and we leave it to the reader. The following observation says that the family $\int_0^t H_s dX_s$ is also a stochastic process.

Proposition 2.3.2 . *Let (X_t) be an adapted process on the filtered space $(\Omega, \mathcal{F}, (\mathcal{F}_t), \mathbb{P})$ and H_t be an elementary adapted process.*

Then $(\int_0^t H_s dX_s)_{t \geq 0}$ is an adapted process.

Proof. From Equation (2.13) it is clear that $\int_0^t H_s dX_s$ is $\mathcal{F}_t$-measurable. We are left to show that the mapping

$$[0, \infty) \times \Omega \ni (t, \omega) \mapsto \left(\int_0^t H_s dX_s \right)(\omega)$$

is $\mathcal{B}_{[0,\infty)} \otimes \mathcal{F}$-measurable.

To see this we first observe that we can assume that H is of the form $H_t = h 1_{[t_1, t_2)}$ with h being $\mathcal{F}_{t_1}$-measurable, since every elementary process is a finite sums of these even simpler processes. Secondly we note that in this case

$$\int_0^t H_s dX_s = \begin{cases} 0 & \text{if } t < t_1 \\ h(X_t - X_{t_1}) & \text{if } t_1 \leq t < t_2 \\ h(X_{t_2} - X_{t_1}) & \text{if } t_2 \leq t \end{cases}$$

$$= 1_{[t_1, t_2]}(t) h(X_t - X_{t_1}) + 1_{(t_2, \infty)}(t) h(X_{t_2} - X_{t_1}),$$

and note that the map $[0, \infty) \ni (t, \omega) \mapsto (\int_0^t H_s dX_s)(\omega)$ can be written as product of sums of $\mathcal{B}_{[0,\infty)} \otimes \mathcal{F}$-measurable maps. $\square$

For the rest of this section we will restrict our attention to stochastic integrals with respect to a Brownian Motion (B_t) and extend the notion $\int_s^t H_u dB_u$ to a more general class of adapted processes H. Rather than thinking of a stochastic process being a family of random variables defined $(\Omega, \mathcal{F}, \mathbb{P})$ indexed by t we will think of a process being a map defined on the set $[0, \infty) \times \Omega$.

For a subset A of $[0, \infty) \times \Omega$ and $t \geq 0$ we call

$$(2.14) \qquad\qquad A_t = \{\omega \in \Omega | (t, \omega) \in A\}$$

the *t-cut of A*.

Proposition 2.3.3 .   *Let $B_{[0,\infty)} \otimes \mathcal{F}$ be the product σ-algebra of $B_{[0,\infty)}$ and $\mathcal{F}$ as defined in Proposition B.2.1 and in the examples mentioned thereafter in Appendix B.2. The set of all $A \in B_{[0,\infty)} \otimes \mathcal{F}$ which have the property that for all $t \geq 0$ the t-cut of A is an element of $\mathcal{F}_t$ forms a sub-σ-algebra of $B_{[0,\infty)} \otimes \Omega$.*

We will call this σ-algebra the set of all progressively measurable sets on $(\Omega, \mathcal{F}, (\mathcal{F}_t), \mathbb{P})$ *and denote it by $\mathcal{P}$.*

Proof. We only need to note that for $A \subset [0, \infty) \times \Omega$ and $t \geq 0$ it follows that $([0, \infty) \times \Omega \setminus A)_t = \Omega \setminus A_t$ and that for a sequence (A^n) of subsets of $[0, \infty) \times \Omega$ it follows that $(\bigcup A^n)_t = \bigcup A_t^n$.   □

Proposition 2.3.4 .

1) *All elementary adapted processes on $(\Omega, \mathcal{F}, (\mathcal{F}_t), \mathbb{P})$ are progressively measurable.*

2) *All continuous adapted processes on $(\Omega, \mathcal{F}, (\mathcal{F}_t), \mathbb{P})$ are progressively measurable.*

Proof. To proof (1) we only need to consider a process H of the form $H_u = h1_{[s,t)}(u)$ with $0 \le s < t < \infty$ and h being $\mathcal{F}_s$-measurable. For a measurable set $B \subset \mathbb{R}$ and a $v \in [0, \infty)$ it follows now that

$$\{(u, \omega)|H_u(\omega) \in B\}_v = \begin{cases} \{\omega|h(\omega) \in B\} & \text{if } s \le v < t \\ \Omega & \text{if } v < s \text{ or } t \le v \text{ and } 0 \in B \\ \emptyset & \text{if } v < s \text{ or } t \le v \text{ and } 0 \notin B \end{cases}$$

which implies that $\{(u, \omega)|H_u(\omega) \in B\}_v \in \mathcal{F}_v$ in all cases.

To show (2) we approximate a continuous adapted process H by elementary ones. For $n \in \mathbb{N}$ define

$$H_u^{(n)} = \sum_{i=0}^{n2^n} H_{i2^{-n}} 1_{[i2^{-n}, (i+1)2^{-n})}(u).$$

It follows that for all $\omega \in \Omega$ and $u \ge 0$ $\lim_{n \to \infty} H_u^{(n)}(\omega) = H_u(\omega)$. Since the pointwise limit of measurable maps is still measurable the claim follows. $\square$

Remark. The reader might ask whether or not every adapted process is progressively measurable. this is in general not true, but under some technical conditions on the filtered space $(\Omega, \mathcal{F}, (\mathcal{F}_t), \mathbb{P})$ there is for every adapted process H a version $\tilde{H}$ (meaning that for all $t \ge 0$: $H_t = \tilde{H}_t$ almost surely) which is progressively measurable. But we do not want to elaborate on that question and note that 2.3.4 provides a big enough class of progressively measurable process.

We will fix a time $T > 0$ and consider only processes indexed over the time $[0, T]$.

Definition. We denote by $\mathcal{H}_2([0,T])$ the set of all progressively measurable processes $(H_t)_{0\le t\le T}$ on the filtered space $(\Omega, \mathcal{F}, (\mathcal{F}_t)_{0\le t\le T}, \mathbb{P})$ for which the paths are square integrable on $[0,T]$ almost surely, i.e. for almost all $\omega \in \Omega$

$$\int_0^T H_t(\omega)^2 dt < \infty,$$

and for which

$$\mathbb{E}\left(\int_0^T H_t^2 dt\right) < \infty.$$

For $H \in \mathcal{H}_2([0,T])$ we put

$$\|H\|_{H_2} = \mathbb{E}^{1/2}\left(\int_0^T H_t^2 dt\right).$$

The set of all elementary processes $H_t = \sum_{i=1}^{n-1} h_i 1_{[t_i,t_{i+1})}$, with $0 = t_i < t_1 < \ldots t_n = T$, which lie in $\mathcal{H}_2([0,T])$ are denoted by $\mathcal{H}_{2,e}([0,T])$.

Note that $H \in \mathcal{H}_{2,e}([0,T])$ if and only if the h_i's are square integrable.

Remark. Let $\lambda_{[0,T]}$ be the uniform distribution on the interval $[0,T]$. Consider the product probability $\mathbb{P} \otimes \lambda_{[0,T]}$ on the set $\Omega \otimes [0,T]$ furnished with the product σ-algebra $\mathcal{F} \otimes \mathcal{B}_{[0,T]}$ (see Proposition B.2.4 in Appendix B.2). For a measurable $f :\ \Omega \otimes [0,T] \to \mathbb{R}$ it follows that

$$\|f(\cdot,\cdot)\|_{L_2} = \mathbb{E}^{1/2}_{\lambda_{[0,T]}\otimes\mathbb{P}}(f^2(\omega,t))$$

$$= \mathbb{E}^{(1/2)}\left(\frac{1}{T}\int_0^T f^2(\omega,t)dt\right) = \frac{1}{\sqrt{T}}\mathbb{E}^{(1/2)}\left(\int_0^T f^2(\omega,t)dt\right).$$

Now we restrict the probablity $\lambda_{[0,T]} \otimes \mathbb{P}$ to the sub algebra of progressively measurable sets. Denote this restriction by $\lambda_{[0,T]} \otimes \mathbb{P}|_{\mathcal{P}}$.

Thus, we observe that $\mathcal{H}_2([0,T])$ is equal to the space $L_2(\mathbb{P} \otimes \lambda_{[0,T]}|_{\mathcal{P}})$, and $\|H\|_{\mathcal{H}_2} = \sqrt{T}\|H_{(\cdot)}(\cdot)\|_{L_2}$ $H \in \mathcal{H}_2([0,T])$. Therefore $\|\cdot\|_{\mathcal{H}_2}$ is a norm on $\mathcal{H}_2([0,T])$ (see Theorem B.4.5 Appendix B.4) and the notion of convergence in $\mathcal{H}_2([0,T])$ will refer to that norm.

We are now in the position to state our key observation.

Theorem 2.3.5 *(The basic Isometry).*

The map

$$\Phi : \mathcal{H}_{2,e}([0,T]) \mapsto L_2(\mathbb{P}), \quad H \mapsto \int_0^T H_t dB_t,$$

is welldefined, meaning that $\int_0^T H_t dB_t$ is an element of $L_2(\mathbb{P})$, the space of square integrable maps on $(\Omega, \mathcal{F}, \mathbb{P})$ and Φ is an isometry on $\mathcal{H}_{2,e}([0,T])$ into $L_2(\mathbb{P})$, meaning that

$$\| \int_0^T H_t dB_t \|_{L_2} = \mathbb{E}^{1/2}\left(\left(\int_0^T H_t dB_t \right)^2 \right) = \|H\|_{\mathcal{H}_2}, \quad \text{for all } H \in \mathcal{H}_{2,e}([0,T]).$$

Secondly, for $0 \le s < t \le T$ the map

$$\Phi_{[s,t]} : \mathcal{H}_{2,e}([0,T]) \mapsto L_2(\mathbb{P}), \quad H \mapsto \int_s^t H_u dB_u,$$

is a contraction, i.e.

$$\| \int_s^t H_u dB_u \|_{L_2} \le \|H\|_{\mathcal{H}_2}, \quad \text{for all } H \in \mathcal{H}_{2,e}([0,T]).$$

Proof. For $H_t = \sum_{i=1}^{n-1} h_i 1_{[t_i,t_{i+1})}$, with $0 = t_i < t_1 < \ldots t_n = T$ we note that

$$\mathbb{E}\left(\left(\int_0^T H_t dB_t \right)^2 \right) = \mathbb{E}\left(\left(\sum_{i=0}^{n-1} h_i(B_{t_{i+1}} - B_{t_i}) \right)^2 \right)$$

$$= \mathbb{E}\left(\sum_{i=0}^{n-1} h_i^2 (B_{t_{i+1}} - B_{t_i})^2 \right)$$

$$[\text{Since} \quad \mathbb{E}(h_i h_j (B_{t_{i+1}} - B_{t_i})(B_{t_{j+1}} - B_{t_j})) =$$

$$\mathbb{E}(h_i(B_{t_{i+1}} - B_{t_i})h_j \mathbb{E}((B_{t_{j+1}} - B_{t_j})|\mathcal{F}_{t_j})) = 0 \text{ if } i < j]$$

$$= \sum_{i=0}^{n-1} \mathbb{E}(h_i^2)(t_{i+1} - t_i)$$

$$= \mathbb{E}\left(\sum_{i=0}^{n-1} h_i^2(t_{i+1} - t_i) \right) = \mathbb{E}\left(\int_0^T H_t^2 dt \right),$$

which implies the claim. $\square$

Theorem 2.3.6 *(Density).*

The set $\mathcal{H}_{2,e}([0,T])$ is dense in $\mathcal{H}_2([0,T])$, i.e. for every $H \in \mathcal{H}_2([0,T])$ there is a sequence $H^{(n)} \subset \mathcal{H}_{2,e}([0,T])$ so that

$$\lim_{n \to \infty} \|H - H^{(n)}\|_{\mathcal{H}_2} = 0.$$

The proof of Theorem2.3.6 is somewhat technical and we will not present it. Secondly it will actually be enough to think of the space $\mathcal{H}_2([0,T])$ being the set of all progressively measurable processes H for which there is a sequence $(H^{(n)}$ in $\mathcal{H}_{2,e}([0,T])$ so that $\lim_{n \to \infty} \|H - H^{(n)}\|_{\mathcal{H}_2} = 0$. We will prove later (see Proposition 2.3.8) that all continuous, bounded and adapted processes are in that set.

Using Theorems 2.3.5 and 2.3.6 we are in the position to define $\int_s^t H_u dB_u$ for all $H \in \mathcal{H}_2([0,T])$.

Theorem 2.3.7 *(Stochastic integrals with repect to (B_t) in $\mathcal{H}_2([0,T])$).*
Given $0 \le s < t \le T$ the map

$$\Phi_{[s,t]} : \mathcal{H}_{2,e}([0,T]) \to L_2(\mathbb{P}), \quad H \mapsto \int_s^t H_u dB_u$$

can be extended in a unique way to a map, still denoted by $\Phi_{[s,t]}$,

$$\Phi_{[s,t]} : H \in \mathcal{H}_2([0,T]) \to L_2(\mathbb{P}),$$

so that $\Phi_{[s,t]}$ is still a contraction on $\mathcal{H}_2([0,T])$.
We denote

$$\int_s^t H_u dB_u = \Phi_{[s,t]}(H), \ \text{for } H \in \mathcal{H}_2([0,T]),$$

and call it also the stochastic integral of H with respect to (B_u) on $[s,t]$.
Moreover, this extension has the following properties,

1) *If $s < t$, H and G are in $\mathcal{H}_2([0,T])$, and α and β are $\mathcal{F}_s$-measurable random variables*
   so that $\alpha H_u 1_{[s,t]}(u)$ and $\beta G_u 1_{[s,t]}(u)$ are still in $\mathcal{H}_2([0,T])$, then

$$\int_s^t \alpha H_u + \beta G_u dB_u = \alpha \int_s^t H_u dB_u + \beta \int_s^t G_u dB_u.$$

2) *If $s < r < t$ and $H \in \mathcal{H}_2([0,T])$ then*

$$\int_s^t H_u dB_u = \int_s^r H_u dB_u + \int_r^t H_u dB_u.$$

3 *For $H \in \mathcal{H}_2([0,T])$ the process*

$$\left(\int_0^t H_u dB_u \right)_{t \in [0,T]}$$

   is a martingale.

Proof. Let $H \in \mathcal{H}_2([0,T])$. By Theorem 2.3.6 we can choose a sequence $H^{(n)} \subset \mathcal{H}_{2,e}([0,T])$

with $\lim_{n\to\infty} \|H - H^{(n)}\|_{\mathcal{H}_2} = 0$. By Theorem 2.3.5 this implies that the sequence $\int_s^t H_u^{(n)} dB_u$ is a Cauchy sequence in $L_2(\mathbb{P})$, and thus by completness of the space $L_2(\mathbb{P})$ convergent to some element $y \in L_2(\mathbb{P})$ (see Appendix B.4). We first note that y does not depend on the choice of the sequence $H^{(n)} \subset \mathcal{H}_{2,e}([0,T])$ as long as it converges to H with respect to $\|\cdot\|_{\mathcal{H}_2}$. Indeed, if $\widetilde{H}^{(n)} \subset \mathcal{H}_{2,e}([0,T])$, with $\lim_{n\to\infty} \|H - \widetilde{H}^{(n)}\|_{\mathcal{H}_2} = 0$, then it follows that $\lim_{n\to\infty} \|H^{(n)} - \widetilde{H}^{(n)}\|_{\mathcal{H}_2} = 0$. Thus it follows from Theorem 2.3.5 that

$$\lim_{n\to\infty} \|\Phi_{[s,t]}(H^{(n)}) - \Phi_{[s,t]}(\widetilde{H}^{(n)})\|_{L_2} = 0$$

which implies that $\lim_{n\to\infty} \|y - \Phi_{[s,t]}(\widetilde{H}^{(n)})\|_{L_2} = 0$.

Letting for $H \in \mathcal{H}_2([0,T])$,

$$\Phi_{[s,t]}(H) = L_2 - \lim_{n\to\infty} \Phi_{[s,t]}(H^{(n)}),$$

we now deduce that $\Phi_{[s,t]}$ is a welldefined map on $\mathcal{H}_2([0,T])$ into $L_2(\mathbb{P})$.

In order to show that $\Phi_{[s,t]}$ is a contraction as well as to show the claims (1) and (2) we let $H, G \in \mathcal{H}_2([0,T])$, and choose $(H^{(n)}), (G^{(n)}) \subset \mathcal{H}_{2,e}([0,T])$ converging to H and G respectively. We note that

$$\begin{aligned}
\|\Phi_{[s,t]}(H) - \Phi_{[s,t]}(G)\| &= \lim_{n\to\infty} \|\Phi_{[s,t]}(H^{(n)}) - \Phi_{[s,t]}(G^{(n)})\|_{L_2} \\
&\le \lim_{n\to\infty} \|H^{(n)} - G^{(n)}\|_{\mathcal{H}_2} \qquad \text{[by Theorem 2.3.5 (2)]} \\
&= \|H - G\|_{\mathcal{H}_2},
\end{aligned}$$

which shows that $\Phi_{[s,t]}$ is a contraction. Secondly, applying Proposition 2.2.1 (1), we get for two $\mathcal{F}_s$-measurable maps α, β satisfying the requirements of the statement of the Theorem

$$\begin{aligned}
\Phi_{[s,t]}(\alpha H + \beta G) &= L_2 - \lim_{n\to\infty} \Phi_{[s,t]}(\alpha H^{(n)} + \beta G^{(n)}) \\
&= L_2 - \lim_{n\to\infty} \alpha\Phi_{[s,t]}(H^{(n)}) + \beta\Phi_{[s,t]}(G^{(n)}) = \alpha\Phi_{[s,t]}(H) + \beta\Phi_{[s,t]}(G),
\end{aligned}$$

which implies (1). For $s < r < t$ we deduce from Proposition 2.2.1 (2) that

$$\Phi_{[s,t]}(H) = L_2 - \lim_{n\to\infty} \Phi_{[s,t]}(H^{(n)}) = L_2 - \lim_{n\to\infty} \Phi_{[s,r]}(H^{(n)}) + \lim_{n\to\infty} \Phi_{[r,t]}(H^{(n)}) = \Phi_{[s,r]}(H) + \Phi_{[r,t]}(H),$$

which implies (2).

In order to proof that $\Phi_{[s,t]}$ is unique we assume that $\widetilde{\Phi}_{[s,t]}$ is also a contractive extension and deduce that for $H \in \mathcal{H}_2([0,T])$ and $(H^{(n)}) \subset \mathcal{H}_{2,e}([0,T])$ converging to H that

$$\Phi_{[s,t]}(H) = L_2 - \lim_{n\to\infty} \Phi_{[s,t]}(H^{(n)}) = L_2 - \lim_{n\to\infty} \widetilde{\Phi}_{[s,t]}(H^{(n)}) = \widetilde{\Phi}_{[s,t]}(H).$$

Finally we show that $(\int_0^t H_u dB_u)_{0 \le t \le T}$ is martingale. If $H \in \mathcal{H}_{2,e}([0,T])$ this can be easily seen (see Exercise....). In the general case we choose $H^{(n)} \subset \mathcal{H}_{2,e}([0,T])$ converging to H and deduce from Proposition B.4.8 in Appendix B.4 for $0 \le s \le t \le T$ that that

$$\mathbb{E}(\Phi_{[0,t]}(H|\mathcal{F}_s) = L_2 - \lim_{n\to\infty} \mathbb{E}(\Phi_{[0,t]}(H^{(n)}|\mathcal{F}_s) = L_2 - \lim_{n\to\infty} (\Phi_{[0,s]}(H^{(n)}) = \gtrless_{[0,s]}(H),$$

which proves (3) and finishes the proof of the Theorem. $\qquad\square$

To get a better feeling for stochastic integrals we want to write the stochastic integral of a continuous and bounded process with respect the Brownian Motion in a more concrete way.

Proposition 2.3.8 . *Let $(H_t)_{t\in[0,T]}$ be a continuous and adapted stochastic process on $(\Omega, \mathcal{F}, (\mathcal{F}_s)_{0 \le s \le T}, \mathbb{P})$. Also assume that $\sup_{t\in[0,T]} |H_t| \le c < \infty$ almost surely. For $n \in \mathbb{N}$ let $P^{(n)} = (t_0^{(n)}, t_1^{(n)}, \ldots, t_1^{(n)})$ be a partition of $[0,T]$, with $\|P^{(n)}\| \to 0$, for $n \to \infty$, and define $H^{(n)}$ by*

$$H_u^{(n)} = \sum_{i=0}^{n-1} H_{t_i} 1_{[t_i^{(n)}, t_{i+1}^{(n)})}(u).$$

Then $H^{(n)}$ converges in $\mathcal{H}_2([0,T])$ to H and, consequently it follows from Theorem 2.3.7 that

$$\int_s^t H_u dB_u = L_2 - \lim_{n\to\infty} \int_s^t H_u^{(n)} dB_u = L_2 - \lim_{n\to\infty} \sum_{i=0}^{n-1} H_{t_i} (B_{(t_{i+1}^{(n)} \vee s)\wedge t} - B_{(t_i^{(n)} \vee s)\wedge t}).$$

Proof. For fixed $\omega \in \Omega$ we deduce from the defintion of Riemann integrals that

$$\lim_{n\to\infty} \int_0^T (H_u(\omega) - H_u^{(n)}(\omega))^2 dt = 0.$$

Thus the sequence of random variables $(\int_0^T (H_u - H_u^{(n)})^2 dt)$ is almost sureley converging to zero. Since $\int_0^T (H_u - H_u^{(n)})^2 dt \leq Tc^2$ the Majorized Convergence Theorem B.2.11 applies and we deduce the claim. $\qquad\square$

We will need one more extension of the stochastic integral.

Defintion. $\mathcal{H}_2^w([0,T])$ is the space of all progressively measurable processes $(H_t)_{t\in[0,T]}$ for which.

$$\mathbb{P}\left(\left\{\omega \in \Omega : \int_0^T H_u^2(\omega)dt < \infty\right\}\right) = 1.$$

Convergence in $\mathcal{H}_2^w([0,T])$ will be defined as follows. A sequence $H^{(n)} \subset \mathcal{H}_2^w([0,T])$ is said to converge to $H \in \mathcal{H}_2^w([0,T])$ if the sequence $\int_0^T (H_t - H_t^{(n)})^2 dt$ converges in probability to 0.

Remark. Note that $\mathcal{H}_2^w([0,T])$ contains all continuous processes.

The following Lemma plays a key role for extending the stochastic integral to processes in $\mathcal{H}_2^w([0,T])$.

Lemma 2.3.9 . *Let $(H_t)_{t\in[0,T]}$ be a process in $\mathcal{H}_2([0,T])$, $0 \leq s < t \leq T$, and $\varepsilon, \delta > 0$.*
Then

$$\mathbb{P}\left(\left\{\left|\int_0^T H_u dB_u\right| \geq \varepsilon\right\}\right) \leq \mathbb{P}\left(\left\{\left|\int_0^T H_u^2 dt\right| \geq \delta\right\}\right) + \frac{\delta}{\varepsilon^2}$$

Proof. First assume that $H \in \mathcal{H}_{2,e}([0,T])$.

Define $\widetilde{H}$ by

$$\widetilde{H}_u(\omega) = \begin{cases} H_u(\omega) & \text{if } u \geq s \text{ and } \int_s^u H_v^2(\omega)d\tilde{v} \leq \delta \\ 0 & \text{otherwise} \end{cases}$$

Note that $\int_s^t \widetilde{H}_u^2 du \leq \delta$. For $\omega \in \Omega$ it follows that either $H_u(\omega) = \widetilde{H}_u(\omega)$ for all $u \in [s,t]$ or that $\int_s^t H_u^2 du \geq \delta$. In the first case it follows from the definition of stochastic integrals for elementary processes that $\int_s^t H_u(\omega)du = \int_s^t \widetilde{H}_u(\omega)du$.

We therefore conclude that

$$\mathbb{P}\left(\left\{\left|\int_0^T H_u dB_u\right| \geq \varepsilon\right\}\right)$$

$$\leq \mathbb{P}\left(\left\{\left|\int_0^T \tilde{H}_u dB_u\right| \geq \varepsilon\right\}\right) + \mathbb{P}\left(\left\{\left|\int_0^T H_u^2 du\right| \geq \delta\right\}\right)$$

$$\frac{1}{\varepsilon^2}\mathbb{E}\left(\left(\int_0^T \tilde{H}_u dB_u\right)^2\right) + \mathbb{P}\left(\left\{\left|\int_0^T H_u^2 du\right| \geq \delta\right\}\right)$$

[Inequality of Tschebyscheff (see Proposition B.4.1 in Appendix B.4)]

$$= \frac{1}{\varepsilon^2}\mathbb{E}\left(\int_0^T \tilde{H}_u^2 du\right) + \mathbb{P}\left(\left\{\left|\int_0^T H_u^2 du\right| \geq \delta\right\}\right)$$

[By Theorem 2.3.5]

$$\leq \frac{\delta}{\varepsilon^2} + \mathbb{P}\left(\left\{\left|\int_0^T H_u^2 du\right| \geq \delta\right\}\right)$$

This proves the claim for elementary processes. In order to generalize it to an arbitrary $H \in \mathcal{H}_2([0,T])$ we first choose a sequence $H^{(n)} \subset \mathcal{H}_{2,e}([0,T])$ converging to H with respect to $\|\cdot\|_{\mathcal{H}_2}$ and note that then

$$\lim_{n\to\infty} \mathbb{P}\left(\left\{\left|\int_0^T H_u^{(n)} dB_u\right| \geq \varepsilon\right\}\right) = \mathbb{P}\left(\left\{\left|\int_0^T H_u dB_u\right| \geq \varepsilon\right\}\right), \text{ and}$$

$$\lim_{n\to\infty} \mathbb{P}\left(\left\{\left|\int_0^T (H_u^{(n)})^2 du\right| \geq \delta\right\}\right) = \mathbb{P}\left(\left\{\left|\int_0^T H_u^2 du\right| \geq \delta\right\}\right). \qquad \square$$

Corollary 2.3.10 . *Assume that $H^{(n)} \subset \mathcal{H}_2([0,T])$ is a Cauchy sequence with respect to the convergence defined in $\mathcal{H}_2^w([0,T])$, i.e. for all $\varepsilon > 0$ there is an $n \in \mathbb{N}$ so that for all $k, m \geq n$*

$$\mathbb{P}\left(\left\{\int_0^T (H_u^{(k)} - H_u^{(m)})^2 du > \varepsilon\right\}\right) < \varepsilon.$$

Then for all $0 \leq s < t \leq T$ the sequence $\int_s^t H_u^{(n)} dB_u$ with respect of convergence in probability in the space $L_0(\mathbb{P})$, the space of all measurable functions on Ω.

Proof. Assume that $H^{(n)}$ is a Cauchy sequence in $\mathcal{H}_2([0,T])$ with respect to the convergence defined in $H \in \mathcal{H}_2^w([0,T])$. Fix $\varepsilon > 0$ and choose $\delta = \varepsilon^3/2$. We can find $n \in \mathbb{N}$ so that for all $m, k \geq n$

$$\mathbb{P}\left(\left\{\int_s^t (H_u(k) - H_u^{(m)})^2 du > \delta\right\}\right) < \varepsilon/2,$$

and deduce from Lemma 2.3.9 that

$$\mathbb{P}\left(\left\{\int_s^t (H_u^{(k)} - H_u^{(m)}) dB_u > \varepsilon\right\}\right) \leq \mathbb{P}\left(\left\{\int_s^t (H_u^{(k)} - H_u^{(m)})^2 du > \delta\right\}\right) + \frac{\delta}{\varepsilon^2} = \varepsilon.$$

This shows that $\int_s^t H_u^{(n)} dB_u$ is a Cauchy sequence with respect to the convergence in probability. Since $L_0(\mathbb{P})$ is complete with respect to convergence in probability (see Proposition B.4.3 in Appendix B.4) the claim follows.   □

Now we are in the position to extend stochastic integration to the space $\mathcal{H}_2^w([0, T])$ using similar arguments as in the proof of Theorem 2.3.7.

Theorem 2.3.11 *(Stochastic integrals with respect to (B_t) on $\mathcal{H}_2^w([0,T])$). Given $0 \leq s < t \leq T$ the map*

$$\Phi_{[s,t]} : \mathcal{H}_2([0,T]) \to L_2(\mathbb{P}), \quad H \mapsto \int_s^t H_u dB_u$$

can be extended in a unique way to a map, still denoted by $\Phi_{[s,t]}$,

$$\Phi_{[s,t]} : H \in \mathcal{H}_2^w([0,T]) \to L_0(\mathbb{P}),$$

so that $\Phi_{[s,t]}$ is continuous with respect to the convergence defined on $\mathcal{H}_2^w([0,T])$ and the convergence in probability on $L_0(\mathbb{P})$ Here $L_0(\mathbb{P})$ denotes the measurable maps defined on $(\Omega, mathcalF)$ with convergence in probabilty.

We denote

$$\int_s^t H_u dBu = \Phi_{[s,t]}(H), \; for \; H \in \mathcal{H}_2^w([0,T]),$$

and call it also the stochastic integral of H with respect to (B_u) on $[s,t]$.

Moreover this extension has the following properties,

1) If $s < t$, α, β are $\mathcal{F}_s$-measurable, and H and G are in $\mathcal{H}_2^w([0,T])$ then

$$\int_s^t \alpha H_u + \beta G_u dB_u = \alpha \int_s^t H_u dB_u + \beta \int_s^t G_u dB_u.$$

2) If $s < r < t$ and $H \in \mathcal{H}_2^w([0,T])$ then

$$\int_s^t H_u dB_u = \int_s^r H_u dB_u + \int_r^t H_u dB_u.$$

Proof. We first show that $\mathcal{H}_2([0,T])$ is dense in $\mathcal{H}_2^w([0,T])$ with respect to the convergence defined in $\mathcal{H}_2^w([0,T])$. For $H \in \mathcal{H}_2^w([0,T])$ define $H^n = \max(n, H) \; (\in \mathcal{H}_2([0,T]))$. Then for fixed $\omega \in \Omega$ and $u \in [0,T]$ $H_u^{(n)}(\omega)$ converges to $H_u(\omega)$. Keeping ω still fixed we deduce from the Majorized Convergence theorem applied to the uniform distribution on $[0,T]$ that $\int_s^t (H_u(\omega) - H_u^{(n)}(\omega))^2 du$ converges to 0. Thus $\int_s^t (H_u - H_u^{(n)})^2 du$ converges in probability to

0.

If $H \in \mathcal{H}_2^w([0,T])$ we can find a sequence $H^{(n)}$ in $\mathcal{H}_2([0,T])$ which converges to H, in particular it is a Cauchy sequence with respect to the convergence defined in $H_2^w([0,T])$. For $s < t$ it follows now from Corollary 2.3.10 that $\int_s^t H_u^{(n)} dB_u$ converges in probability to some element y in $L_0(\mathbb{P})$.

From now on the proof is similar to the proof of Theorem 2.3.7, and we will therefore only sketch the remaining part. The norm $\| \cdot \|_{L_2}$ used in the proof of Theorem 2.3.7 has to be replaced by the metric $d(f,g) = \mathbb{E}(\min\{(|f - g|, 1\})$ which characterizes convergence in probability in the space $L_0(\mathbb{P})$.

We first will have to note that above limit y does not depend on the chosen approximating sequence $H^{(n)}$ and therefore we can put $\int_s^t H dB_u = y$.

The continuity of $\Phi_{[s,t]}$ on $H_2^w([0,T])$ follows from the continuity of $\Phi_{[s,t]}$ on $H_2([0,T])$ as shown in Corollary 2.3.10, and claim (1) and (2) follow as in the proof of Theorem 2.3.7. $\square$

2.4 Stochastic Calculus, the Ito Formula

In this section we want to develop some basic principles of "Stochastic Calculus". More precisely we want to formulate a version of the Fundamental Theorem of Calculus for stochastic processes.

Let us first recall the Fundamental Theorem of Calculus and its proof.

Theorem 2.4.1 *(The Fundamental Theorem of Calculus).*
Assume $f \colon [0, T] \to \mathbb{R}$ is continuously differentiable.
Then $f(T) - f(0) = \displaystyle\int_0^T f'(t)dt$.

Proof. Let $P = \{t_0, t_1, \ldots, t_n\}$ be a partition of $[0, T]$, $(0 = t_0 < t_1, \ldots, t_n = T)$. Then

$$f(T) - f(0) = \sum_{i=1}^n f(t_i) - f(t_{i-1})$$

$$= \sum_{i=1}^n \Delta t_i \frac{f(t_i) - f(t_{i-1})}{\Delta t_i}$$

$$[\Delta t_i = t_i - t_{i-1}]$$

$$= \sum_{i=1}^n \Delta t_i f'(t_i^*)$$

[with $t_i^* \in [t_{i-1}, t_i]$ chosen by the Mean Value Theorem].

From the definition of Riemann integrals we deduce on the other hand that

$$\int_0^T g(t)dt = \lim_{\|P\| \to 0} \sum_{i=1}^n \Delta t_i g(t_i^*) \quad \text{[with } t_i^* \in [t_{i-1}, t_i] \text{ arbitrary]}.$$

Thus, we get

$$f(T) - f(0) = \lim_{\|P\| \to 0} \sum_{i=1}^n \Delta t_i f'(t_i^*) = \int_0^T f'(t)dt. \qquad \square$$

We are given now a function $g\colon \mathbb{R} \to \mathbb{R}$, and a Brownian motion on $(\Omega, \mathcal{F}, (\mathcal{F}_s)_{0 \leq s < \infty}, \mathbb{P})$ and want to write

$$g(B_T) - g(B_0)$$

as a stochastic integral. But in this case we encounter some differences to the deterministic case.

Note that $g(B_t)$ is a random variable on Ω i.e. $g(B_t)\colon \Omega \ni \omega \longmapsto g(B_t(\omega))$. Assuming g being twice differentiable and bounded we obtain for a partition $P = \{t_0, t_1, \dots, t_n\}$ of $[0, T]$ from Taylor's expansion that

$$g(B_T) - g(0) = \sum_{i=1}^{n} g(B_{t_i}) - g(B_{t_{i-1}})$$

$$= \sum_{i=1}^{n} g'(B_{t_{i-1}})(B_{t_i} - B_{t_{i-1}}) + \sum_{i=1}^{n} \frac{1}{2} g''(\xi_i)(B_{t_i} - B_{t_{i-1}})^2,$$

with ξ_i being an appropriately chosen random variable assuming its values between $B_{t_{i-1}}$ and B_{t_i}. If we let $\|P\| \to 0$ then $\sum_{i=1}^{n} g'(B_{t_{i-1}})(B_{t_i} - B_{t_{i-1}})$ converges by Proposition 2.3.8 in L_2 to

$$\int_0^T g'(B_t)dB_t.$$

The problem is now the following: contrary to the deterministic case $\left(\text{i.e. } \sum_{i=1}^{n}(t_i - t_{i-1})^2 g''(t_i^*)\right)$

$$\sum_{i=1}^{n}(B_{t_i} - B_{t_{i-1}})^2 g''(B_{t_i})$$

does in general not converge in L_2 to zero. Indeed, by Theorem 2.2.5 it follows that

$$\sum_{i=1}^{n}(B_{t_i} - B_{t_{i-1}})^2 \longrightarrow T \quad \text{in} \quad L_2.$$

Thus, we will have supplementary terms in the stochastic version of the Fundamental Theorem of Calculus.

In order to simplify as much as possible the following analysis, let us assume for the moment that $g\colon \mathbb{R} \to \mathbb{R}$ is three times continuously differentiable and has a bounded first, second and third derivative, say

$$\sup_{x \in \mathbb{R}} \max\{|g'(x)|, |g''(x)|, |g'''(x)|\} = c < \infty.$$

This will make the derivations easier and more transparent. Later we will state more general results.

Using Taylor's expansion up to the third term we can write

$$(2.15) \qquad g(B_T) - g(0) = \sum_{i=1}^{n} g(B_{t_i}) - g(B_{t_{i-1}})$$

$$= \sum_{i=1}^{n} g'(B_{t_{i-1}})[B_{t_i} - B_{t_{i-1}}] \qquad \text{(I)}$$

$$+ \frac{1}{2} \sum_{i=1}^{n} g''(B_{t_{i-1}})[B_{t_i} - B_{t_{i-1}}]^2 \qquad \text{(II)}$$

$$+ \frac{1}{6} \sum_{i=1}^{n} g'''(\xi_i)(B_{t_i} - B_{t_{i-1}})^3 \qquad \text{(III)}$$

where $P = \{t_0, t_1, \ldots, t_n\}$ is a partition of $[0, T]$ and the ξ_i's are appropriately chosen random variables between $B_{t_{i-1}}$ and B_{t_i}.

We consider a sequence of partitions of $[0, T]$ $(P^{(n)})_{n \in \mathbb{N}}$, $P^{(n)} = (t_0^{(n)}, t_1^{(n)}, \ldots t_n^{(n)})$, with $\|P^{(n)}\| \to 0$, and analyse what happens to the terms I, II, and III if n tends to ∞.

First we note that by Proposition 2.2.6 in Section 2.2 it follows that

$$(2.16) \qquad \mathbb{E}\left(\left(\sum_{i=1}^{n} |g''(\xi_i)||B_{t_i^{(n)}} - B_{t_{i-1}^{(n)}}|^3\right)^2\right) \le c^2 \mathbb{E}\left(\left(\sum_{i=1}^{n} |B_{t_i^{(n)}} - B_{t_{i-1}^{(n)}}|^3\right)^2\right) \to 0, \text{ if } n \to \infty.$$

This means that the third term (III) in (2.15) vanishes.

Secondly, it follows from Proposition 2.3.8 of Section 2.3 that

$$(2.17) \qquad L_2 - \lim_{n \to \infty} \sum_{i=1}^{n} g'(B_{t_{i-1}^{(n)}})[B_{t_i^{(n)}} - B_{t_{i-1}^{(n)}}] = \int_0^T g'(B_t)dB_t,$$

The following Lemma will handle the term (II) in (2.15). It can be seen as a generalization of Theorem 2.2.5 in Section 2.2.

Lemma 2.4.2 .   Let $f : \mathbb{R} \to \mathbb{R}$ be continuous and bounded.

Then

$$L_2 - \lim_{n \to \infty} \sum_{i=0}^{n-1} f(B_{t_i^{(n)}})(B_{t_{i+1}^{(n)}} - B_{t_i^{(n)}})^2 = \int_0^T f(B_t)dt.$$

Note that the left side of the equation has to be understood pointwise in the Riemann sense: for $\omega \in \Omega$ $\left(\int_0^T f(B_t)dt\right)(\omega)$ is the integral of the continuous function $[0, T] \ni t \mapsto f(B_t(\omega))$.

Proof of Lemma 2.4.2. Assume $|f(x)| \le c$, whenever $x \in \mathbb{R}$, for some $c > 0$. For $\in \mathbb{N}$ define the following two random variables.

$$Y^{(n)} = \sum_{i=0}^{n-1} f(B_{t_i^{(n)}})(B_{t_{i+1}^{(n)}} - B_{t_i^{(n)}})^2 \text{ and}$$

$$Z^{(n)} = \sum_{i=0}^{n-1} f(B_{t_i^{(n)}})(t_{i+1}^{(n)} - t_i^{(n)})$$

Since for $i < j$ we deduce that

$$\mathbb{E}\Big(f(B_{t_i^{(n)}})\big[(B_{t_{i+1}^{(n)}} - B_{t_i^{(n)}})^2 - (t_{i+1}^{(n)} - t_i^{(n)})\big]f(B_{t_j^{(n)}})\big[(B_{t_{j+1}^{(n)}} - B_{t_j^{(n)}})^2 - (t_{j+1}^{(n)} - t_j^{(n)})\big]\Big)$$

$$= \mathbb{E}\Big(f(B_{t_i^{(n)}})\big[(B_{t_{i+1}^{(n)}} - B_{t_i^{(n)}})^2 - (t_{i+1}^{(n)} - t_i^{(n)})\big]f(B_{t_j^{(n)}})\mathbb{E}\Big(\big[(B_{t_{j+1}^{(n)}} - B_{t_j^{(n)}})^2 - (t_{j+1}^{(n)} - t_j^{(n)})\big]\Big|\mathcal{F}_{t_j^{(n)}}\Big)\Big) = 0,$$

it follows that

$$\mathbb{E}\Big((Y^{(n)} - Z^{(n)})^2\Big) = \mathbb{E}\Big(\big(\sum_{i=0}^{n-1} f(B_{t_i^{(n)}})[(B_{t_{i+1}^{(n)}} - B_{t_i^{(n)}})^2 - (t_{i+1}^{(n)} - t_i^{(n)})]\big)^2\Big)$$

$$= \mathbb{E}\Big(\sum_{i=0}^{n-1} f^2(B_{t_i^{(n)}})[(B_{t_{i+1}^{(n)}} - B_{t_i^{(n)}})^2 - (t_{i+1}^{(n)} - t_i^{(n)})]^2\Big)$$

$$\le c^2\mathbb{E}\Big(\sum_{i=0}^{n-1}[(B_{t_{i+1}^{(n)}} - B_{t_i^{(n)}})^2 - (t_{i+1}^{(n)} - t_i^{(n)})]^2\Big)$$

$$\to 0, \text{ as shown in the proof of Theorem 2.2.5.}$$

Secondly, we note that by the definition of Riemann integrals, it follows that for each $\omega \in \Omega$ $Z^{(n)}(\omega)$ converges to $\int_0^T f(B_t(\omega))dt$. Since $|Z^{(n)}(\omega)| \le cT$ for all $\omega \in \Omega$ we deduce from the Theorem of Majorized Convergence that $Z^{(n)}$ converges in L_2 to $\int_0^T f(B_t(\omega))dt$.

Thus by the triangle inequality

$$\|Y^{(n)} - \int_0^T f(B_t)dt\|_{L_2} \le \|Y^{(n)} - Z^{(n)}\|_{L_2} + \|Z^{(n)} - \int_0^T f(B_t)dt\|_{L_2} \to 0, \text{ for } n \to \infty. \qquad \square$$

Using now the equations (2.16) and (2.17) as well as the result of Lemma 2.4.2 we deduce from equation (2.16) that

$$g(B_T) - g(0) = \int_0^T g'(B_s)dB_s + \frac{1}{2}\int_0^T g''(B_s)ds$$

for functions $g \colon \mathbb{R} \to \mathbb{R}$ being 3 times continuously differentiable with bounded third and second derivatives.

Using now the more general stochastic integral as defined in Theorem 2.3.11 for elements of $\mathcal{H}_2^w([0,T])$ we deduce with a little more work but essentially the same ideas the following formula.

Theorem 2.4.3 *(Special Ito-formula).*
Assume $g(\cdot, \cdot) : [0, \infty) \times \mathbb{R} \to \mathbb{R}$ *is* $(t, x) \mapsto g(t, x)$ *is once continuously differentiable in* t *and twice continuously differentiable in* x *then*

$$g(t, B_t) - g(0, B_0) = \int_0^t \frac{\partial g}{\partial s}(s, B_s)ds + \int_0^t \frac{\partial g}{\partial x}(s, B_s)dB_s + \frac{1}{2}\int_0^t \frac{\partial^2 g}{\partial x^2}(s, B_s)ds$$

Remark. Ito's formula allows us to find $\int_0^t g(B_s)dB_s$ as follows.

Assume g is continuously differentiable, and let G be an antiderivative of g. Then the formula of Ito implies that

$$G(B_t) - G(0) = \int_0^t g(B_s)dB_s + \frac{1}{2}\int_0^t g'(B_s)ds.$$

Thus

$$\int_0^t g(B_s)dB_s = G(B_t) - G(0) - \frac{1}{2}\int_0^t g'(B_s)ds.$$

We now want to generalize the notion of stochastic integrals. Instead of integrating with respect to only the Brownian Motion we introduce integration with respect to "diffusion processes", a class of processes we will use to model stock prices.

Definition. Let (X_t), and (Y_t) be two processes so that their restriction to $[0,T]$ is in $\mathcal{H}_2^w([0,T])$ for any $T \geq 0$. Recall that this means that they are progressively measurable and

$$\mathbb{P}\left(\left\{\int_0^T X_u^2 du < \infty\right\}\right) = \mathbb{P}\left(\left\{\int_0^T Y_u^2 du < \infty\right\}\right) = 1.$$

Let Z_0 be $\mathcal{F}_0$-measurable.

The process Z_t with

(2.18) $$Z_t = Z_0 + \int_0^t X_u du + \int_0^t Y_u dB_u.$$

is called a *diffusion process*.

We also write instead of (2.18)

(2.19) $$dZ_t = X_t dt + Y_t dB_t.$$

Remark. Formally the definition of Equation (2.19) is given by Equation (2.18). Nevertheless (2.19) has a more intuitive interpretation: Changes of Z_t over small time periods consist on the one hand of the deterministic "drift term" $X_t dt$ and on the other hand of the random "diffusion term" $Y_t dB_t$.

As already mentioned, diffusion processes will be our model for stock prices. Therefore we will have to define stochastic integration with respect to these processes.

Definition. A progressively measurable process (H_t) is called weakly square integrable with respect to a diffusion process (Z_t), were Z_t is given by

$$Z_t = Z_0 + \int_0^t X_u du + \int_0^t Y_u dB_u$$

if for all $T > 0$ it follows that

$$\mathbb{P}\left(\left\{\int_0^T (H_u X_u)^2 du < \infty\right\}\right) = \mathbb{P}\left(\left\{\int_0^T (H_u Y_u)^2 du < \infty\right\}\right) = 1.$$

Note that this means that for all $T > 0$ the processes $(H_u X_u)$ and $(H_u Y_u)$ are elements of $\mathcal{H}_2^w(0, T])$.

Therefore we can define the *stochastic integral of* (H_u) *with respect to* (Z_u) *on the interval* $[s, t]$ by

(2.20)
$$\int_s^t H_u dZ_u = \int_s^t H_u X_u du + \int_s^t H_u Y_u dB_u$$

Theorem 2.3.11 of Section 2.3 can be easily extended.

Proposition 2.4.4 . *Given a diffusion process* $dZ_t = X_t dt + Y_t dB_t$,

1) *If* $s < t$, α, β *are* $\mathcal{F}_s$-*measurable, and* H *and* G *are weakly square integrable with respect to* Z_t *then*

$$\int_s^t \alpha H_u + \beta G_u dZ_u = \alpha \int_s^t H_u dZ_u + \beta \int_s^t G_u dZ_u.$$

2) *If* $s < r < t$ *and* H *is square integrable with respect to* Z_t *then*

$$\int_s^t H_u dZ_u = \int_s^r H_u dZ_u + \int_r^t H_u dZ_u.$$

Remark. On one hand we defined in Equation (2.13) of Section 2.3 the stochastic integral of an elemantary adapted process with respect to a general adapted process. We have to verify that in the case of H being an elemntary process and Z being a diffusion process the definition in (2.13) coincides with the definition given in Equation (2.20). Secondly, the definition of Equation (2.13) was derived from our intuition on how gains and losses should be defined for a strategy H and we have to make sure that Equation (2.20) still coincides with that intuition.

Thus let $H_u = \sum_{i=0}^{n-1} h_i 1_{[t_i, t_{i+1})}$ be an elementary adapted process being square integrable with respect to Z. We observe that

$$\int_s^t H_u dZ_t = \int_s^t H_u X_u du + \int_s^t H_u Y_u dB_u$$

[in the sense of Equation (2.20)]

$$= \sum_{i=0}^{n-1} \int_{(t_i \vee s) \wedge t}^{(t_{i+1} \vee s) \wedge t} h_i X_u du + \int_{(t_i \vee s) \wedge t}^{(t_{i+1} \vee s) \wedge t} h_i Y_u dB_u$$

$$= \sum_{i=0}^{n-1} h_i \int_{(t_i \vee s) \wedge t}^{(t_{i+1} \vee s) \wedge t} X_u du + h_i \int_{(t_i \vee s) \wedge t}^{(t_{i+1} \vee s) \wedge t} Y_u dB_u$$

$$= \sum_{i=0}^{n-1} h_i (Z_{(t_{i+1} \vee s) \wedge t} - Z_{(t_i \vee s) \wedge t})$$

$$= \int_s^t H_u dZ_t$$

[in the sense of Equation (2.13)]

Now we can state the Ito Formula for diffusion processes.

Theorem 2.4.5 *(General Ito formula).*

Assume Z_t is a diffusion process $dZ_t = X_t\, dt + Y_t\, dB_t$, $(X_t)_{t \geq 0}$, and $g: [0, \infty) \times \mathbb{R} \to \mathbb{R}$ $(t, x) \mapsto g(t, x)$ is continuously differentiable in t and twice continuously differentiable in x then

$$g(T, Z_T) - g(0, Z_0) = \int_0^T \frac{\partial g}{\partial t}(t, Z_t) dt + \int_0^T \frac{\partial g}{\partial x}(t, Z_t) dZ_t + \frac{1}{2} \int_0^T \frac{\partial^2 g}{\partial x^2}(t, Z_t) Y_s^2\, ds$$

with

$$\int_0^T \frac{\partial g}{\partial x}(t, Z_t) dZ_t = \int_0^T \frac{\partial g}{\partial x}(t, Z_t) X_t\, dt + \int_0^t \frac{\partial g}{\partial x}(t, Z_t) Y_t\, dB_t.$$

Remark: Here is an informal way to remember the laws of stochastic calculus:

Now using the second Taylor expansion in differential form for $dZ_t = X_t \, dt + Y_t \, dB_t$

$$d(g(t, Z_t)) = \frac{\partial}{\partial t}g(t, Z_t)dt + \underbrace{\frac{\partial}{\partial x}g(t, Z_t)dZ_t}_{=\frac{\partial}{\partial x}g(t,Z_t)X_t dt + \frac{\partial}{\partial x}g(t,Z_t)Y_t dB_t}$$

$$+ \underbrace{\frac{1}{2}\frac{\partial^2}{\partial t^2}g(t, Z_t)d^2 t}_{=0} + \underbrace{\frac{\partial^2}{\partial t \partial x}g(t, Z_t)dt \, dZ_t}_{=0}$$

$$+ \underbrace{\frac{1}{2}\frac{\partial^2}{\partial x^2}g(t, Z_t)d^2 Z_t}_{=\frac{1}{2}\frac{\partial^2}{\partial x^2}g(t,Z_t)Y_t^2 \, dt} .$$

Law:　　　　　　　　　　　precise meaning:

$$(dt)^2 = 0 \qquad \lim_{\substack{\|P_n\| \to 0 \\ s=t_0^{(n)}<t_1^{(n)}<\cdots<t_n^{(n)}=t}} \sum_{i=1}^{n} (t_i^{(n)} - t_{i-1}^{(n)})^2 = 0$$

$$dt\, dB_t = 0 \qquad \lim_{\substack{\|P_n\| \to 0 \\ s=t_0^{(n)}<t_1^{(n)}<\cdots<t_n^{(n)}=t}} \sum_{i=1}^{n} |t_i^{(n)} - t_{i-1}^{(n)}|\, |B_{t_i^{(n)}} - B_{t_{i-1}^{(n)}}| = 0$$

$$(dB_t)^2 = dt \qquad \lim_{\substack{\|P_n\| \to 0 \\ s=t_0^{(n)}<t_1^{(n)}<\cdots<t_n^{(n)}=t}} \sum_{i=1}^{n} (B_{t_i^{(n)}} - B_{t_{i-1}^{(n)}})^2 = t - s.$$

After this rather abstract and technical introduction of the basics of stochastic processes we are in the position to introduce a model for the stock price (S_t). We are given a probability space $(\Omega, \mathcal{F}, \mathbb{P})$ and a filtration $(\mathcal{F}_t)_{t\geq 0}$.

$(S_t)_{t\geq 0}$ is then a stochastic process satisfying a "stochastic differential equation" of the following form

$$dS_t(\omega) = \mu(t, \omega, S_t(\omega))S_t(\omega)dt + \nu(t, \omega, S_t(\omega))S_t(\omega)dB_t.$$

Or, in integral form is equation can be written as:

$$S_t(\omega) - S_0 = \int_0^t \mu(s, \omega, S_s(\omega))S_s(\omega)ds + \int_0^t \nu(s, w, S_s(\omega))S_s(\omega)dB_s.$$

where $(\mu(t, \cdot, S_t(\cdot))_{t\geq 0}$ (the drift) and $(\nu(t, \cdot, S_t(\cdot))_{t\geq 0}$ (volatility) are adapted piecewise continuous processes whenever $(S_t(\cdot))_{t\geq 0}$ has these properties.

Note, that we haven't given an "explicit model" for the stock price yet. Since "S_t" appears on both sides of the equation, it is only an "implicit" description. The following theorem on stochastic differential equations gives conditions which insure the uniqueness and existence of a solution:

Theorem 2.4.6 . *Assume $(\mu(t, \cdot, X_t(\cdot)))_{t\geq 0}$ and $\nu(t, \cdot, (X_t(\cdot)))_{t\geq 0}$ are $(\mathcal{F}_t)_{t\geq 0}$ adapted piecewise continuous, locally square integrable, whenever $(X_t)_{t\geq 0}$ has these properties. Also assume the following "Lipschitz condition" in the third argument, i.e. $\exists K > 0$ so that for all $t \geq 0$, $\omega \in \Omega$*

$$|x\mu(t,\omega,x) - y\mu(t,\omega,y)| \leq K|x-y|$$
$$|x\nu(t,\omega,x) - y\nu(t,\omega,y)| \leq K|x-y|.$$

Then the stochastic differential equation

$$dX_t = \mu(t, \cdot, X_t)X_t \, dt + \nu(t, \cdot, X_t)X_t \, dB_t$$

has a unique solution $(X_t)_{t\geq 0}$

$$\left[i.e. \ X_t - X_0 = \int_0^t \mu(s, \cdot, X_s)X_s \, ds + \int_0^t \nu(s, \cdot, X_s)X_s \, dB_s \right].$$

Example: Let us assume the drift μ and the volatility ν being constant. What is the solution of the following SDE ?

(*) $$dS_t = \mu S_t \, dt + \nu S_t \, dB_t$$

We apply Ito's formula to $g(t, x) = \ln x$

$$d\ln(S_t) = \frac{dS_t}{S_t} - \frac{1}{2}\frac{1}{S_t^2}\nu^2 S_t^2 \, dt = \frac{dS_t}{S_t} - \frac{\nu^2}{2}dt$$

Thus by solving for $\frac{dS_t}{S_t}$ and integrating we derive that

$$\int_0^t \frac{dS_s}{S_s} = \ln(S_t) - \ln(S_0) + \frac{\nu^2}{2}t.$$

On the other hand (*) implies that

$$\int_0^t \frac{dS_t}{S_s} = \mu t + \nu B_t.$$

which implies that

$$\ln(S_t) - \ln(S_0) + \frac{\nu^2}{2}t = \mu t + \nu B_t$$

or

$$S_t = S_0 \cdot e^{\nu B_t + (\mu - \frac{\nu^2}{2})t}.$$

Chapter 3

The Black-Scholes Model

3.1 The Black-Scholes Equation

In this section we want to solve the following problem:

Consider a general derivative, which pays $F(S_T)$ at time T, if the price of the underlying asset (we call it stock) at time T is S_T. We assume that the price of the stock satisfies the models we described in the previous sections. What is an arbitrage free value of the derivative at previous times t, $0 \leq t < T$?

Let us first precisely state our assumptions.

We denote the stock price at time $t, 0 \leq t \leq T$, by S_t, S_0 being a constant and we assume S_t satisfies the following stochastic differential equation

(A1) $$dS_t = \mu_t S_t \, dt + \nu_t S_t \, dB_t,$$

in integral form this means:

(A1') $$S_t - S_0 = \int_0^t \mu_u S_u du + \int_0^t \nu_u S_u \, dB_u.$$

$(B_t)_{t \geq 0}$ is a Brownian motion, with respect to a filtration $(\mathcal{F}_t)_{t \geq 0}$, and μ_t and ν_t are stochastic processes, adapted to $(\mathcal{F}_t)$, and possibly depending on t as well as on S_t, i.e.

$$\mu_t = \mu(S_t, t) \text{ and } \nu_t = \nu(S_t, t).$$

We assume (A1) respectively (A1') have a unique solution. Conditions for the existence of unique solutions were given in Theorem 2.4.6

Secondly there is a riskless bond with fixed interest rate r which is continuously compounded. If β_t denotes the value of the bond at, time $0 \leq t \leq T$, it follows that

(A2) $$d\beta_t = r\beta_t \, dt, \text{ or } \beta_t = \beta_0 e^{rt}.$$

Finally, we are given a derivative which pays $F(S_T)$ at time T. For the moment we only assume that $F : \mathbb{R} \to \mathbb{R}$ is measurable. A further growth condition on F will be introduced later. We want to find an arbitrage free price of this derivative at any time $0 \leq t < T$.

We have to make the following further assumptions :

(A3) For each time $0 \leq t \leq T$ there exists a unique arbitrage-free price for the derivative, which we denote by V_t. Furthermore, V_t can be written as

$$V_t = f(S_t, t)$$

(i.e. V_t depends only on t and the stock price S_t at time t) and

$$f : [0, \infty) \times [0, T) \to \mathbb{R}$$

is twice continuously differentiable in the first and once continuously differentiable in the second variable.

We will use the following notation for derivatives often used in physics :

$$f'(x, u) = \frac{\partial}{\partial x} f(x, u)$$
$$f''(x, u) = \frac{\partial^2}{\partial x^2} f(x, u)$$
$$\dot{f}(x, u) = \frac{\partial}{\partial u} f(x, u).$$

Finally, we have to clarify the possibilities of an investor. An investor can purchase any real number of bonds and units of the underlying stock. His portfolio at time t is a pair (a_t, b_t), where a_t denotes the number of shares of a stock and b_t denotes the number of bonds he owns at time t. The process of pairs $(a_t, b_t)_{0 \leq t \leq T}$ is called a strategy. Since decisions on investments can not depend on future events we have to assume that

(A4) $(a_t)_{0 \leq t \leq T}$ and $(b_t)_{0 \leq t \leq T}$ are processes on $(\Omega, \mathcal{F}, \mathbb{P})$ which are adapted to the filtration $(\mathcal{F}_t)_{0 \leq t \leq T}$.

Secondly we assume (in order to be able to apply stochastic calculus)

(A5) $(a_t)_{0 \leq t \leq T}$ is wekly square integrable with respect to S_t (as introduced in Section 2.4 and $(b_t)_{0 \leq t \leq T}$ is integrable with respect to db_t (in the usuual sense).

Therefore the integrals

$$\int_s^t a_u \, dS_u, \quad \text{and} \int_s^t b_u \, d\beta_u, \quad 0 \leq s < t \leq T,$$

exist and represent the gains/losses during the timeperiod $[s, t]$, caused generated by the holdings in stocks and bonds respectively.

Definition: A strategy $(a_t, b_t)_{0 \leq t \leq T}$ is called *self-financing* if the value of the portfolio at any time t equals to the value of the portfolio at time 0 augmented by gains or decreased by losses up to time t. In a formula that means

(1)
$$\underbrace{(a_t S_t + b_t \beta_t)}_{\text{value at } t} - \underbrace{(a_0 S_0 + b_0 \beta_0)}_{\text{value at } 0} = \underbrace{\int_0^t a_u \, dS_u + \int_0^t b_u \, d\beta_u}_{\text{gain/loss}}$$

or in differential form

(2)
$$d(a_t S_t + b_t \beta_t) = a_t \, dS_t + b_t \, d\beta_t.$$

I.e. whenever the investor increases his position in stocks he will decrease his position in bonds by exactly the same value and vice versa. Now, we are in the position to formulate our last assumption

(A6) There is a self-financing strategy $(a_t, b_t)_{0 \leq t \leq T}$, satisfying (A4) and (A5) which *replicates* the derivative, i.e. at any time $0 \leq t \leq T$.

$$V_t = \text{Value of portfolio } (a_t, b_t)$$

$$= a_t S_t + b_t \beta_t.$$

Remark: Up to this point, the reader might not see the justification of the above introduced assumptions. Why for instance, should it be possible to replicate the derivative? Why should a replicating strategy satisfy the conditions in (A5)? Why should the value V_t of the derivative at time t only depend on t and S_t but not on S_u, for some other time $u < t$? Why should this dependence be differentiable? At this time, we cannot give a satisfying answer to these questions yet. But, under the assumption that the stock price (S_t) satisfies (A1), that the bond price satifies (A2), and that the function F satisfyes a certain growth condition, we will find a function $f(S,t)$ satisfying (A3) and a replicating and self financing strategy (a_t, b_t). From the existence of such a strategy it follows that $V_t = f(S_t, t) = a_t S_t + b_t \beta_t$ is the only arbitragefree price of our derivative.

After this set-up we are ready for the computations. First we use Ito's formula for $dV_t = df(S_t, t)$.

(3.1) $dV_t = df(S_t, t)$

$$= f'(S_t, t)dS_t + \dot{f}(S_t, t)dt + \frac{1}{2}f''(S_t, t)(dS_t)^2$$

$$= f'(S_t, t)\nu(S_t, t)S_t \, dB_t + [f'(S_t, t)\mu(S_t, t)S_t + \dot{f}(S_t, t) + \frac{1}{2}f''(S_t, t)\nu(S_t, t)^2 S_t^2]dt$$

[by (A1), note $(dS_t)^2 = \nu^2(S_t, t)S_t^2 \, dt$].

On the other hand it follows from (A6) that

(3.2) $$V_t - V_0 = a_t S_t + b_t \beta_t - (a_0 S_0 + b_0 \beta_0)$$

$$= \int_0^t a_u \, dS_u + \int_0^t b_u \, d\beta_u$$

[using (A1)].

In differential form,

$$(3.3) \qquad dV_t = a_t \, dS_t + b_t d\beta_t$$

$$= a_t \mu(S_t, t) S_t \, dt + a_t \nu(S_t, t) S_t \, dB_t + b_t r \beta_t \, dt$$

$$= a_t \nu(S_t, t) S_t \, dB_t + [a_t \mu(S_t, t) S_t + r b_t \beta_t] dt.$$

Comparing Equation 3.1 with Equation 3.3, we observe that these equation are satisfied if we demand that

$$(3.4) \quad f'(S_t, t) \nu(S_t, t) S_t = a_t \nu(S_t, t) S_t \qquad \text{[the "dB_t-term" of (3.1) and (3.2) respectively]}$$

and

$$(3.5) \qquad f'(S_t, t) \mu(S_t, t) S_t + \dot{f}(S_t, t) + \frac{1}{2} f''(S_t, t) \nu(S_t, t)^2 S_t^2 = a_t \mu(S_t, t) S_t + b_t r \beta_t$$

$$\text{[the "dt-term" of of (3.1) and (3.2) respectively].}$$

Equation 3.4 cancels to

$$(3.6) \qquad a_t = f'(S_t, t).$$

This is the *hedging* equation. Once f is known $f'(S_t, t)$ is the number of shares of the stock the investor has to buy in order to replicate the derivative. Solving equation (A6) for b_t we obtain

$$(3.7) \qquad b_t = \frac{1}{\beta_t} [f(S_t, t) - a_t S_t] = \frac{1}{\beta_t} [f(S_t, t) - f'(S_t, t) S_t]$$

Inserting (3.6) and (3.7) into (3.5) we derive that

$$\dot{f}(S_t, t) + \frac{1}{2} f''(S_t, t) \nu(S_t, t)^2 S_t^2 = r f(S_t, t) - r f'(S_t, t) S_t,$$

or

$$(3.8) \qquad \frac{1}{2} \nu(S_t, t)^2 S_t^2 f''(S_t, t) + r S_t f'(S_t, t) + \dot{f}(S_t, t) - r f(S_t, t) = 0.$$

Thus, in order to find the function $F(t, S)$ satisfying (3.8) we will have to solve the following *initial value problem* (BSE) (the Black-Scholes Equation).

(BSE) Find $f\colon [0,\infty) \times [0,T] \longrightarrow \mathbb{R}$ satisfying the *partial differential equation*:

$$\frac{1}{2}\nu(S,t)^2 S^2 f''(S,t) + rSf'(S,t) + \dot{f}(S,t) - rf(S,t) = 0,$$

assuming for $t = T$ the values $f(S,T) = F(S)$.

Conclusion. We reduced the problem of finding the arbitrage free value of a derivative to the problem of solving the (deterministic) initial value problem (BSE). Secondly, we deduce that once we found $f(\cdot,\cdot)$, we can hedge (replicate) the derivative by the following self-financing strategy:

$$a_t = f'(S_t,t), \quad \text{and} \quad b_t = \frac{1}{\beta_t}[f(S_t,t) - f'(S_t,t)S_t].$$

3.2 Solution of the Black-Scholes Equation

In this section we want to solve the initial value problem (BSE) obtained in the previous section. We will assume that the volatility ν is constant.

(BSE) $\quad \frac{1}{2}\nu^2 S^2 f''(S,t) + rS f'(S,t) + \dot{f}(S,t) - rf(S,t) = 0, \quad 0 \le t \le T, \quad 0 < S$

with $f(S,T) = F(S)$.

We will proceed in the following way. Substituting the variables appropriately we will transform (BSE) into the well known Heat Equation (HE).

(HE) $$h''(x,\tau) = \dot{h}(x,\tau)$$
$$h(x,0) = h_0(x).$$

Then we will present the methods to solve the Heat equation. Finally, reversing all the substitutions will lead us to a solution of (BSE). We first make the following a change of variables:

(3.9) $$S = S(x) = e^x \quad \text{(or } x = \ln(S))$$
$$t = t(\tau) = T - \frac{2\tau}{\nu^2} \quad \left(\text{or } \tau = \frac{1}{2}\nu^2(T-t)\right).$$

Note that the second equation in 3.9 means that we "inverted time".

We let

(3.10) $$g(x,\tau) = f(S(x),t(\tau)) = f\left(e^x, T - \frac{2\tau}{\nu^2}\right),$$

and note that the initial conditions becomes

(3.11) $$g(x,0) = f(S(x),T) = F(e^x).$$

Computing the relevant derivatives of $g(x,t)$ we obtain

$$g'(x,\tau) = f'(S,t)S,$$

$$g''(x,\tau) = f'(S,t)S + f''(S,t)S^2,$$

$$quad[\text{Note that } \frac{\partial S}{\partial x} = S]$$

$$\dot{g}(x,\tau) = -\frac{2}{\nu^2}\dot{f}(e^x,t).$$

The partial differential equation written in terms of x, τ and $g(x,\tau)$ becomes

$$\frac{\nu^2}{2}g''(x,\tau) - \frac{\nu^2}{2}g'(x,\tau) + rg'(x,\tau) - \frac{\nu^2}{2}\dot{g}(x,\tau) - rg(x,\tau) = 0$$

or after multiplication by $\frac{2}{\nu^2}$

$$g''(x,\tau) + \left(\frac{2r}{\nu^2} - 1\right)g'(x,\tau) - \frac{2r}{\nu^2}g(x,\tau) = \dot{g}(x,\tau).$$

Putting $k = \frac{2r}{\nu^2}$ we obtain

(3.12) $$g''(x,\tau) + (k-1)g'(x,\tau) - kg(x,\tau) = \dot{g}(x,\tau).$$

Secondly we let

(3.13) $$g(x,\tau) = e^{\alpha x + \beta \tau} h(x,\tau)$$

and try to find the right choice for α and β in order to obtain (HE).

The relevant derivatives of $g(x,\tau)$ can be written as follows

$$g'(x,\tau) = e^{\alpha x + \beta \tau}[\alpha h(x,\tau) + h'(x,\tau)]$$

$$g''(x,\tau) = e^{\alpha x + \beta \tau}[\alpha^2 h(x,\tau) + 2\alpha h'(x,\tau) + h''(x,\tau)]$$

$$\dot{g}(x,\tau) = e^{\alpha x + \beta \tau}[\beta h(x,\tau) + \dot{h}(x,\tau)].$$

The partial differential equation (3.12) becomes (after cancelling the factor $e^{\alpha x + \beta \tau}$ on both sides)

$$\alpha^2 h(x,\tau) + 2\alpha h'(x,\tau) + h''(x,\tau) + (k-1)\alpha h(x,\tau) + (k-1)h'(x,\tau) - kh(x,\tau)$$
$$= \beta h(x,\tau) + \dot{h}(x,\tau)$$

or

$$h''(x,\tau) + (2\alpha + k - 1)h'(x,\tau) + (\alpha^2 + (k-1)\alpha - k - \beta)h(x,\tau) = \dot{h}(x,\tau).$$

Now we can choose α, β so that the factors of h' and h vanish, i.e.

(3.14) $$\alpha = -\frac{k-1}{2}, \quad \text{and}$$

$$\beta = \alpha^2 + (k-1)\alpha - k = \left(\frac{k-1}{2}\right)^2 - (k-1)^2 - k = -\frac{1}{4}(k+1)^2.$$

We now arrived to the Heat Equation

(3.15) $$h''(x,\tau) = \dot{h}(x,\tau)$$

with the initial function

(3.16) $$h(x,0) = h_0(x) = e^{-\alpha x}g(x,0) = e^{-\alpha x}F(e^x)$$

This is the "one dimensional heat-equation" (in one variable x).

Interpretation: Insulated wire has at time 0 the temperature distribution $T_0(x)$

One wants to know the temperature distribution $T(x,t)$ at some time $t > 0$. From laws in physics one can deduce that $T(x,t)$ has to satisfy

$$T''(x,t) = c\dot{T}(x,t),$$

where c is called the conductivity of the wire.

Proposition 3.2.1 . $h(x,t) = \frac{1}{2\sqrt{\pi t}}e^{-x^2/4t}$, *i.e. the density of* $N(0,2t)$ *is a solution of* $h''(x,t) = \dot{h}(x,t)$.

Proof. Simply compute the derivatives

$$\dot{h}(x,t) = \frac{1}{2\sqrt{\pi t}} \left[\frac{x^2}{4t^2} - \frac{1}{2t} \right] e^{-x^2/4t}$$

$$h'(x,t) = \frac{1}{2\sqrt{\pi t}} \left[-\frac{x}{2t} \right] e^{-x^2/4t}$$

$$h''(x,t) = \frac{1}{2\sqrt{\pi t}} \left[\frac{x^2}{4t^2} - \frac{1}{2t} \right] e^{-x^2/4t}$$

and realize that $h''(x,t) = \dot{h}(x,t)$.   □

Proposition 3.2.2 .

  a) *If $h(x,t)$ is a solution of the equation $h'' = \dot{h}$ and $c \in \mathbb{R}$ then its translation by c,*
  i.e. the function $(x,t) \mapsto h(x-c,t)$ is also a solution.

  b) *If $h_1(x,t), h_2(x,t), \dots, h_n(x,t)$ are solutions of $h'' = \dot{h}$ and if $\alpha_1, \alpha_2, \dots, \alpha_n \in \mathbb{R}$,*
  then $\sum_{i=1}^{n} \alpha_i h_i(x,t)$ is also a solution.

In particular $\sum_{i=1}^{n} \alpha_i h(x-c_i,t)$ is solution if $h(x,t)$ is one.

Proposition 3.2.3 .   *Let $h_0 : \mathbb{R} \to \mathbb{R}$ be continuous and assume that*

$$\int_{-\infty}^{\infty} c^2 |h_0(c)| \cdot e^{-\frac{(x-c)^2}{4t}} dc < \infty \quad \text{for all } t > 0.$$

Then $\frac{1}{2\sqrt{\pi t}} \int_{-\infty}^{\infty} h_0(c) \cdot e^{-\frac{(x-c)^2}{4t}} dc$ is solution of $h'' = \dot{h}$.

Proof. Define

$$h(x,t) = \int_{-\infty}^{\infty} h_0(c) \frac{1}{2\sqrt{\pi t}} e^{-\frac{(x-c)^2}{4t}} dc.$$

The integrability condition on h_0 allows us to interchange $\frac{\partial}{\partial t}$ as well as $\frac{\partial}{\partial x}$ and $\frac{\partial^2}{\partial x^2}$ and $\int \ldots dc$ with taking the integral with respect to c (see Exercis.....). This means together with Proposition 3.2.1 that

$$\dot{h}(x,t) = \frac{1}{2\sqrt{\pi t}} \int_{-\infty}^{\infty} \frac{d}{dt} h_0(c) e^{-\frac{(x-c)^2}{4t}} dc$$

$$= \frac{1}{2\sqrt{\pi t}} \int_{-\infty}^{\infty} h_0(c) \left[\frac{(x-c)^2}{4t^2} - \frac{1}{2t} \right] e^{-(x-c)^2/4t} dc \text{ and}$$

$$h''(x,t) = \frac{1}{2\sqrt{\pi t}} \int_{-\infty}^{\infty} \frac{d^2}{dx^2} h_0(c) e^{-\frac{(x-c)^2}{4t}} dc$$

$$= \frac{1}{2\sqrt{\pi t}} \int_{-\infty}^{\infty} h_0(c) \left[\frac{(x-c)^2}{4t^2} - \frac{1}{2t} \right] e^{-(x-c)^2/4t} dc \quad \text{for} \quad t > 0 \text{ and } x \in \mathbb{R},$$

Proposition 3.2.4 . *Assume $h_0 : \mathbb{R} \to \mathbb{R}$ is continuous and assume that*

$$\frac{1}{2\sqrt{\pi t}} \int_{-\infty}^{\infty} |h_0(c)| e^{-\frac{(x-c)^2}{4t}} dc < \infty \quad \text{for all} \quad t > 0$$

then $\lim\limits_{t \to 0} \frac{1}{2\sqrt{\pi t}} \int_{-\infty}^{\infty} h_0(c) e^{-\frac{(x-c)^2}{4t}} dc = h_0(x)$ *for all $x \in \mathbb{R}$.*

Proof. Let $\varepsilon > 0$ and $x \in \mathbb{R}$. Using the continuity of h_0 we find $\delta > 0$ so that for all $\tilde{x} \in \mathbb{R}$ with $|\tilde{x} - x| < \delta$ it follows that $|h_0(x) - h_0(\tilde{x})| < \varepsilon$. We write

$$\int_{-\infty}^{\infty} h_0(c) \frac{1}{2\sqrt{\pi t}} e^{-(x-c)^2/4t} dc$$

$$= \int_{x-\delta}^{x+\delta} h_0(c) \frac{1}{2\sqrt{\pi t}} e^{-(x-c)^2/4t} dc$$

$$+ \int_{x+\delta}^{\infty} h_0(c) \frac{1}{2\sqrt{\pi t}} e^{-(x-c)^2/4t} dc \quad + \int_{-\infty}^{x-\delta} h_0(c) \frac{1}{2\sqrt{\pi t}} e^{-(x-c)^2/4t} dc.$$

Now, whenever $\eta \geq \delta^2$, it follows that $\frac{1}{2\sqrt{\pi t}}e^{-\eta/4t} \downarrow 0$, whenever $t \downarrow 0$. Thus

$$(3.17) \qquad \int_{x+\delta}^{\infty} |h_0(c)| \frac{1}{2\sqrt{\pi t}} e^{-(x-c)^2/4t} dc \xrightarrow[t\to 0]{} 0 \text{ and } \int_{-\infty}^{x-\delta} |h_0(c)| \frac{1}{2\sqrt{\pi t}} e^{-(x-c)^2/4t} dc \xrightarrow[t\to 0]{},$$

by monotone convergence. In particular (replace $h_0(c)$ by the constant 1) it follows that
$\int_{x+\delta}^{\infty} \frac{1}{2\sqrt{\pi t}} e^{-(x-c)^2/4t} dc \xrightarrow[t\to 0]{} 0$ and $\int_{-\infty}^{x-\delta} \frac{1}{2\sqrt{\pi t}} e^{-(x-c)^2/4t} dc \xrightarrow[t\to 0]{} 0$. Thus we conclude that

$$\limsup_{t\to 0} \left| \frac{1}{2\sqrt{\pi t}} \int_{x-\delta}^{x+\delta} h_0(c) e^{-\frac{(x-c)^2}{4t}} dc - h_0(x) \right|$$

$$= \limsup_{t\to 0} \left| \frac{1}{2\sqrt{\pi t}} \int_{x-\delta}^{x+\delta} h_0(c) e^{-\frac{(x-c)^2}{4t}} dc - \frac{1}{2\sqrt{\pi t}} \int_{x-\delta}^{x+\delta} h_0(x) e^{-\frac{(x-c)^2}{4t}} dc \right|$$

$$[\text{We are using that} \frac{1}{2\sqrt{\pi t}} e^{-\frac{(x-c)^2}{4t}} \text{ is a density}]$$

$$\leq \limsup_{t\to 0} \frac{1}{2\sqrt{\pi t}} \int_{x-\delta}^{x+\delta} |h_0(c) - h_0(x)| e^{-\frac{(x-c)^2}{4t}} dc$$

$$+ \limsup_{t\to 0} \frac{1}{2\sqrt{\pi t}} \int_{x+\delta}^{\infty} |h_0(x)| e^{-(x-c)^2/4t} dc$$

$$+ \limsup_{t\to 0} \frac{1}{2\sqrt{\pi t}} \int_{-\infty}^{x-\delta} |h_0(x)| e^{-(x-c)^2/4t} dc$$

$$\leq \varepsilon.$$

Since $\varepsilon > 0$ arbitrary claim follows.   □

Conclusion

The solution of the heat equation

$$h''(x,t) = \dot{h}(x,t) \ with h(x,0) = h_0(x)$$

is

$$h(x,t) = \frac{1}{2\sqrt{\pi t}} \int_{-\infty}^{\infty} h_0(c) e^{-\frac{(x-c)^2}{4t}} dc,$$

Assuming the integrability condition

$$\frac{1}{2\sqrt{\pi t}} \int_{-\infty}^{\infty} |h_0(c)| c^2 e^{-\frac{(x-c)^2}{4t}} \, dc < \infty \quad \text{for all } t < \infty.$$

Remark: Given two functions f, g the function $x \mapsto \int_{-\infty}^{\infty} f(z) g(x-z) dz$ is called the convolution of f and g denoted by $f * g$.

Using convolutions one can write the solution to the heat equation as

$h(x,t) = h_0 * \rho_{2t}(x)$ where $\rho_{2t} = \frac{1}{2\sqrt{\pi t}} e^{-\frac{x^2}{4t}}$ (density of $N(0, 2t)$). For $t = 0$ "$h_0 * \rho_0$" has to be interpreted as h_0 (which is justified by Proposition 3.2.4).

We now turn to the computation of $f(s, t)$ by tracing back our substitutions

$$f(S,t) = g\left(\ln(S), \frac{1}{2} \nu^2 (T-t) \right) \quad \text{[by (3.10)]}$$

$$\underset{[(6)]}{=} e^{\alpha \ln(S)} e^{\frac{1}{2}\beta \nu^2 (T-t)} h\left(\ln(S), \frac{1}{2} \nu^2 (T-t) \right) \text{ [by (3.13)]}$$

$$= e^{\alpha \ln(S)} e^{\frac{1}{2}\beta \nu^2 (T-t)} \frac{1}{\sqrt{2\pi \nu^2 (T-t)}} \cdot \int_{-\infty}^{\infty} h_0(\xi) \cdot e^{-\frac{(\xi - \ln(S))^2}{2\nu^2(T-t)}} \, d\xi \quad \text{[Proposition (3.2.4)]}$$

$$= e^{\alpha \ln(S)} e^{\frac{1}{2}\beta \nu^2 (T-t)} \frac{1}{\sqrt{2\pi \nu^2 (T-t)}} \int_{-\infty}^{\infty} e^{-\alpha \xi} F'(e^{\xi}) \cdot e^{-\frac{(\xi - \ln(S))^2}{2\nu(T-t)}} \, d\xi$$

$$= e^{\frac{1}{2}\beta \nu^2 (T-t)} \frac{1}{\sqrt{2\pi \nu^2 (T-t)}} \int_{-\infty}^{\infty} F(Se^{\eta}) \cdot e^{-\alpha \eta - \frac{\eta^2}{2\nu^2(T-t)}} \, d\eta$$

[Substitute $\eta = \xi - \ln(S)$]

$$= e^{\frac{1}{2}\beta \nu^2 (T-t)} \cdot e^{\frac{1}{2}\alpha^2 \nu^2 (T-t)} \frac{1}{\sqrt{2\pi \nu^2 (T-t)}} \int_{-\infty}^{\infty} F(Se^{\eta}) e^{-\frac{[\eta + \alpha \nu^2 (T-t)]^2}{2\nu^2(T-t)}} \, d\eta$$

[Quadratic completion]

$$= e^{-r(T-t)} \frac{1}{\sqrt{2\pi \nu^2 (T-t)}} \int_{-\infty}^{\infty} F(S \cdot e^{r(T-t)} e^{-\frac{\nu^2}{2}(T-t)+z}) e^{-\frac{z^2}{2\nu^2(T-t)}} \, dz$$

$$\left[\text{Substitute } \eta = z - \alpha \nu^2 (T-t) = z + \frac{2r - \nu^2}{2\nu^2} \nu^2 (T-t) = z + \left(r - \frac{\nu^2}{2} \right)(T-t) \right]$$

Now we deduce from the choice of α and β (3.14) that $\beta + \alpha^2 = \frac{1}{4}(-(k+1)^2 + (k-1)^2) = -k = -\frac{2r}{\nu^2}$ and obtain

$$(3.18) \qquad V_t = f(S_t, t) = \frac{e^{-r(T-t)}}{\sqrt{2\pi\nu^2(T-t)}} \int_{-\infty}^{\infty} F(S_t e^{r(T-t)} e^{-\frac{\nu^2}{2}(T-t)} \cdot e^z) e^{-\frac{z^2}{2\nu^2(T-t)}} dz$$

We can represent V_t as an expected value involving the Browinan Motion. For that note that

$$\frac{1}{\sqrt{2\pi\nu^2(T-t)}} e^{-\frac{z^2}{2\nu^2(T-t)}}$$

is the density of the distribution of $\nu(B_T - B_t)$. Thus we deduce that

$$(3.19) \qquad V_t = f(S_t, t) = e^{-r(T-t)} \mathbb{E}\left(F(S_t e^{r(T-t)} e^{-\frac{\nu^2}{2}(T-t)+\nu(B_T - B_t)}) \right).$$

in particular for $t = 0$ we obtain

$$(3.20) \qquad V_0 = e^{-rT} \mathbb{E}(F(S_0 e^{rT} e^{-\frac{\nu^2}{2}T+\nu B_T})) = \frac{e^{-rT}}{\sqrt{2\pi\nu^2 T}} \int_{-\infty}^{\infty} F(S_0 e^{rT} e^{-\frac{\nu^2}{2}T} \cdot e^z) e^{-\frac{z^2}{2\nu^2 T}} dz.$$

3.3 Discussion and Application of the Black-Scholes Formula

Let us first observe that as in the case of futures (Section 0.2) and as in the case of the log-binomial model (Section 1.3)we arrived to the follwoing conclusion. The value of a derivative in the Black Scholes Model can be interpreted as the discounted expected value of the pay-off function with respect to a risk neutral distribution. Indeed, the value of a derivative, paying $F(S_T)$ at time T, is at time 0 worth

$$(3.21) \qquad V_0 = e^{-rT}\mathbb{E}(F(e^{rT}S_0 \cdot e^{-\frac{1}{2}\nu^2 T + \nu B_T})).$$

We define $\widetilde{S}_t = e^{rt}S_0 e^{-\frac{1}{2}\nu^2 t + \nu B_t}$, $0 \le t \le T$. This is the log-normal process with the same volatility ν as S_t but with the drift r, the drift of a riskless bond. Since the process $M_t = S_0 e^{-\frac{1}{2}\nu^2 t + \nu B_t}$ is a martingale (see Proposition 2.2.3), we deduce that for $0 \le t < u \le T$

$$\mathbb{E}(\widetilde{S}_u | \mathcal{F}_t) = e^{r(u-t)}\widetilde{S}_t.$$

Thus the expected yield of $\widetilde{S}_t$ equals to the yield of the riskless bond. We call therefore $(\widetilde{S}_t)$ the *riskneutral version of* (S_t). Using $\widetilde{S}_t$ the value of a derivative can now be writeen as

$$(3.22) \qquad V_0 = e^{-rT}\mathbb{E}(F(\widetilde{S}_T)).$$

Using Equation 3.20 of Section 3.2 we can compute the value of a European call ($F(S) = (S - K)^+$) and a European put ($F(S) = (K - S)^+$) (Exercise....).

Proposition 3.3.1 .   *For a European call and put, with expiration date T and exercise price K, the value at time $0 \le t \le T$ is*

$$C(S,t) = SN(d) - Ke^{-r(T-t)}N(d - \nu\sqrt{T-t})$$

and

$$P(S,t) = Ke^{-r(T-t)}N(-d + \nu\sqrt{T-t}) - SN(-d) \quad respectively,$$

where

$$N(d) = \frac{1}{\sqrt{2\pi}} \int_{-\infty}^{d} e^{-x^2/2}dx, \ and$$

$$d = \frac{\log(S/K) + \left(r + \frac{1}{2}\nu^2\right)(T-t)}{\nu\sqrt{T-t}}.$$

Proposition 3.3.2   *(Asymptotic behavior of C(S,t))).*

a) *If $S \ll K$ (call is "out of money"), thus $\log(S/K) \ll 0$ and $d \ll 0$, and we deduce $C(S,t) \approx 0$.*

b) *If $S \gg K$ (call is "in the money") then $\log(S/K) \gg 0$, $d \gg 0$ and $N(d) \approx 1$. In that case we deduce $C(S,t) \approx S - Ke^{-r(T-t)}$, which is the value of a future with the same expiration date and exercise price.*

We now turn to four important functions associated with a derivative paying $F(S)$ if at time T the stock price is S.

First note that the value of a derivative

$$V_t = f(S_t, t) = e^{-r(T-t)}\mathbb{E}(F(S_t e^{r(T-t)}e^{-\frac{\nu^2}{2}(T-t)+\nu(B_T-B_t)}))$$

does not only depend on t and S_t but also on the interest rate r and the volatility ν and we can think of f being a function of t, S, but also of the interstrate r and the volatility ν, $f(S_t, t, r, \nu) = f(S_t, t)$. 1) The "delta" of F:

$$\Delta_F(S, t) = \frac{\partial}{\partial S} f(S, t, r, \nu)$$

2) the "gamma" of F:

$$\Gamma_F(S, t) = \frac{\partial^2}{\partial S^2} f(S, t, r, \nu)$$

3) the "theta" of F

$$\theta_F(S, t) = -\frac{\partial}{\partial t} f(S, t, r, \nu)$$

4) the "vega" of F:

$$v_F(S, t) = \frac{\partial}{\partial \nu} f(S, t, r, \nu)$$

5) the "rho" of F:

$$\rho_F(S, t) = \frac{\partial}{\partial r} f(S, t, r, \nu).$$

We already encountered Δ_F during the derivation of the Black-Scholes formula: $a_t = \Delta_F(S, t)$ is the number of shares of a stock, an investor has to hold at time t, together with $b_t = (V_t - a_t S_t)/\beta_t$ bonds, if he wants to replicate the derivative.

Any two of the considered three securities (bond, stock, derivative) form a complete market, which means as in the discrete case that we can replicate any of these three securities by the two others. If he wants to replicate the bond for example, one needs to hold $\frac{V_t}{b_t}$ units of the derivative and $-\frac{a_t S_t}{b_t}$ units of the stock (solve $V_t = a_t S_t + b_t \beta_t$ for β_t). These strategies are called "Δ-hedging". They have one big problem: they demand a continuous, practically impossible, adaptation of the portfolio. Thus, one has to approximate the Δ-hedging by only finitely many portfolios. There is a trade off between increased number of transactions, which on one hand increases the accuracy, but also increases on the other hand the transaction costs. The function Γ_F represents the curvature of f as a function on S and can be used for refined hedging strategies.

Finally ρ_F and v_F represent the dependence of f on r and ν. Usually the interest rate r and the volatility ν are only known up to errors Δr and $\Delta \nu$. The interest rate could for example change before the exercise date and also the volatility can only be estimated from past data. Thus ρ_F and υ_F can be used to estimate the possible error of f

$$f(S, t, r + \Delta r, \nu + \Delta\nu) - f(S, t, r, \nu) \approx \rho_F \Delta r + \upsilon_F \Delta\nu.$$

We finally want to compute the "Δ of a call"

$$\Delta_{call}(S, t) := \frac{\partial}{\partial S} C(S, t).$$

Proposition 3.3.3 .

$$\Delta_{call}(S, t) = N(d)$$

$$= \frac{1}{\sqrt{2\pi}} \int_{-\infty}^{[\log(S/K) + (r + \frac{1}{2}\nu^2)(T-t)]/\nu\sqrt{T-t}} e^{-x^2/2} \, dx.$$

Proof.

$$\frac{\partial}{\partial S} C(S, t) = \frac{\partial}{\partial S}[SN(d) - Ke^{-r(T-t)}N(d - \nu\sqrt{T-t})]$$

$$= N(d) + SN'(d)\frac{\partial}{\partial S}d - Ke^{-r(T-t)}N'(d - \nu\sqrt{T-t})\frac{\partial}{\partial S}(d - \nu\sqrt{T-t})$$

$$= N(d) + \frac{\partial d}{\partial S}[SN'(d) - Ke^{-r(T-t)}N'(d - \nu\sqrt{T-t})].$$

In order to verify the formula we will show that the term in above brackets vanishes. Note that $N'(d) = \frac{1}{\sqrt{2\pi}}e^{-d^2/2}$.

Dividing [......] by

$$N'(d - \nu\sqrt{T-t}) = \frac{1}{\sqrt{2\pi}}e^{-\frac{[d-\nu\sqrt{T-t}]^2}{2}} = \frac{1}{\sqrt{2\pi}}e^{-\frac{d^2}{2} + d\nu\sqrt{T-t} - \frac{\nu^2}{2}(T-t)}$$

we get:

$$[\ldots]/N'(d - \nu\sqrt{T-t}) = Se^{-d\nu\sqrt{T-t}+\frac{\nu^2}{2}(T-t)} - Ke^{-r(T-t)}$$

$$= Se^{-\log(S/K)-(r+\frac{1}{2}\nu^2)(T-t)+\frac{\nu^2}{2}(T-t)} - Ke^{-r(T-t)}$$

$$\left[\text{recall that } d = \frac{\log(S/K) + (r + \frac{1}{2}\nu^2)(T-t)}{\nu\sqrt{T-t}}\right]$$

$$= Ke^{-r(T-t)} - Ke^{-r(T-t)} = 0.$$

3.4   Black-Scholes Formula for Dividend Paying Assets

A. Continuous dividends

Let us first consider the simplest payment structure. Suppose that in a time dt the stock pays out a dividend $D_0 S_t dt$, with D_0 being a constant. Using the arbitrage argument the price must fall by the amount of the dividend payment, S_t satisfies the following modified stochastic differential equation:

$$dS_t = (\mu_t - D_0)S_t \ dt + \nu_t S_t \ dB_t.$$

One might expect that since μ_t does not effect the option price, and that since S_t satisfies the same equation with $\mu_t - D_0$ instead of μ_t we will arrive to the same option-price. This is not the case. Indeed our replicating portfolio $(a_t, b_t)_{0 \le t \le T}$ satisfies now the following equation

$$V_t - V_0 = \underbrace{\int_0^t a_s dS_s}_{\substack{\text{gain/loss} \\ \text{from} \\ \text{stock}}} + \underbrace{\int_0^t b_s r \beta_s ds}_{\substack{\text{gain/loss} \\ \text{from} \\ \text{bonds}}} + \underbrace{\int_0^t D_0 S_s a_s e^{r(t-s)} ds}_{\substack{\text{gains from} \\ \text{reinvested dividends}}}$$

or, in differential form,

$$dV_t = a_t \ dS_t + b_t \ d\beta_t + D_0 S_t a_t \ dt.$$

This looks like Equation 3.3 of Section 3.1 containing the additional term $D_0 S_t a_t \ dt$.

Using now exactly the same arguments as in Section 3.1 we arrive to the following partial differential equation

$$\frac{1}{2}\nu^2 S^2 f'' + (r - D_0)S f' + \dot{f} - rf = 0,$$

and using the same techniques as in Section 3.2 we derive the value of a derivative:

$$(3.23) \qquad V_t = f(S_t, t) = \frac{e^{-(r-D_0)(T-t)}}{\sqrt{2\pi\nu^2(T-t)}} \int_{-\infty}^{\infty} F(S_t e^{(r-D_0)(T-t)} e^{-\frac{\nu^2}{2}(T-t)} \cdot e^z) e^{-\frac{z^2}{2\nu^2(T-t)}} dz$$

and for $t = 0$:

$$(3.24) \qquad V_0 = f(S_0, 0) = \frac{e^{-(r-D_0)T}}{\sqrt{2\pi\nu^2 T}} \int_{-\infty}^{\infty} F(S_t e^{(r-D_0)T} e^{-\frac{\nu^2}{2}T} \cdot e^z) e^{-\frac{z^2}{2\nu^2 T}} dz$$

B. Discrete dividend payments

Suppose now that during the life time of an option there is one dividend payment at time $0 < t_d < T$ which is $d \cdot S_{t_d^-}$ where $S_{t_d^-}$ is the price of the underlying asset just before time t_d. If we denote by $S_{t_d^+}$ the price of the underlying asset right after the payment we conclude

$$S_{t_d^-} = S_{t_d^+} + dS_{t_d^-},$$

otherwise there would be an arbitrage possibility.

Now let $f(S_t, t)$ be the value of the option at time t. Since the owner of an option does not receive a dividend we must have

$$f(S_{t_d^-}, t_d^-) = f(S_{t_d^+}, t_d^+),$$

otherwise there would be again a arbitrage possibility.

So we have for any S

$$f(S, t_d^-) = \lim_{t \uparrow t_d} f(S, t) = f(S(1-d), t_d^+) = \lim_{t \downarrow t_d} f(S(1-d), t).$$

In other words, since the path

$$t \mapsto f(S_t, t)$$

is almost surely continuous, the function in two variables

$$(S, t) \mapsto f(S, t)$$

cannot be continuous at $t = t_d$.

We can find the solution in two steps, each time using the methods of solutions presented in the Sections 3.1 and 3.2

① For $t_d \le t < T$ we find $f(S, t)$ as explained in Sections 3.1 and 3.2.

② Then we define a new options whose exercise date is t_d and whose payoff function is

$$\widetilde{F}(S) := f(S(1-d), t_d).$$

For this derivative we find the value $\tilde{f}(S,t)$, $0 \leq t \leq t_d$.

Finally we put for $0 \leq t \leq T$

$$f(S,t) = \begin{cases} \tilde{f}(S,t) & \text{if } t < t_d \\ f(S,t) & \text{if } t \geq t_d. \end{cases}$$

Note that

(3.25) $$\lim_{t \uparrow t_d} f(S,t) = \widetilde{F}(S) = f(S(1-d), t_d) = \lim_{t \downarrow t_d} f(S(1-d), t).$$

Chapter 4

Interest Derivatives

Chapter 5

Martingale Method, Stopping Times and American Options

We start in this chapter with a more general and abstract approach to evaluate claims. A general claim will be simply a function $f : \Omega \to \mathbb{R}$ and $f(\omega)$ represents the payoff if $\omega \in \Omega$ happens. A Valuation assigns to each such claim a number, its value at time 0. We will specify some reaonable conditions on valuations and will conclude that evaluating claims is equivalent to find equivalent probabilities which turn the price processes of the underlying assets into risk neutral processes. This generalizes observations we already made in the log-binomial and the log-normal case.

In the following sections we concerned with pricing American style options. Thes options allow the holder to choose the exercise date within a specified exercise period. In order to define mathematically allowable exercise strategies we need the concept of *stopping times*. Stopping times will be introduced and discussed in section 5.2. In the sections 5.3 and 5.4 we finally develope a pricing theory for American style options.

5.1   Martingales and Option Pricing

In this section we want to present a general approach to determine arbitrage free values of options. We will deduce the following principle:

> The problem of finding arbitrage free values of options is equivalent to the problem of finding an equivalent probability which turns the discounted prices of the underlying assets into martingales.

The notions of *equivalent probabilities* and *discounted price processes* will be introduced later. In order to formulate and prove this principle we will loosely follow ideas first developped by Harrison and Kreps [HK], Harrison and Pliska [HP] and Kreps [K]. Inspired by Black's and Schole's formula for options for log-normal processes they formulated a pricing theory for contingent claims within a more general frame.

We consider several stochastic adapted processes $(S_t^{(1)})_{0 \le t \le T}$, $(S_t^{(2)})_{0 \le t \le T}, \ldots (S_t^{(n)})_{0 \le t \le T}$ on a filtered probability space $(\Omega, \mathcal{F}\mathbb{P}, (\mathcal{F}_t)_{0 \le t \le T})$. We assume that $\mathcal{F} = \mathcal{F}_T$. We think of these processes being the prices of n underlying assets. As usual $\mathcal{F}_t$ represents the σ-algebra of all events whose outcome is known by the time t. Since $\mathcal{F}_0$ represents the presence we assume that for all $A \in \mathcal{F}_0$ either $\mathbb{P}(A) = 0$ (A did not happen) or $\mathbb{P}(A)$ (A happened).

In order to simplify computations we will first introduce a "change of currency". We denote by $r > 0$ the, continuously compounded, interest rate of a riskless bond during the time period $[0, T]$. Our new currency is a "riskless bond which pays one Euro at the end of the considered time period". We will represent prices using the correct number of these *zero bonds*. Only at the very end of our discourse we will translate our results back into the usual currency. The "new prices" of our underlying assets are now given by

$$(5.1) \qquad \widehat{S}_t^{(i)} = e^{r(T-t)} S_t^{(i)}.$$

A *general claim or option* is now simply a function $f \colon \Omega \to \mathbb{R}$, which we assume to be $\mathcal{F}_T$-measurable and bounded. Later we will pass to unbounded claims. Note that for example the pay-off of a call within the Black Scholes model is unbounded from above, since a log-normal random variable is unbounded. We think of $f(w)$, $w \in \Omega$, being the pay-off (or liability) at time T, if w occurs.

Remark. If f is $\mathcal{F}_t$-measurable for some $t < T$, then the gain/loss caused by f will be already determined at time t and we might distinguish between "the option which pays $f(w)$ at time t" and "the option which pays $f(w)$ at some other time $\tilde{t} > t$". But in our new bond-currency this distinction is unnecessary since the interest rate (in terms of bonds) is zero.

Defintion. For $t \in [0, T]$ the vectorspace of all bounded $\mathcal{F}_t$ measurable functions $f : \Omega \to \mathbb{R}$ is denoted by

$$L_\infty(\Omega, \mathcal{F}_t).$$

A valuation at time 0 is defined to be a map

$$V_0 : L_\infty(\Omega, \mathcal{F}_T) \to \mathbb{R}.$$

The interpretation is as follows: $V_0(f)$ is the value assigned to the security f at time 0.

We want to enumerate some reasonable properties a valuations should have. As we will see, these properties are dictated by the fact that we want to avoid arbitrage possibilities.

(V1) Linearity

If $f_1, f_2 \in L_\infty(\Omega, \mathcal{F}_T)$, $\alpha_1, \alpha_2 \in \mathbb{R}$, and $0 \le t \le T$ then

$$V_0(\alpha_1 f_1 + \alpha_2 f_2) = \alpha_1 V_0(f_1) + \alpha_2 V_0(f_2).$$

(V2) Positivity

If $f \in L_\infty(\Omega, \mathcal{F}_T)$ and $0 \le t \le T$, then

(a) $f \ge 0$ a.s. $\Rightarrow V_0(f) \ge 0$.

(b) $f \ge 0$ a.s. and $\mathbb{P}(\{f > 0\}) > 0 \Rightarrow V_0(f) > 0$.

An element $A \in \mathcal{F}_T$ with $\mathbb{P}(A) = 0$ has the property that $\chi_A \ge 0$ a.s. and $\chi_A \le 0$ a.s. Thus condition (V1) implies that

(5.2) $$V_0(\chi_A) = 0 \iff \mathbb{P}(A) = 0$$

Remark. Let us derive for example (V1) from basic arbitrage arguments:

Assume that for some choice of α_1, α_2 $f_1, f_2 \in L_\infty(\Omega, \mathcal{F}_T)$

$$V_0(\alpha_1 f_1 + \alpha_2 f_2) \neq \alpha_1 V_0(f_1, t) + \alpha_2 V_0(f_2, t).$$

Then an investor could proceede in the following way.

- Case 1: $V_0(\alpha_1 f_1 + \alpha_2 f_2) < \alpha_1 V_0(f_1, t) + \alpha_2 V_0(f_2, t).$

    Go short α_1 times the option f_1 and α_2 times the option f_2 and buy one unit of $(\alpha_1 f_1 + \alpha_2 f_2)$.

- Case 2: $V_0(\alpha_1 f_1 + \alpha_2 f_2) > \alpha_1 V_0(f_1, t) + \alpha_2 V_0(f_2, t).$

    Go short one unit of $(\alpha_1 f_1 + \alpha_2 f_2)$ and buy α_1 times the option (f_1) and α_2 times the option (f_2).

In both cases the riskless gain is $|V_0(\alpha_1 f_1 + \alpha_2 f_2) - \alpha_1 V_0(f_1, t) + \alpha_2 V_0(f_2, t)|.$

The next condition simply says that a zero bond is allways worth a zero bond.

(V3) Normalization $V_0(1) = 1.$

Finally we need a condition which cannot be deduced completely from a simple arbitrage argument.

(V4) Monotone Continuity

Assume $f_1, f_2, \ldots$ are in $L_\infty(\Omega, \mathcal{F}_T)$ and $f_1 \leq f_2 \leq f_3 \leq \cdots$. Furthermore assume that $f = \lim_{n \to \infty} f_n = \sup_{n \in \mathbb{N}} f_n$ is also bounded. Then

$$\sup_{n \in \mathbb{N}} V_0(f_n) = V_0(f).$$

Remark.

Assume $f_1, f_2, \ldots$ are in $L_\infty(\Omega, \mathcal{F}_T)$ and $f_1 \leq f_2 \leq f_3 \leq \cdots$ and $f = \lim_{n \to \infty} f_n$ exists a.s. and is an element of $L_\infty(\Omega, \mathcal{F}_t)$.

Already (V2) implies that $\sup_{n \in \mathbb{N}} V_0(f_n) \leq V_0(f)$. Indeed, since $f > f_n$, for all n, it follows that $V_0(f_n) \leq V_0(f)$, and thus $\sup_{n \in \mathbb{N}} V_0(f_n) \leq V_0(f)$

Let us discuss what it would mean if this inequality were strict and $\Delta = V_0(f) - \sup_{n \in \mathbb{N}} V_0(f_n) > 0$.

In that case an investor could take an arbitrarily small $\varepsilon > 0$ (much smaller than Δ) and choose $N \in \mathbb{N}$ so large that $\mathbb{E}_\mathbb{P}(f - f_N) < \varepsilon$. The strategy of selling at $t = 0$ one unit of f and buying one unit of f_N would lead to a fixed gain of at least Δ at time $t = 0$ and a liability of $f - f_N$ at time T whose expected value is smaller than ε.

In other words he or she could make a fixed gain at time 0, namely at least $V(f,t) - \sup_{n \in \mathbb{N}} V(f_n, t)$ with a risk of having a loss at time T whose expected value he or she can choose to be as small as he or she wants it to be. Following Kreps [K] this condition (V4) is referred to as "No Free Lunch".

We will now show that a valuation at time 0 is given by an equivalent probability $\mathbb{Q}$.

Definition.   A probability $\mathbb{Q}$ on $(\Omega, \mathcal{F}_T)$ is called *equivalent to* $\mathbb{P}$ if for any set $A \in \mathcal{F}_T$

$$\mathbb{P}(A) = 0 \iff \mathbb{Q}(A) = 0.$$

We say that $\mathbb{P}$ and $\mathbb{Q}$ are *equivalent* if $\mathbb{P}$ is absolutely continuous to $\mathbb{Q}$ and $\mathbb{Q}$ is absolute continuous to $\mathbb{P}$, i.e. if for any $A \in \mathcal{F}$

$$\mathbb{P}(A) = 0 \Leftrightarrow \mathbb{Q}(A) = 0.$$

In that case we can apply the Theorem of Radon-Nikodym (Theorem B.3.1 in Appendix B.3) and deduce that there is a $\mathbb{P}$ integrable $g : \Omega \to \mathbb{R}$ so that

$$\mathbb{Q}(A) = \mathbb{E}_\mathbb{P}(g\chi_A), \quad \text{for all} A \in \mathcal{F}.$$

Proposition 5.1.1 .   *There is a one to one correspondance between all valuations at 0 satisfying (V1)-(V4) and all probabilities $\mathbb{Q}$ on $\mathcal{F}_T$ which are equivalent to $\mathbb{P}$. This correspondance is given by*

$$\mathbb{Q}(A) = V_0(\chi_A), \quad A \in \mathcal{F}_T,$$

if V_0 is a valuation at 0 satisfying (V1)-(V4), and by

$$V_0(f) = \mathbb{E}_\mathbb{Q}(f), \quad f \in L_\infty(\Omega, \mathcal{F}_T),$$

if $\mathbb{Q}$ is a probability equivalent to $\mathbb{P}$.

Proof of Proposition 5.1.1.   For $A \in \mathcal{F}$ we put

$$\mathbb{Q}(A) = V_0(A)$$

and have first to show that $\mathbb{Q}$ is a probability on $\mathcal{F}$ which is $\mathbb{P}$-equivalent.

By (V2) and the following remark it follows that $\mathbb{Q}(\phi) = V_0(\chi_\phi) = 0$, (V3) implies that $\mathbb{Q}(\Omega) = V_0(1) = 1$, and by (V2), $0 \le \mathbb{Q}(A) \le 1$, for all $A \in \mathcal{F}$. If $A_1, A_2, A_3, \ldots \in \mathcal{F}$ are disjoint it follows

$$\mathbb{Q}\left(\bigcup_{n\in\mathbb{N}} A_n\right) = V_0(\chi_{\cup_{n\in\mathbb{N}}A_n})$$

$$= \sup_{N\in\mathbb{N}} V_0(\chi_{\cup_n^N A_n}) \quad [\text{by (V4)}]$$

$$= \sup_{N\in\mathbb{N}} \sum_{n=1}^N V_0(\chi_{A_n}) \quad [\text{by (V2)}]$$

$$= \sup_{N\in\mathbb{N}} \sum_{n=1}^N \mathbb{Q}(A_n) = \sum_{n=1}^\infty \mathbb{Q}(A_n).$$

The fact that $\mathbb{Q}$ is $\mathbb{P}$-equivalent follows again from (V1) and the observation 5.2.

Conversely if $\mathbb{Q}$ is a probabilty equivalent to $\mathbb{P}$, we put $V_0(f) = \mathbb{E}_\mathbb{Q}(f)$, for $f \in L_\infty(\Omega, \mathcal{F}_T)$, and deduce (V1) from the linearity of expected values, (V2) from the monotonicity of expected values and the assumption that $\mathbb{Q}$ is equivalent, (V3) from the fact that $\mathbb{Q}(\Omega) = 1$, and fianlly we deduce (V4) from the Monoton Convergence Theorem (Theorem B.2.10 in Appendix B.2). □

Until now, we did not use the (discounted) stock prices $(\widehat{S}_t^{(i)})_{0 \leq t \leq T}$. We have to formulate a condition which states that the valuation at 0 of an option is *consistent with the stock prices*. Therefore we want to consider for $t \in [0,T]$ the random variable $\widehat{S}_t^{(i)}$ as an option, namely the claim which pays $\widehat{S}_t^{(i)}$. Since $\widehat{S}_t^{(i)}$ might not be bounded (like in the log-normal case for example) we will first extend V_0 to a larger class of functions.

Let $f : \Omega \to \mathbb{R}$ be measurable, and *bounded from below almost surely* which means that there is a $c \in \mathbb{R}$ so that $f \geq c$ almost surely. If V_0 is a valuation at 0 satisfying (V1)-(V4) we put

$$\widetilde{V}_0(f) = \sup_{g \in L_\infty(\Omega, \mathcal{F}_T), g \leq f} V_0(g).$$

Remark.

This supremum could be $+\infty$. Secondly, we note that $\widetilde{V}_0(f) = \lim_{n \to \infty} V_0(\max(f,n))$ (Exercise....). And thirdly we note that one can deduce from condition (V4) that $\widetilde{V}_0 = V_0$ on the space $L_\infty(\Omega, \mathcal{F}_T)$ (Execise....), i.e. $\widetilde{V}_0$ is an extension of V_0 onto the set of all measurable functions whith are bounded from below. Therefore we will continue to denote $\widetilde{V}_0$ simply by V_0.

Since V_0 is determined by an equivalent probability $\mathbb{Q}$ it follows that

$$V_0(f) = \sup_{g \in L_\infty(\Omega, \mathcal{F}_T), g \leq f} \mathbb{E}_\mathbb{Q}(g) = \lim_{n \to \infty} \mathbb{E}_\mathbb{Q}(\max(f,n)) = \mathbb{E}_\mathbb{Q}(f).$$

We will now assume that our discounted stock prices $(\widehat{S}_t^{(i)})$ are bounded from below (usually by 0) and consider the following condition on V_0.

(V5) If $0 \leq u \leq t \leq T$, $i = 1, 2 \ldots n$ and $A \in \mathcal{F}_u$ it follows that $V_0(\chi_A \widehat{S}_t^{(i)}) = V_0(\chi_A \widehat{S}_u^{(i)})$.

Remark. Let us give an argument why the absence of (V5) would lead to arbitrage possibilities. Assume for example $V_0(\chi_A \widehat{S}_u^{(i)}) < V_0(\chi_A \widehat{S}_t^{(i)})$. An investor would buy one unit of $\chi_A \widehat{S}_u^{(i)}$ and sell one unit of $\chi_A \widehat{S}_t^{(i)}$ at time 0 and have a gain of $V_0(\chi_A \widehat{S}_t^{(i)}) - V_0(\chi_A \widehat{S}_u^{(i)})$. In the future he can avoid any loss by proceeding as follows. If at time t A does not happens the option he bought becomes worthless, but also his liability towards the buyer of the option he sold vanishes. If A happens he recieves at time u the amount of $\widehat{S}_u^{(i)}$ which he can use to buy one unit of the $i - th$ stock, and cover therefore his liability at time t.

Theorem 5.1.2 .   *There is a one to one correspondance between all valuations at 0 satisfying (V1)-(V5) and the set of all equivalent probabilities $\mathbb{Q}$ under which the discounted stock prices are martingales.*

This correspondance is the same as in Proposition 5.1.1.

A probability $\mathbb{Q}$ which is equivalent to $\mathbb{P}$ and turns the discounted stock prices into martingales will be called a equivalent martingale probability *for the processes* $(\widehat{S}_t^{(i)})$, $i = 1, 2, \ldots n$.

Remark. Note that we did not assume that the stock prices $(\widehat{S}_t^{(i)})$ are integrable with respect to $\mathbb{P}$. This is not necessary. But they turn out to be integrable with respect to any equivalent martingale probability.

Proof of Theorem 5.1.2. Assume V_0 satisfies (V1)-(V5) and let $\mathbb{Q}$ be the corresponding probability given by Proposition 5.1.1. First we have to show that $(\widehat{S}_t^{(i)})$ is integrable with respect to $\mathbb{Q}$. Indeed choose $-c$, $c > 0$, to be a lower bound of $(\widehat{S}_t^{(i)})$ and note that

$$\mathbb{E}_{\mathbb{Q}}(|\widehat{S}_t^{(i)}|) \leq c + \mathbb{E}_{\mathbb{Q}}(\widehat{S}_t^{(i)})$$
$$= c + \lim_{n \to \infty} \mathbb{E}_{\mathbb{Q}}(\min(\widehat{S}_t^{(i)}, n)) \text{ [Monoton Convergence]}$$
$$= c + \lim_{n \to \infty} V_0(\min(\widehat{S}_t^{(i)}, n))$$
$$= c + V_0(\widehat{S}_t^{(i)})$$
$$= c + S_0^{(i)} < \infty \text{ [Apply (V5) to } u = 0, \text{ and } A = \Omega]$$

For $u < t$ and $A \in \mathcal{F}_u$ it follows now from (V5) that

$$\mathbb{E}_{\mathbb{Q}}(\chi_A \widehat{S}_t^{(i)}) = V_0(\chi_A \widehat{S}_t^{(i)}) = V_0(\chi_A \widehat{S}_u^{(i)}) = \mathbb{E}_{\mathbb{Q}}(\chi_A \widehat{S}_u^{(i)}).$$

Since $\widehat{S}_u^{(i)}$ is $\mathcal{F}_u$-measurable this implies by the definition of conditional expectations that
$\mathbb{E}_{\mathbb{Q}}(\widehat{S}_t^{(i)} | \mathcal{F}_u) = \widehat{S}_u^{(i)}$ almost surely.   □

We now want to describe valuations for other times t and define a *valuation process* to be a map

$$V : L_\infty(\Omega, \mathcal{F}_t) \times [0, T] \rightarrow L_\infty(\Omega, \mathcal{F}_T), \quad (f, t) \mapsto V_t(f),$$

so that for $t \in [0, T]$ the function $V_t(f)$ is $\mathcal{F}_t$-measurable. $V_t(f)$ has to interpreted as the value of the claim f given all information up to time t. For $t = 0$ $V_0(f)$ has to be a constant almost surely and will therefore be identified with this constant.

The following condition can easily be deduced from an arbitrage argument (see Exercise...)

(V6) For $t \in [0, T]$ and $f \in L_\infty(\Omega, \mathcal{F}_T)$ it follows that

$$V_0(\chi_A V_t(f)) = V_0(\chi_A f).$$

I.e. at time 0 a claim which pays f if $A \in \mathcal{F}_t$ occured must have the same value as a claim which pays $V_t(f)$ if A occured.

Similar as in Theorem 5.1.2 we can prove the following statement.

Theorem 5.1.3 .   *Assume* $V : L_\infty(\Omega, \mathcal{F}_T) \times [0, T] \rightarrow L_\infty(\Omega, \mathcal{F}_T)$ *is a valuation process which satisfies (V6) and for which V_0 satisfies (V1)-(V5).*

Let $\mathbb{Q}$ be the corresponding equivalent martingale measure. Then it follows for $f \in L_\infty(\Omega, \mathcal{F}_T)$ and $t \in [0, T]$:

$$V_t(f) = \mathbb{E}_{\mathbb{Q}}(f | \mathcal{F}_t).$$

We finally want to translate our formula for pricing options back to the case where our currency are Euros and not bonds. We consider an option which pays at time $t \leq T$ the amount $g(\omega)$ in Euros, where g is $\mathcal{F}_t$-measurable. Since our currency consists of Euros, the time of the pay-off becomes relevant. In terms of bonds this amount equals to $f(\omega) = e^{r(T-t)}g(\omega)$ bonds. If $W(g, t, s)$ is the value of this option at time $s \leq t$ measured in Euros, its value measured in bonds is denoted by $V(f, s) = V(f, t, s)$. Now let $\mathbb{Q}$ be the $\mathbb{P}$-equivalent probability measure associated to V, turning $\widehat{S}_t^{(i)} = e^{r(T-t)}S_t^{(i)}$ into a martingale. Then it follows

$$(5.3) \qquad W(g, t, s) = e^{-r(T-s)}V(f, s)$$

$$= e^{-r(T-s)}\mathbb{E}_{\mathbb{Q}}(f|\mathcal{F}_s)$$

$$= e^{-r(T-s)}\mathbb{E}_{\mathbb{Q}}(e^{r(T-t)}g|\mathcal{F}_s) = e^{-r(t-s)}\mathbb{E}_{\mathbb{Q}}(g|\mathcal{F}_s).$$

For evaluating American options it will turn out that we are in particular interested in derivatives of the form

$$g = 1_A G(S_t)$$

with $A \in \mathcal{F}_t$ and with pay-off taking place at time t. In that case

$$(5.4) \qquad W(f, t, s) = e^{-r(t-s)}\mathbb{E}_{\mathbb{Q}}(1_A G(S_t)|\mathcal{F}_s) = e^{-r(t-s)}\mathbb{E}_{\mathbb{Q}}(1_A G(e^{-r(T-t)}\widehat{S}_t)|\mathcal{F}_s).$$

Remark. Theorems 5.1.2 and 5.1.3 leave the following two questions unanswered:

1) Given the stock prices, is it always possible to find a valuation satisfying (V1)-(V5), or equivalently is there always an equivalent martingale measure?

   The answer to this question depends on the model we are considering. Within the discrete model we showed that the existence of an equivalent martingale probability is equivalent to the absence of arbitrage (this is how Theorem 1.1.3. can be interpreted). We actually computed the (unique) equivalent martingale probability for the Binomial model. Also, it can be shown that our results on option pricing in the Black Scholes model can be interpreted as a result on existence and uniqueness of equivalent martingale measures. In the literature we find more results connecting the absence of arbitrage to the existance of equivalent martingale measures. Here are some examples:

   a) For finitely many trading times: Dalang, Morton, and Willinger (1989) [DMW]

   b) For continuous trading times and continuous and bounded price processes: Delbaen (1992) [D1]

c) For continuous trading time and bounded price processes with right continuous paths having left limits: Delbaen and Schachermayer [DS2].

d) For continuous trading time and unbounded price proccesses with right continuous paths having left limits: Delbaen and Schachermayer [DS3] .

The second question which comes in mind is the following:

2) Are the equivalent martingale probabilities unique? Equivalently: are arbitrage-free option prices unique?

Unfortunately, only in few cases they are unique, the most important examples are the log-binomial and the Black Scholes model. This is the reason why, despite all its flaws, the Black-Scholes model is still the best and the most often used model.

There are several attempts to force uniqueness of $\mathbb{Q}$ by requiring some functionals $\Phi(\mathbb{Q})$ to be minimal. These functionals for example measure the "distance between $\mathbb{P}$ and $\mathbb{Q}$". Here is an example of such a result.

Theorem 5.1.4 . *Assume $(\widehat{S}_t^{(j)})$, $j \in J$ is a family of processes for which there is an equivalent martingale measure such that the density f of $\mathbb{Q}$ with respect to $\mathbb{P}$ is square $\mathbb{P}$-integrable. Assume also that $\frac{1}{f}$ (which is the density of $\mathbb{P}$ with respect of $\mathbb{Q}$) is square $\mathbb{Q}$-integrable.*

Then there is a unique martingale measure for which

$$\Phi(\mathbb{Q}) = ||f||_{L_2(\mathbb{P})} + ||\frac{1}{f}||_{L_2(\mathbb{Q})}$$

is minimal.

Other results of these type can for example be found in Delbaen and Schachermayer (1996) [DS4]. and in Schweizer [Sch]. But there is one main problem in all of these approaches: As much as it they might make sense mathematically, there is no compelling economic reason why the "right option price" should be given by minimizing a certain functional Φ.

5.2   Stopping Times

Let $(S_t)_{0 \leq t \leq T}$ be a stochastic process on a filtered space $(\Omega, \mathcal{F}, \mathbb{P}, (\mathcal{F}_t)_{0 \leq t \leq T})$ describing the price of a stock during the time period $[0, T]$. *An American style option contingent to that stock* is a security which guarantees a payment of $F(S_t)$ whenever the holder chooses to exercise his or her option during the time period $[0, T]$. Thus, studying American options we are facing the additional problem that the holder has more freedom in exercising his or her option. We first will have to study the *possible* or *admissible* rules the holder can apply to determine when to exercise the option. In probability theory such *admissible rules* are referred to as stopping times, they can be seen as strategies "for stopping or starting certain processes". Before we present the mathematical rigorous definition let us consider some examples. Stopping times can be used for

1) determining when to sell or buy a stock.

2) when to quit playing a certain game.

3) when, playing Black Jack, to tell the dealer that one does not want more cards.

4) when to exercise an American option.

Examples. Consider the following strategies. Which of them should be called admissible?

1) Sell a stock once it got over 100 Euros.

2) At Black Jack: stop buying cards once one has at least 16 points.

3) At Black Jack: stop buying if the next card would get you over 21.

4) Play roulette until you made a gain of at least 1000 Euros or you lost all your money.

5) Sell a stock at the day its value is maximal over a given period $[0, T]$.

There is a crucial difference between the strategies (1), (2), and (4), on one hand and (3), and (5) on the other hand: For (1), (2) and (4) the decision to stop at a certain time t

depends only on events happening before or at time t. On the other hand in (3), and (5), the decision of stopping at a certain time depends on future events: in (3) the decision to stop depends on the value of the next card, and in (5) the decision to sell a stock at a time t depends on whether or not all future values $(S_u)_{t<u\leq T}$ are smaller or equal to S_t.

Conclusion: A stopping time should be seen as a map $\tau\colon \Omega \to [0,\infty)$ or $\tau\colon \Omega \to [0,T]$ (if the considered time period is finite) for which the event $\{\tau = t\}$, or $\{\tau \leq t\}$ only depends on events happened at time t or before. Thus, the events $\{\tau \leq t\}$, $\{\tau = t\}$ must be $\mathcal{F}_t$ measurable. This leads us to the following precise definition.

Definition. Given a filtered probability space $(\Omega, \mathcal{F}, \mathbb{P}, (\mathcal{F}_t)_{t\in I})$ where I is an index set like $I = [0,\infty)$, $I = [0,T]$, or I is discrete like $I = \{0, t_1, t_2, \ldots, t_n\}$ or $I = \{0, t_1, t_2, t_3, \ldots\}$.

A stopping time is then a map:

$$\tau\colon \ \Omega \to I,$$

or, if I is an unbounded indexset, τ can assume the value ∞

$$\tau\colon \ \Omega \to I \cup \{\infty\},$$

having the property that the set $\{\omega \in \Omega \mid \tau \leq t\} \in \mathcal{F}_t$ for all $t \in I$. A map $\tau\colon \Omega \to I$, respectively $\tau\colon \Omega \to I \cup \{\infty\}$, with countable range, say $\{\tau(w)\colon w \in \Omega\} = \{t_0, t_1, t_2, \ldots\}$ is a stopping time if and only if

$$\{\tau = t_i\} \in \mathcal{F}_{t_i} \quad \text{for} \quad i = 1, 2, \ldots .$$

It is often much easier, but enough for our purposes, to consider only stopping times with countable ranges.

Proposition 5.2.1 .

a) *Constant random variables $\tau \equiv t$ are stopping times.*

b) *If τ, σ are stopping times then $\max(\tau, \sigma)$ and $\min(\tau, \sigma)$ are stopping times.*

c) *Suppose $I = [0, \infty)$ or $I = \mathbb{N}_0$. If τ is stopping time and $t \in I$, then $\tau + t$ is stopping time.*

But: $\tau - t$ not necessarily stopping time.

Proof of Proposition 5.2.1. We will only show (b) for $\max(\tau, \sigma)$ and leave the rest as an exercise. For $t \in I$ note that

$$\{\max(\tau, \sigma) \leq t\} = \{\tau \leq t\} \cup \{\sigma \leq t\} \in \mathcal{F}_t.$$

☐

The following Proposition exhibits some important examples of stopping times. They can be formulated in financial terms as follows: Telling your broker to sell a stock at the time it surpasses a certain value is an admissible strategy. We first need some technical conditions on the filtration and the stochastic processes.

If the index set I is continuous, i.e. of the form $I = [0, T]$ or $I = [0, \infty)$ we will say that a stochastic process $(S_t)_{t \in I}$ on the filtered space $(\Omega, \mathcal{F}, \mathbb{P}, (\mathcal{F}_t)_{t \in I})$ satisfies the *usual conditions* if

1) $\mathcal{F}_0$ consists of all sets A for which $\mathbb{P}(A) = 0$ or $\mathbb{P}(A) = 1$. This means that an $\mathcal{F}_0$-measurable random variable is almost surely a constant and conversely each random variable which is almost surely a constant is $\mathcal{F}_0$-measurable.

2) For $t, \mathcal{F}_t = \bigcap_{u > t} \mathcal{F}_u.$

3) The paths of (S_t) are right continuous having limits to the left, i.e. for $w \in \Omega$

$$\lim_{u \nearrow t} S_u(w) \text{ exists and } \lim_{u \searrow t} S_u(w) = S_t(w).$$

If I is discrete above assumptions (2) and (3) are meaningless, and in that case we mean by the usual conditions only above condition (1).

Proposition 5.2.2 . *Assume that for the stochastic process on $(\Omega, \mathcal{F}, \mathbb{P}, (\mathcal{F}_t)_{t \in I})$ the usual conditions are satisfied. Let $a \in \mathbb{R}$ and define for $w \in \Omega$:*

a) $\tau(w) = \inf\{t \in I | S_t(w) \geq a\}$

b) $\sigma(w) = \inf\{t \in I | S_t(w) > a\}$

(with $\inf(\emptyset) = \sup I$ or ∞ depending whether or not I is bounded)

Then τ and σ are stopping times.

Proof. We assume $I = [0, \infty)$. The other cases can be handled similarly.
For $t \in I$ we deduce from the right continuity that

$$\{\tau \leq t\} = \bigcup_{u \leq t} \{w \in \Omega \mid S_u(w) \geq a\}$$

$$= \bigcap_{n \in \mathbb{N}} \bigcup_{\substack{u < t \\ u \text{ rational}}} \{w \in \Omega \mid S_u(w) \geq a - \frac{1}{n}\} \cup \{w \in \Omega \mid S_t(w) \geq a\}.$$

Note that the first union is uncountable. Thus although all the sets of the form $\{w \in \Omega \mid S_u(w) \geq a\}$, $u \leq t$, lie in $\mathcal{F}_t$ we cannot yet deduce that the union of these uncountable many sets is in $\mathcal{F}_t$. But using the fact that the paths of S_t are right continuous we can reduce it to a countable union of elements of $\mathcal{F}_t$.

The proof of part (b) is left as an exercise. $\qquad\square$

Defintion. If $(S_t)_{t \in I}$ is an adapted process and τ a stopping time on $(\Omega, \mathcal{F}, \mathbb{P}, (\mathcal{F}_t)_{t \in I})$ we call the process $(S_{t \wedge \tau})_{t \in I}$ with

$$S_{t \wedge \tau}(w) := \begin{cases} S_t(w) & \text{if } t < \tau(w) \\ S_{\tau(w)}(w) & \text{if } t \geq \tau(w) \end{cases}$$

the *process* (S_t) *stopped by* τ and $S_\tau : \Omega \to \mathbb{R}$, with $S_\tau(\omega) = S_{\tau(\omega)}(\omega)$ is called terminal element .

As we observed before "events happening before a fixed time t" are elements of $\mathcal{F}_t$. We now want to define what it means for an event *to happen before a stopping time τ.*

Proposition 5.2.3 .   *Let $\tau \colon \Omega \to I$ be a stopping time on $(\Omega, \mathcal{F}, \mathbb{P}, (\mathcal{F}_t)_{i \in I})$. Then the set of all elements A of $\mathcal{F}$ which have the property that*

$$A \cap \{\tau \leq t\} \in \mathcal{F}_t$$

form a σ-algebra, it is called the σ-algebra of events before τ and is denoted by $\mathcal{F}_\tau$.

Proof.   We verify the properties of σ-algebras:

1) $\phi \in \mathcal{F}_\tau$ since $\phi \cap \{\tau \leq t\} \in \mathcal{F}_t$ for all $t \in I$.

2) If $A \in \mathcal{F}_\tau$, then

$$(\Omega \backslash A) \cap \{\tau \leq t\} = \Omega \cap \{\tau \leq t\} \backslash A \cap \{\tau \leq t\} \in \mathcal{F}_t$$

for all $t \in I$, then $\Omega \backslash A \in \mathcal{F}_\tau$.

3) If $A_1, A_2, \ldots \in \mathcal{F}_\tau$, then

$$\bigcup_{i \in \mathbb{N}} A_i \cap \{\tau \leq t\} = \bigcup_{i \in \mathbb{N}} \underbrace{(A_i \cap \{\tau \leq t\})}_{\in \mathcal{F}_t} \in \mathcal{F}_t$$

for all $t \in I$. Thus $\bigcup_{i \in \mathbb{N}} A_i \in \mathcal{F}_\tau$. $\square$

Proposition 5.2.4 . *Assume $(S_t)_{t \in I}$ is an adapted process and τ a stopping time on $(\Omega, \mathcal{F}, \mathbb{P}, (\mathcal{F}_t)_{t \in I})$ satisfying the usual conditions (if $I = [0, \infty)$ or $I = [0, T]$). Let τ be a stopping time and assume $\tau < \infty$ a.s.*

Then S_τ is $\mathcal{F}_\tau$ measurable.

Proof. We assume $I = [0, \infty)$. In the case that $I = [0, T]$ the proof is the same, if $I = \{t_1, t_2, \dots\}$ the proof is simpler.

Given $a \in \mathbb{R}$ we have to show that $\{S_\tau < a\} \in \mathcal{F}_\tau$. This means that for given $t \in [0, \infty)$ we have to show that

$$\{S_\tau < a\} \cap \{\tau \leq t\} \in \mathcal{F}_t.$$

For let $n \in \mathbb{N}$ $P_n = (t_0^{(n)}, t_1^{(n)}, \dots t_n^{(n)})$ be a partition of $[0, t]$ $(0 = t_0^{(n)} < t_1^{(n)} < \dots < t_n^{(n)} = t)$ for which $\lim_{n \to \infty} ||P_n|| = 0$. Using the fact that S_t is right continuous we note that

$$\{S_\tau < a\} \cap \{\tau \leq t\}$$

$$= \left[\{\tau = t\} \cap \{S_t < a\} \right] \cup \bigcap_{n \in \mathbb{N}} \bigcup_{i=1}^{n} \left[\{t_{i-1}^{(n)} < \tau \leq t_i^{(n)}\} \cap \bigcup_{\substack{q \in [t_{i-1}^{(n)}, t_i^{(n)}) \\ q \text{ rational}}} \{S_q < a \text{ and } \tau < q\} \right].$$

Thus we wrote the set $\{S_\tau < a\} \cap \{\tau \leq t\}$ as countable unions and intersections of sets in $\mathcal{F}_t$, from which we deduce the claim. □

Proposition 5.2.5 .

Suppose σ and τ are stopping times on $(\Omega, \mathcal{F}, \mathbb{P}, (\mathcal{F}_t)_{t \in I})$.

a) *If $\sigma \leq \tau$ then $\mathcal{F}_\sigma \subset \mathcal{F}_\tau$.*

b) *If $A \in \mathcal{F}_\sigma$ then $A \cap \{\sigma \leq \tau\} \in \mathcal{F}_\tau$.*

Proof.   a) Suppose that $A \in \mathcal{F}_\sigma$, then

$$A \cap \{\sigma \le t\} \in \mathcal{F}_t \quad \text{all} \quad t \in I.$$

This implies for all t

$$A \cap \{\tau \le t\} = \underbrace{A \cap \{\sigma \le t\}}_{\in \mathcal{F}_t} \cap \underbrace{\{\tau \le t\}}_{\in \mathcal{F}_t} \in \mathcal{F}_t.$$

b) Suppose that $A \in \mathcal{F}_\sigma$, then for $t \in I$

(5.5) $A \cap \{\sigma \le \tau\} \cap \{\tau \le t\} = (A \cap \{\sigma \le t\}) \cap \{\tau \le t\} \cap \{\min(\sigma, t) \le \min(\tau, t)\}.$

By Proposition 5.2.1 follows that $\min(\sigma, t)$ and $\min(\tau, t)$ are also stopping times, and from part (a) follows that $\mathcal{F}_{\min(\sigma,t)} \subset \mathcal{F}_{\min(\tau,t)} \subset \mathcal{F}_t$ Therefore each of the three sets on the right side of (5.5) lies in $\mathcal{F}_t$. Since $t \in I$ was arbitrary it follows, that $A \cap \{\sigma \le \tau\} \in \mathcal{F}_\tau$.   □

We now come to our key result in this section. Roughly it says the following: If $(S_t)_{t \in I}$ is a martingale, a submartingale or a supermartingale, i.e. for $s < t$

$$\mathbb{E}(S_t | \mathcal{F}_s) = S_s, \text{ respectively}$$
$$\mathbb{E}(S_t | \mathcal{F}_s) \ge S_s, \text{ respectively}$$
$$\mathbb{E}(S_t | \mathcal{F}_s) \le S_s,$$

then the above inequalities are preserved if one replaces s and t by two bounded stopping times σ and τ with $\sigma \le \tau$.

Theorem 5.2.6 *(Optional Sampling Theorem).*

Assume $(S_t)_{t \in I}$ is an adapted process on the filtered space $(\Omega, \mathcal{F}, \mathbb{P}, (\mathcal{F}_t)_{t \in I})$ and assume the usual condition (at the beginning of the section) are satisfied. Let σ, τ be the stopping times with $\sigma \leq \tau$ and $\tau \leq N$ for some $N \in I$ if

a) $(S_t)_{t \in I}$ is a martingale, then

$$\mathbb{E}(S_\tau | \mathcal{F}_\sigma) = S_\sigma \quad a.s.$$

b) $(S_t)_{t \in I}$ is a submartingale, then

$$\mathbb{E}(S_\tau | \mathcal{F}_\sigma) \geq S_\sigma \quad a.s.$$

c) $(S_t)_{t \in I}$ is a supermartingale, then

$$\mathbb{E}(S_\tau | \mathcal{F}_\sigma) \leq S_\sigma \quad a.s.$$

Proof. In the case that $I = [0, \infty)$ or $I = [0, T)$ the proof would need some technical tools going beyond the scope of this text. Therefore we will prove the statement only in the discrete case and will assume without loss of generality that $I = \mathbb{N}_0$. Nevertheless the proof can easily be adapted to the continuous case if one assumes that the stopping times σ and τ achieve only finitely many values.

We only need to show b) because if (S_t) is a supermartingale then $(-S_t)$ is a submartingale and if (S_t) is a martingale it is both a sub- and a super-martingale.

Let $\sigma \leq \tau \leq N$ be two stopping times. We will first define "intermediate stopping times"

$$\sigma_0 = \sigma$$

$$\sigma_1 = \min(\tau, \sigma + 1)$$

$$\vdots$$

$$\sigma_N = \min(\tau, \sigma + N).$$

Since $\tau \leq N$ it follows that $\sigma_N = \tau$. Secondly, it follows that for any $i = 0, 1, 2, \ldots, N-1$ we have $\sigma_i \leq \sigma_{i+1}$ and σ_{i+1} and σ_i differ by at most 1.

It is enough to show that for $i = 0, 1, \ldots, N-1$

$$\mathbb{E}(S_{\sigma_{i+1}}|\mathcal{F}_{\sigma_i}) \geq S_{\sigma_i} \quad \text{a.s.}$$

which means by the definition of conditional expectations that for any given $A \in \mathcal{F}_{\sigma_i}$ we have to show that

$$\mathbb{E}(1_A S_{\sigma_{i+1}}) \geq \mathbb{E}(1_A S_{\sigma_i}).$$

Indeed

$$\mathbb{E}(1_A S_{\sigma_{i+1}}) = \sum_{j=0}^{N} \mathbb{E}(1_{A \cap \{\sigma_i = j\}} S_{\sigma_{i+1}})$$

$$= \sum_{j=0}^{N} \mathbb{E}(1_{A \cap \{\sigma_i = j\} \cap \{\sigma_{i+1} = j\}} S_j) + \mathbb{E}(1_{A \cap \{\sigma_i = j\} \cap \{\sigma_{i+1} = j+1\}} S_{j+1})$$

$$[\sigma_i \leq \sigma_{i+1} \leq \sigma_i + 1]$$

$$= \sum_{j=0}^{N} \mathbb{E}(1_{A \cap \{\sigma_i = j\} \cap \{\sigma_{i+1} = j\}} S_j) + \mathbb{E}(1_{A \cap \{\sigma_i = j\} \cap \{\sigma_{i+1} > j\}} S_{j+1})$$

$$[\{\sigma_{i+1} > j\} = \Omega \backslash \{\sigma_{i+1} \leq j\} \in \mathcal{F}_j]$$

$$\geq \sum_{j=0}^{N} \mathbb{E}(1_{A \cap \{\sigma_i = j\} \cap \{\sigma_{i+1} = j\}} S_j) + \mathbb{E}(1_{A \cap \{\sigma_i = j\} \cap \{\sigma_{i+1} > j\}} S_j)$$

[Since $\mathbb{E}(S_{j+1}|\mathcal{F}_j) \geq S_j$ a.s., it follows for $B \in \mathcal{F}_j$, $\mathbb{E}(1_B S_{j+1}) \geq \mathbb{E}(1_B S_j)$]

$$= \sum_{j=0}^{N} \mathbb{E}(1_{A \cap \{\sigma_i = j\}} S_j)$$

$$= \mathbb{E}(1_A S_{\sigma_i})$$

$\square$

The following example shows that the boundedness condition "$\tau \leq N$" in Theorem is necessary. It formulates the well known "doubling strategy" in roulette for example: Bet on red, doubling each time the stake, until red appears.

Example. Assume $X_1, X_2, X_3, \ldots$ are independent random variables with $\mathbb{P}(X_i = 1) = p > 0$, and $\mathbb{P}(X_i = -1) = (1-p)$. Define

$$S_n = \sum_{i=1}^{n} 2^{i-1} X_i$$

and $\tau(w) = \min\{n \in \mathbb{N}, X_n = 1\}$. Note $\tau < \infty$ almost surely and note that for $w \in \Omega$

$$
\begin{aligned}
S_{\tau(w)}(w) &= \sum_{i=1}^{\tau(w)} 2^{i-1} X_i(w) \\
&= 2^{\tau(w)-1} - \sum_{i=1}^{\tau(w)-1} 2^{i-1} \\
&= 2^{\tau(w)-1} - \left(1 + 2 + 4 + \cdots + 2^{\tau(w)-2}\right) \\
&= 1 \quad \text{[geometrical sequence]}.
\end{aligned}
$$

Thus $\mathbb{E}(S_\tau) = 1$. On the other hand, (S_n) is a martingale if $p = \frac{1}{2}$ and a supermartingale if $p < \frac{1}{2}$. Moreover, if $p \leq \frac{1}{2}$

$$\mathbb{E}(S_n) = \sum_{i=1}^{n} 2^{i-1}(p - (1-p)) \leq 0. \qquad \square$$

5.3   Valuation of American Style Options

We now turn to the problem of finding arbitrage free prices for American style options. Recall that an American style option contingent to a security S with pay-off function F and exercise period $[0, T]$ pays $F(S_t)$ dollars, if the holder of the option decides to exercise the option at time $t \in [0, T]$ and the price of the underlying security is S_t. As discussed in the previous section the holder is allowed to use any strategy defined by a stopping time.

We will, at least for the moment, only consider finitely many trading times $0, 1, 2, \ldots, N$, with $N \in \mathbb{N}$ and American style options which are exercisable only at these times. We also assume for the moment that all prices are given in zero bonds paying one Euro at time N. This forces us to let the payoff function F also depends on the exercise date n (chosen by the holder). Indeed, let $g(S_n)$ be the payoff in Euros if the holder exercises at time n. Then the payoff in terms of zero bonds at this time would be $F_n = e^{r(N-n)}g(S_n)$, where $r > 0$ denotes the interest paid between the times i and $i + 1$, $i = 0, 1, \ldots N - 1$. Thus, although $g(S_n)$ is only a function of S_n a dependence on the exercise date will be unavoidable if we translate this amount into zero bonds .

Therefore we will work within the following frame.

We think of an American option as a sequence of $N + 1$ functions on Ω, and we denote them as $F_0, F_1, \ldots, F_{N+1}$. The vector function $(F_0, F_1, \ldots, F_N)$ will be denoted by F. For $\omega \in \Omega$ the number $F_n(\omega)$ represents the payoff if the holder decides to exercise at time n assuming ω happens. Because of some technical reasons we will assume that the holder can exercise the option at time 0.

F_i, $i = 0, 1, \ldots N$, is defined on some filtered probability space $(\Omega, \mathcal{F}, \mathbb{P}, (\mathcal{F}_i)_{i=0,1,\ldots N})$. $\mathcal{F}_0$ consists of all sets $A \in \mathcal{F}$ with $\mathbb{P}(A) = 0$ or $\mathbb{P}(A) = 1$, and $\mathcal{F}_n$ represents as usual the set of all events for which it is known by the time n whether or not they happened. Since by time n it should be determined how much the holder of an option receives if he decides to exercise the option we will require that F_n is $\mathcal{F}_n$-measurable, for $n = 0, 1, \ldots N$.

An American style option $F = (F_0, F_1, \ldots, F_n)$ is called *contingent* to a price process $(S_i)_{i=0,1,\ldots N}$ if F_n is of the form $F_n(\omega) = f_n(\widehat{S}_n(\omega))$, where $f_n : \mathbb{R} \mapsto \mathbb{R}$ is measurable. We could write in this case F_n as a function of S_n instead of a function of $\widehat{S}_n$. But we want to keep all prices in a given formula in the same currency. We will also continue with the convention to denote payoff functions in zero bonds by the letter F and payoff functions in Euros by the letter G or g.

Example. An American call.

The payoff function of a call is $g(S) = (S - E)^+$. If $(S_n)_{n=0,...N}$ is the price process for the underlying asset it follows that

$$(5.6) \qquad F_n = e^{r(N-n)}(S_n - E)^+ = (e^{r(N-n)}S_n - e^{r(N-n)}E)^+ = (\widehat{S}_n - \widehat{E}_n)^+,$$

with $\widehat{E}_n = e^{r(N-n)}E$.

As in Section 5.1 we are given several processes describing the prices of the underlying assets. We will fix an equivalent probablity $\mathbb{Q}$ which turn the discounted prices of these assets into martingales. As discussed in Section 5.1 the value of a general claim paying $f(\omega)$ is given by

$$(5.7) \qquad\qquad\qquad V_e(f, t) = \mathbb{E}_\mathbb{Q}(f \mid \mathcal{F}_t)$$

where in this section t runs only over the discrete values $0, 1, \ldots N$. We will use the subscript "e" for European style options.

We will prove in this section that once an equivalent martingale probability is chosen and the value of each European style option determined by the formula (5.7), the arbitrage free price of each American style option is also determined.

If F is the sequence of pay-off functions we denote by $V_a(F, n)$, $n \in \{0, 1, \ldots, N\}$, the value of the American style option at time n. Here we assume that the holder is still able to exercise at time n. Therefore $V_a(F, n)$ is at least the *intrinsic value* of the option, i.e.

$$(V_a 1) \qquad\qquad\qquad V_a(F, n) \geq F_n$$

It is clear that $V_a(F, N) = F_N$, and the following principle is a key observation and will enable us to trace back the value at the American style option until the time 0.

For $n = 0, 1, \ldots, N - 1$

$(V_a 2)$ $V_a(F, n) = \max\big(F_n, V_e(V_a(F, n+1), n)\big) = \max\big((F_n, \mathbb{E}_\mathbb{Q}(V_a(F, n+1)|\mathcal{F}_n)\big)$

Note that $V_e(V_a(F, n+1), n)$ is the value, at time n, of a claim which pays the amount $V_a(F, n+1)$ in zerobonds.

Remark. The principle $(V_a 2)$ follows from the following arbitrage argument.

Assume first that $V_a(F, n) < \max(F_n, V_e(V_a(F, n+1), n))$. At time n we could proceed as follows: Buy an American style option F and sell short an option paying $V_a(F, n+1)$ at time $n+1$. From the inequality $(V_a 1)$ we deduce that $V_a(F, n) < V_e(V_a(F, n+1), n)$ and therefore the transactions at time n generates an income of $V_e(V_a(F, n+1), n) - V_a(F, n)$. At time $n+1$, we sell the American option receiving the amount of $V_a(F, n+1)$ which can be used to close the short position.

If $V_a(F, n) > \max(F_n, V_e(V_a(F, n+1), n))$ we could sell at time n an American style option F and receive the amount $V_a(F, n)$.

Then we are faced with two possibilities:

Either the buyer of that option exercises it right at time n (which would not be very smart given the price difference) and we would make a profit of $V_a(F, n) - F_n > 0$. Or the buyer does not exercise at time n. In that case we would buy at time n an option which pays at time $n+1$ the amount of $V_a(F, n+1)$ and at time $n+1$ we could close the short position using the amount $V_a(F, n+1)$. Nevertheless, we end up with a sure profit of $V_a(F, n) - V_e(V_a(F, n+1), n) > 0$.

$\square$

Using $(V_a 2)$ we are able to compute $V_a(F, n)$ similar to the computation of option prices within the log binomial model by tracing back the price starting with the final time N back to the time 0.

$$V_a(F, N) = F_N, \text{ and}$$
$$V_a(F, N - 1) = \max\big(F_{N-1}, V_e(V_a(F, N), N - 1)\big)$$
$$= \max\big(F_{N-1}), \mathbb{E}_\mathbb{Q}(F_N|\mathcal{F}_{N-1})\big)$$

and, if $V_a(F, n)$, $n \geq 1$, is already computed, then

$$(5.8) \qquad V_a(F, n-1) = \max\big(F_{n-1}, V_e(V_a(F, n), n-1)\big)$$

$$= \max\left(F_{n-1}, \mathbb{E}_\mathbb{Q}(V_a(F, n)|\mathcal{F}_{n-1}).\right)$$

As mentioned at the beginning of this section the holder of an American option can choose a strategy, in mathematical terms a stopping time, to determine the time at which the option should be exercised. What is the best exercise strategy?

To answer this question consider for a fixed stopping time $\tau\colon \Omega \to \{0, 1, \ldots, N\}$ the claim which pays F_τ. Thus $F_\tau(\omega) = F_{\tau(\omega)}(\omega)$, which is the process (F_n) stopped at τ (see Section 5.2). For example a European style option with fixed exercise date N can be seen as an option with $\tau \equiv N$. Using our result of Section 5.1 we can compute its value as follows

$$V(F_\tau, 0) = \mathbb{E}_\mathbb{Q}(F_\tau) = \sum_{n=0}^{N} \mathbb{E}_\mathbb{Q}(1_{\{\tau=n\}} F_n).$$

Theorem 5.3.1 . *For $n \in \{0, 1, \ldots, N\}$ it follows that*

$$(5.9) \qquad V_a(F, n) = \sup_{\substack{n \leq \tau \leq N \\ \tau \text{ stopping time}}} \mathbb{E}_\mathbb{Q}(F_\tau | \mathcal{F}_n).$$

Furthermore the "sup" in Equation (5.9) is attained for the following stopping time τ_n:

$$\tau_n = \min\{\ell \geq n \mid F_\ell \geq V_e(V_a(F, \ell+1), \ell)\}.$$

where for $\ell = N$, we put $V_e(V_a(F, N+1), N) = F_N$.

In particular,

$$V_a(F, 0) = \sup_{\substack{0 \leq \tau \leq N \\ \tau \text{ stopping time}}} \mathbb{E}_\mathbb{Q}(F_\tau)$$

and the optimal stopping time is in this case

$$\tau_0 = \min\{\ell \geq 0 \mid F_\ell(\widehat{S}_\ell) \geq V_e(V_a(F, \ell+1), \ell)\}.$$

Remark. Note that the optimal stopping time can be described as follows: "Exercise the option once its value equals its intrinsic value".

Proof of Theorem 5.3.1. By reversed induction we prove for each $n = N, N - 1, \ldots, 0$ the following 3 claims

claim 1: τ_n is a stopping time.

claim 2: $V_a(F, n) \geq \sup_{n \leq \tau \leq N} \mathbb{E}_{\mathbb{Q}}(F_\tau \mid \mathcal{F}_n)$.

claim 3: $V_a(F, n) \leq \mathbb{E}_{\mathbb{Q}}(F_{\tau_n} \mid \mathcal{F}_n)$.

For $n = N$ all three claims are trivial: $\tau_n \equiv N$, and $V_a(F, N) = F_N = \mathbb{E}_{\mathbb{Q}}(F_N \mid \mathcal{F}_N)$.

Assume now claim 1, claim 2 and claim 3 are true for $n + 1$. We need to verify them for n. First note that for $\omega \in \Omega$

$$(5.10) \qquad \tau_n(\omega) = \begin{cases} n & \text{if } F_n \geq V_e(V_a(F, n+1), n) \\ \tau_{n+1}(\omega) & \text{if } F_n < V_e(V_a(F, n+1), n). \end{cases}$$

Thus $\{\tau_n = n\} = \{F_n \geq V_e(V_a(F, n+1), n)\} \in \mathcal{F}_n$ and for $\ell > n$ we observe that

$$\{\tau_n = \ell\} = \underbrace{\{F_n < V_e(V_a(F, n+1), n)\}}_{\in \mathcal{F}_n} \cap \underbrace{\{\tau_{n+1} = \ell\}}_{\in \mathcal{F}_\ell} \in \mathcal{F}_\ell.$$

In particular, claim 1 follows from the induction hypothesis.

Claim 2 could be explained intuitively: an American style option should be worth at least as much as an option with the same pay-off function and fixed exercise strategy. But let us give a rigorous argument.

For any stopping time $n \leq \tau \leq N$ it follows that

$$\mathbb{E}_{\mathbb{Q}}(F_\tau \mid \mathcal{F}_n) = \mathbb{E}_{\mathbb{Q}}(1_{\{\tau=n\}} F_n + 1_{\{\tau>n\}} F_\tau \mid \mathcal{F}_n)$$

$$= 1_{\{\tau=n\}} F_n + 1_{\{\tau>n\}} \mathbb{E}_{\mathbb{Q}}(F_\tau \mid \mathcal{F}_n)$$

$$[1_{\{\tau=n\}}, 1_{\{\tau>n\}} \text{ and } F_n \text{ are } \mathcal{F}_n\text{-measurable}]$$

$$\leq \max(F_n, \mathbb{E}_{\mathbb{Q}}(F_{\tau \vee (n+1)} \mid \mathcal{F}_n)).$$

Using the induction hypothesis and $(V_a 2)$ we derive that

$$
\begin{aligned}
\mathbb{E}_{\mathbb{Q}}(F_{\tau \vee (n+1)} \mid \mathcal{F}_n) &= \mathbb{E}_{\mathbb{Q}}(\mathbb{E}_{\mathbb{Q}}(F_{\tau \vee (n+1)} \mid \mathcal{F}_{n+1}) \mid \mathcal{F}_n) \\
&\leq \mathbb{E}_{\mathbb{Q}}(V_a(F, n+1) \mid \mathcal{F}_n) \quad [\text{Inductionhypothesis}] \\
&= V_e(V_a(F, n+1), n) \\
&\leq V_a(F, n). \quad [\text{By } (V_a 2)]
\end{aligned}
$$

¿From both inequalities we now deduce claim 2 for n.

We finally have to show claim 3.

$$
\begin{aligned}
V_a(F, n) &= \max(F_n, V_e(V_a(F, n+1), n)) \quad [\text{by } (V_a 2)] \\
&= \max(F_n, \mathbb{E}_{\mathbb{Q}}(\mathbb{E}_{\mathbb{Q}}(F_{\tau_{n+1}} \mid \mathcal{F}_{n+1}) \mid \mathcal{F}_n)) \quad [\text{Induction hypothesis}] \\
&= \begin{cases} F_n & \text{if } \tau_n = n \\ \mathbb{E}_{\mathbb{Q}}(F_{\tau_{n+1}} \mid \mathcal{F}_n) & \text{if } \tau_n > n \end{cases} \\
&= \mathbb{E}_{\mathbb{Q}}(1_{\{\tau_n = n\}} F_{\tau_n} + 1_{\{\tau_n > n\}} F_{\tau_n} \mid \mathcal{F}_n) \\
&\quad [\text{if } \tau_n > n \text{ then } \tau_n = \tau_{n+1}] \\
&= \mathbb{E}_{\mathbb{Q}}(F_{\tau_n} \mid \mathcal{F}_n).
\end{aligned}
$$

$\square$

The price process of a European style option $V_e(F, n) = \mathbb{E}_{\mathbb{Q}}(F_N \mid \mathcal{F}_n)$ is a martingale. The next result describes the process $V_a(F, n)$ as a supermartingale.

Theorem 5.3.2 .   *The process $V_a(F, n)$ is a supermartingale. Furthermore it is* the smallest supermartingale *with the property that $V_a(F, n) \geq F_n$. This means that for any* supermartingale X_n *with the property that*

$$X_n \geq F_n \ a.s.$$

it follows that

$$X_n \geq V_a(F, n) \ a.s.$$

Proof.   By $(V_a 2)$ it follows for $n = 0, 1, \ldots, N - 1$ that

$$\mathbb{E}_{\mathbb{Q}}(V_a(F, n+1) \mid \mathcal{F}_n) = V_e(V_a(F, n+1), n) \leq \max(F_n, V_e(V_a(F, n+1), n)) = V_a(F, n),$$

which proves that $(V_a(F, n))_{n=0,1,\ldots,N}$ is a supermartingale.

If $X_n \geq F_n$ is a supermartingale we will prove by reversed induction that $X_n \geq V_a(F, n)$ a.s. for all $n = N, \ldots, 0$. For $n = N$, $X_N \geq F_N = V_a(F, N)$. Assume we showed the claim for $n + 1$, then it follows that

$$X_n \geq \mathbb{E}_{\mathbb{Q}}(X_{n+1} \mid \mathcal{F}_n)$$

$$[X_n \text{ is a supermartingale}]$$

$$\geq \mathbb{E}_{\mathbb{Q}}(V_a(F, n+1) \mid \mathcal{F}_n)$$

$$[\text{Using the inductionhypothesis}]$$

$$= V_e(V_a(F, n+1), n)$$

since also $X_n \geq F_n$ we deduce from $(V_a 2)$ that

$$X_n \geq \max(F_n, V_e(V_a(F, n+1), n))) = V_a(F, n).$$

$\square$

Example.

We want to consider the log-binomial model with length N, a model for which we know the equivalent martingale probability $\mathbb{Q}$ (which is unique). We assume that F_n is contingent to a process $(S_n)_{n=0,\ldots,N}$ which is log-binomial distributed. Therefore we write $F_n = f_n(\widehat{S}_n)$. If U and D are the factors by which S_n goes up or down (with $D < R = e^r < U$), then $\widehat{S}_n$ goes either up by the factor $e^{-r}U$ or down by the factor $e^{-r}D$ (since the price of the zerobond in terms of Euros increases by the factor e^r between the times n and $n+1$

In terms of zero bonds we deduce

$$\mathbb{Q}(\widehat{S}_{n+1} = e^{-r}U\widehat{S}_n \mid \mathcal{F}_n) = \frac{e^r - D}{U - D}$$

$$\mathbb{Q}(\widehat{S}_{n+1} = e^{-r}D\widehat{S}_n \mid \mathcal{F}_n) = \frac{U - e^r}{U - D}.$$

We let $V_a(F,n)(\widehat{S}_n)$ be the value of an American style option. The discounted stock price $\widehat{S}_n$ can assume the values $U^i D^{n-i}\widehat{S}_0$, $i = 0, 1, \ldots, n$. Strictly speaking, $V_a(F,n)$ depends on $\omega \in \Omega$, but it can be seen easily that $V_a(F,n)$ depends only on the value of $\widehat{S}_n(\omega)$. Thus we can write $V_a(F,n)(\widehat{S}_n)$ for the value of the option at time n if the stockprice is $\widehat{S}_n$.

From $(V_a 2)$ we deduce the following recursive formula

$$V_a(F,n)(\widehat{S}_n) = \max(f_n(\widehat{S}_n), \mathbb{E}_{\mathbb{Q}}(V_a(F,n+1) \mid \mathcal{F}_n)(\widehat{S}_n))$$

$$= \max\left(f_n(\widehat{S}_n), V_a(F,n+1)(\widehat{S}_n e^{-r}U)\frac{e^r - D}{U - D} + V_a(F,n+1)(\widehat{S}_n e^{-r}D)\frac{U - e^r}{U - D}\right).$$

How should somebody hedge his/her portfolio after selling an American style option?

For $n = 0, 1, \ldots, N - 1$ define

$$\Delta_n(\widehat{S}_n) = \frac{V_a(F,n+1)(\widehat{S}_n e^{-r}U) - V_a(F,n+1)(\widehat{S}_n D)}{\widehat{S}_n e^{-r}U - \widehat{S}_n e^{-r}D}$$

$$C_n(\widehat{S}_n) = V_a(F,n)(\widehat{S}_n) - \mathbb{E}_{\mathbb{Q}}(V_a(F,n+1) \mid \mathcal{F}_n)(\widehat{S}_n).$$

¿From $(V_a 2)$ follows that $C_n \geq 0$ and $C_n > 0$ only if $V_a(F,n) = F_n > V_e(V_a(F,n+1),n)$. Now define the following adapted process (X_n) in bond prices :

$$X_0 = V_a(F,0)$$

(which is the amount the seller receives at time 0) and recursively

$$X_{n+1} = \Delta_n(\widehat{S}_n) \cdot \widehat{S}_{n+1} + X_n - C_n - \Delta_n(\widehat{S}_n) \cdot \widehat{S}_n.$$

This is the value of the portfolio at time $n+1$ if at time n the investor bought $\Delta_n(\widehat{S}_n)$ shares of the stock, took $C_n \geq 0$ out of the portfolio and invested the rest in bonds.

We claim that

$$X_n = V_a(F, n),$$

i.e. the investor has at all times the short position of one unit of an American style option covered.

We prove the claim by induction for each $n = 0, 1, \ldots, N$. For $n = 0$ this follows from the choice of X_0.

Assume the claim is correct for some time n.

If at time $n + 1$, $\widehat{S}_{n+1} = e^{-r} U \widehat{S}_n$ we deduce (we suppress the dependence on $\widehat{S}_n$ of Δ_n, X_n and C_n)

$$
\begin{aligned}
X_{n+1} &= \Delta_n(\widehat{S}_n e^{-r} U - \widehat{S}_n) + X_n - C_n \\
&= \frac{V_a(F, n+1)(\widehat{S}_n e^{-r} U) - V_a(F, n+1)(\widehat{S}_n e^{-r} D)}{e^{-r} U - e^{-r} D}(e^{-r} U - 1) + V_a(F, n)(\widehat{S}_n) - C_n \\
&= q_D[V_a(F, n+1)(\widehat{S}_n e^{-r} U) - V_a(F, n+1)(\widehat{S}_n e^{-r} D)] + V_a(F, n)(\widehat{S}_n) - C_n \\
&\quad \left[q_D = \mathbb{Q}(\widehat{S}_{n+1} = e^{-r} D \widehat{S}_n \mid \mathcal{F}_n) = \frac{U - 1}{U - D} \right] \\
&= q_D[V_a(F, n+1)(\widehat{S}_n e^{-r} U) - V_a(F, n+1)(\widehat{S}_n e^{-r} D)] \\
&\quad + q_U V_a(F, n+1)(\widehat{S}_n e^{-r} U) + q_D V_a(F, n+1)(\widehat{S}_n e^{-r} D) \\
&\quad [\text{Recall that by definition of } C_n \text{ that } \mathbb{E}_{\mathbb{Q}}(V_a(F, n+1) \mid \mathcal{F}_n)(\widehat{S}_n) = V_a(F, n)(\widehat{S}_n) - C_n] \\
&= V_a(F, n+1)(e^{-r} U \widehat{S}_n) \\
&\quad [q_U + q_D = 1].
\end{aligned}
$$

If at time $n + 1$, $\widehat{S}_{n+1} = e^{-r} D \widehat{S}_n$ the claim follows from a similar computation.

Remark. Looking at the last hedging argument one might get the impression that the seller of the American option has an arbitrage opportunity since he/she can withdraw the amount C_n, and still cover the short position. But note that C_n only becomes strictly positive if $V_a(F, n) > \mathbb{E}_{\mathbb{Q}}(V_a(F, n+1) \mid \mathcal{F}_n) = V_e(V_a(F, n+1), n)$ and thus by $(V_a 2)$ we deduce that

$V_a(F, n) = F_n(\widehat{S}_n)$. If the buyer chooses to pursue the optimal strategy as determined in Theorem 5.3.1 he/she will exercise at time n and stop the process. If the buyer chooses not to persue the optimal strategy the seller will actually make a profit.

Let us rewrite the (V_a1) and (V_a2) in terms of fixed currencies and consider an American style option contingent to an asset S. It pays $g(S_n)$ Euros if the holder chooses to exercise at time n. The corresponding payoff functions in zero bonds are therefore $F_n = e^{r(N-n)}g(S_n)$, $n = 0, 1, \ldots N$. Denoting the value in Euros of the considered option at time n by $W_a(g, n)$ we deduce that $W_a(g, n) = e^{-(N-n)}V_a(F, n)$ and then observe that the conditions (V_a1) and (V_a2) translate into

$$(W_a1) \qquad W_a(g, n) = e^{-r(N-n)}V_a(F, n) \geq e^{-r(N-n)}F_n = g(S_n)$$

and

$$(W_a2) \qquad W_a(g, n) = e^{-r(N-n)}V_a(F, n)$$
$$= e^{-r(N-n)} \max\left(F_n, \mathbb{E}_\mathbb{Q}(V_a(F, n+1)|\mathcal{F}_n)\right)$$
$$= \max\left(g(S_n), e^{-r}\mathbb{E}_\mathbb{Q}(W_a(F, n+1)|\mathcal{F}_n)\right).$$

In the next section we will derive that for a wide class of payoff functions the value of a European option equals to the value of the corresponding American style option. I.e. there is no benefit for the holder in being able to choose the exercise date. In the following example we will verify this claim for a call in the log-binomial model.

Example. In the log-binomial model is the value of an American call equal to the value of the corresponding European call.

Let $g(S) = (S - E)^+$ and $F_n = e^{r(N-n)}(S_n - E)^+ = (\widehat{S}_n - \widehat{E}_n)^+$, with $\widehat{E} = e^{r(N-n)}E$, for $n = 0, 1, \ldots N$. We assume that S_n is log-binomial distributed and denote the ups by U and the downs by D.

By reversed induction we will show for every $n = N, N-1, \ldots, n$ that $F_n \leq \mathbb{E}_\mathbb{Q}(F_N|\mathcal{F}_n)$. For $n = N$ the claim is clear, and assuming the claim being true for $n+1$ we first not that the function g is convex, meaning that $g(\alpha x + \beta y) \leq \alpha g(x) + \beta g(y)$, whenever $x, y \in \mathbb{R}$ and $\alpha, \beta \geq 0$ with $\alpha + \beta = 1$

Therefore we deduce that

$$
\begin{aligned}
\mathbb{E}_{\mathbb{Q}}(F_N|\mathcal{F}_n) &= \mathbb{E}_{\mathbb{Q}}\big(\mathbb{E}_{\mathbb{Q}}(F_N|\mathcal{F}_{n+1})|\mathcal{F}_n\big) \\
&\geq \mathbb{E}_{\mathbb{Q}}(F_{n+1}|\mathcal{F}_n) \quad \text{[induction hypothesis]} \\
&= \mathbb{E}_{\mathbb{Q}}(g(S_{n+1})e^{r(N-n-1)}|\mathcal{F}_n) \\
&= e^{r(N-n-1)}\big(q_D g(DS_n) + q_U g(US_n)\big) \\
&\geq e^{r(N-n-1)}g\big(q_D DS_n + q_U US_n\big) \quad \text{[Convexity]} \\
&= e^{r(N-n-1)}g(e^r S_n) = e^{r(N-n)}(S_n - e^{-r}E)^+ \geq e^{r(N-n)}(S_n - E)^+ = F_n.
\end{aligned}
$$

Secondly we prove, again by reversed induction, that $V_a(F,n) = V_e(F_N)$. For $n = N$ the claim is trivial and assuming we have shown the claim for $n+1$ we deduce that

$$
\begin{aligned}
V_a(F,n) &= \max\big(F_n, V_e(V_a(F,n+1),n)\big) \\
&= \max\big(F_n, \mathbb{E}_{\mathbb{Q}}(F_N|\mathcal{F}_n)\big) \quad \text{[induction hypothesis]} \\
&= \mathbb{E}_{\mathbb{Q}}(F_N|\mathcal{F}_n) = V_e(F_N,n).
\end{aligned}
$$

$\square$

5.4 For which Payoff Functions do American and European Options have the same Values?

In Section 5.3 we derived the value of American style options assuming only finitely many trading times. Letting the number of trading times increase and the distance between them decrease it is reasonable to assume that the formula (5.9) in Theorem 5.3.1 can be generalized to the continuous time setting. Let $\mathbb{Q}$ be an equivalent probability turning all discounted price processes of the underlying assets into martingales, and assume that $(F_t)_{0 \le t \le T}$ is a family of payoff functions of an American style option. As before we we assume that (F_t) is an adapted process on the filtered probability space $(\Omega, \mathcal{F}, \mathbb{P}, (\mathcal{F}_t)_{0 \le t \le T})$. We think of F_t being the payoff in zerobonds if the holder decides to exercise at time t.

Assuming that all European style options are priced using the equivalent probability $\mathbb{Q}$ in the pricing formula of Theorem 5.1.3, we deduce the price of an American option is given by

$$(5.11) \qquad V_a(F, t) = \sup_{\substack{t \le \tau \le T \\ \tau \text{ stopping time}}} \mathbb{E}_{\mathbb{Q}}(F_\tau \mid \mathcal{F}_t).$$

We omitt a proof of Equation (5.11) for the continuous time case, and refere to .... instead.

Let us first convert Equation (5.11) into our fixed currency. We consider an American style option paying $g(S_t)$ Euros if the holder decides to exercise at time t. Its pay off functions in terms of zerobonds are therefore $F_t = e^{r(T-t)}g(S_t) = e^{r(T-t)}g(e^{-r(T-t)}\widehat{S}_t)$, $0 \le t \le T$. The value $W_a(g, t)$ of the option in terms of Euros is then

$$(5.12) \qquad W_a(g, t) = e^{-r(T-t)}V_a(F, t)$$

$$= e^{-r(T-t)} \sup_{\substack{t \le \tau \le T \\ \tau \text{ stopping time}}} \mathbb{E}_{\mathbb{Q}}(F_\tau) \mid \mathcal{F}_t)$$

$$= \sup_{\substack{t \le \tau \le T \\ \tau \text{ stopping time}}} \mathbb{E}_{\mathbb{Q}}(e^{-r(\tau-t)}g(S_\tau)|\mathcal{F}_t).$$

The following Theorem states a general situation for which the value of an American style option equals to its European version.

Theorem 5.4.1 .   *If g is a convex function with $g(0) = 0$ then*

$$W_a(g, t) = V_e(g, t), \quad whenever \ t \in [0, T].$$

Theorem 5.4.1 will be a consequence of the Optional Sampling Theorem 5.2.6 and the inequality of Jensen (see Theorem B.3.7 in Appendix B.3).

Proof of Theorem 5.4.1.   According to 5.12 we have to show that for two stopping times σ and τ so that $t \leq \sigma \leq \tau \leq T$ it follows that

$$\mathbb{E}_{\mathbb{Q}}(e^{-(\tau-t)r}g(S_\tau)|\mathcal{F}_t) \geq \mathbb{E}_{\mathbb{Q}}(e^{-r(\sigma-t)}g(S_\sigma)|\mathcal{F}_t).$$

Then it would follow that the supremum in 5.12 is achieved for the constant stopping time $\tau \equiv T$. For that, note that

$$
\begin{aligned}
\mathbb{E}_{\mathbb{Q}}(e^{-(\tau-t)r}g(S_\tau)|\mathcal{F}_t) \quad &= \mathbb{E}_{\mathbb{Q}}\big(\mathbb{E}_{\mathbb{Q}}(e^{-r(\tau-t)}g(S_\tau)|\mathcal{F}_\sigma)|\mathcal{F}_t\big) \quad [\mathcal{F}_t \subset \mathcal{F}_\sigma] \\
&= \mathbb{E}_{\mathbb{Q}}\big(e^{-(\sigma-t)r}\mathbb{E}_{\mathbb{Q}}(e^{-(\tau-\sigma)r}g(S_\tau) \mid \mathcal{F}_\sigma) \mid \mathcal{F}_t\big) \\
&\quad [\text{Write } e^{-(\tau-t)r} = e^{-(\sigma-t)r}e^{-(\tau-\sigma)r}] \\
&\geq \mathbb{E}_{\mathbb{Q}}\big(e^{-(\sigma-t)r}\mathbb{E}_{\mathbb{Q}}(g(S_\tau e^{-(\tau-\sigma)r}) \mid \mathcal{F}_\sigma) \mid \mathcal{F}_t\big) \\
&\quad [\text{Note that } a = e^{-(\tau-\sigma)r} \leq 1 \text{ and } ag(x) = ag(x) + (1-a)g(0) \geq g(ax)] \\
&= \mathbb{E}_{\mathbb{Q}}\big(e^{-(\sigma-t)r}\mathbb{E}_{\mathbb{Q}}(g(\widehat{S}_\tau e^{-r(T-\sigma)}) \mid \mathcal{F}_\sigma) \mid \mathcal{F}_t\big) \\
&\geq \mathbb{E}_{\mathbb{Q}}\Big((e^{-(\sigma-t)r}g\big(\mathbb{E}_{\mathbb{Q}}(\widehat{S}_\tau e^{-r(T-\sigma)}) \mid \mathcal{F}_\sigma\big))|\mathcal{F}_t\Big) \\
&\quad [\text{Inequality of Jensen}] \\
&\geq \mathbb{E}_{\mathbb{Q}}(e^{-(\sigma-t)r}g(\widehat{S}_\sigma e^{-r(T-\sigma)})|\mathcal{F}_t) \\
&\quad [\text{Optional Sampling Theorem, } \widehat{S}_t \text{ is a } \mathbb{Q}\text{-martingale}] \\
&= \mathbb{E}_{\mathbb{Q}}(e^{-(\sigma-t)r}g(S_\sigma)|\mathcal{F}_t)
\end{aligned}
$$

which verifies the claim. $\square$

□

Corollary 5.4.2 . *An American call has the same value as the corresponding (i.e. same strike price and same exercise date) European call, assuming the underlying asset does not pay dividends.*

In the following example we consider the case that the underlying asset pays dividends at time t_D, $0 < t_D < T$.

Example. We compare an American to an European call with strike price K and exercise date T assuming the underlying asset follows the Black Scholes model and pays at time $t_D \in (0,T)$ a dividend of the amount $DS_{t_D^-}$. Following the arguments in Section 3.4B and using the formula for European calls in Proposition 3.3.1 of Section 3.3 we deduce for $t_D < t \le T$

$$V_e((S_T - K)^+, t) = S_t N(d) - K e^{-r(T-t)} N(d - \nu\sqrt{T-t}),$$

where $N(d) = \frac{1}{\sqrt{2\pi}} \int\limits_{-\infty}^{d} e^{-x^2/2} dx$, $d = [\log(S_t/K) + (r + \frac{1}{2}\nu^2)(T-t)]/\nu\sqrt{T-t}$, and where ν is the volatility.

Since no dividend is paid out during $(t_D, T]$ it follows from Theorem 5.4.1 that $V_a((S_T - K)^+, t) = V_e((S_T - K)^+, t)$. We observed in Section 3.4B, Equation (3.25), that right before time t_D the value of an European call is

$$V_e\left((S_{t_D^-} - K)^+, t_D^-\right) = V_e\left((S_{t_D^-}(1 - D) - K)^+, t_D^+\right)$$
$$= S_{t_D^-}(1 - D)N(d^*) - K e^{-r(T-t_D)} N(d^* - \nu\sqrt{T-t_D}),$$

with

$$d^* = \frac{\log(S_{t_D^-}(1 - D)/K) + (r + \frac{1}{2}\nu^2)(T-t_D)}{\nu\sqrt{T-t_D}}.$$

Now consider the following situation: the call is very heavy "in the money", meaning that $S_{t_D^-} \gg K$ and thus $N(d) \approx N(d - \nu\sqrt{T - t_D}) \approx 1$. In this case

$$V_e\left((S_{t_D^-}(1 - D) - K)^+, t_D^-\right) \approx S_{t_D^-}(1 - D) - Ke^{-(T-t_D)r}$$

$$= S_{t_D^-} - K + [(1 - e^{-(T-t_D)r})K - DS_{t_D^-}].$$

If secondly $(1 - e^{-(T-t_D)})K < DS_{t_D^-}$, it follows that $V_e((S_{t_D^-} - K)^+, t_D^-)$ is less than its intrinsic value $(S_{t_D^-} - K)^+$, thus the value of the corresponding American style option must be higher.

Chapter 6

Path Dependent Options

6.1   Introduction of Path Dependent Options

In Section 5.1 we developed a theory to price a general option paying $f(\omega)$ at time $t \in [0, T]$, where $f : \Omega \to \mathbb{R}$ was an $\mathcal{F}_t$-measurable map. According to Equation (5.3) in Section 5.1 the value of such an option at time $0 \le s \le t$ is

$$W(g, t, s) = e^{-r(t-s)} \mathbb{E}_{\mathbb{Q}}(g | \mathcal{F}_s),$$

where $\mathbb{Q}$ is a probability measure equivalent to $\mathbb{P}$, for which the underlying assets are martingales if priced in zero-bonds. If we assume the log-binomial model (in the discrete time case) or the Black Scholes model (in the continuous time case) this probability $\mathbb{Q}$ is unique, and thus, prices of options are uniquely determined in this case. Unfortunately, this does not mean that we have already a way to compute these prices. In this chapter we want to find numerically computable formulae or algorithms for option prices. By this we mean for example an integral (the lower the dimension the better), similar to the formula we obtained for European style options within the Black Scholes formula (compare Section 3.2), or at least an algorithm which can be implemented on a computer, like the procedure to find option prices in the log-binomial model (compare Section 1.3), or the procedure of pricing American style option based on the key equality $(V_a 2)$ which leads to an iterative formula if the time is discrete and if we assume expected values with respect to $\mathbb{Q}$ are computable.

The options we are interested in this part, are so called *path dependent options*. For these options the payoff does not only depend on the value of the underlying asset at a certain time t (either to be fixed as in the European style or choosable by the holder as in the American style option), but its payoff also depends on "how the price behaved during the whole time period". Let us give the formal definition.

We will assume that the process describing the value of the underlying asset is continuous. This is true within the Black Scholes model (which will be assumed in this part most of the times) if the asset does not pay out dividends.

Definition. (Path dependent options)

Let $C[0,T]$ be the vectorspace of all continuous functions

$$\varphi : \quad [0,T] \to \mathbb{R},$$

and let F be a function on $C[0,T]$

$$F : \quad C[0,T] \to \mathbb{R}.$$

Now an *option with payoff F contingent to an asset whose price is given by the stochastic process* $(S_t)_{0 \leq t \leq T}$ is a security which pays $F(\varphi)$ at time T if the path of S_t was φ, i.e. if an ω occured for which $S_t(\omega) = \varphi(t)$, for all $t \in [0,T]$.

We will denote such a derivative by $F(S_{(\cdot)})$.

We can think of $S_{(\cdot)}$ being an "infinite dimensional random variable", which assigns to each $\omega \in \Omega$ an element in $C[0,T]$, namely the path $[0,T] \ni t \mapsto S_t(\omega)$. We will have to discuss in Section 6.2 some of the technical points involving distributions on infinite dimensional spaces like $C[0,T]$ in more detail. Let us first enumerate some important classes of path dependent options.

Options depending on finitely many predetermined times

These are options of the form

$$F(S_{(\cdot)}) = F(S_{t_1}, S_{t_2}, \ldots, S_{t_n}),$$

with $0 \le t_1 < t_2 < \ldots < t_n = T$.

The following options can be seen as elements of that class:

a) Options on options: at some predetermined time $0 < t_1 < T$ the holder can decide whether or not to purchase an option with exercise date T.

b) The chooser option: at some predetermined time $0 < t_1 < T$ the holder can decide to either buy a put or a call with given strike price K and exercise date T.

Barrier style options

The payoff of these options depends on the maximal value of the asset price over a given time interval $[0, T]$, i.e.

$$F(S_{(\cdot)}) = g(\max_{0 \le t \le T} S_t),$$

where g is a functions on $\mathbb{R}$.

Asian style options

The payoff of these options depends on the average value of the asset price or a function or the average value of a function of that price i.e.

$$F(S_{(\cdot)}) = G(\frac{1}{T} \int_0^T S_t dt), \text{ or more generally } F(S_{(\cdot)}) = G(\frac{1}{T} \int_0^T g(S_t) dt),$$

Options depending on only finitely many predetermined times can be treated within the usual Black Scholes theory developed in Chapter 3. The idea is the following: We first compute the value of the option in the last time interval $[t_{n-1}, T]$. Since in this time interval the values $S_{t_1}, S_{t_2}, \ldots, S_{t_{n-1}}$ are realized we can treat them as constants, pricing of the option F is then the same as pricing a European style option paying $f(S_T) = F(S_{t_1}, \ldots, S_{t_{n-1}}, S_T)$ at time T. Once we found the price of the option at time t_{n-1} we use this value as the payoff function for a new option and will be able to price our option within the time period $[t_{n-2}, t_{n-1}]$. We can continue this way until we arrive at 0. In order to see which kind of formulae we get let us compute the option value if the payoff depends on two times.

Proposition 6.1.1 .   *We assume that the asset price satisfies the Black Scholes model with constant drift μ and constant volatility ν. Let $0 < t_1 < t_2 = T$ and consider an option paying $F(S_{t_1}, S_T)$ at time T.*
Then the value V_t of this option at time t

   a) for $t \in [t_1, T]$ is:

$$\frac{e^{-r(T-t)}}{\sqrt{2\pi\nu^2(T-t)}} \int\limits_{-\infty}^{\infty} F(S_{t_1}, S_t e^{r(T-t)} e^{-\frac{\nu^2}{2}(T-t)} \cdot e^z) e^{-\frac{z^2}{2\nu^2(T-t)}} dz$$

   b) for $t \in [0, t_1]$ is:

$$\frac{e^{-r(T-t)}}{2\pi\nu^2\sqrt{t_1-t}\sqrt{T-t_1}} \int_{-\infty}^{\infty} \int_{-\infty}^{\infty} F(S_t e^{(r-\frac{\nu^2}{2})(t_1-t)}e^x, S_t e^{(r-\frac{\nu^2}{2})(T-t)}e^{z+x})$$
$$\cdot e^{-\frac{z^2}{2\nu^2(T-t_1)} - \frac{x^2}{2\nu^2(t_1-t)}} dz dx.$$

Proof.   We first compute the value of the option for $t_1 \leq t \leq T$. At that time S_{t_1} is realized and will be treated as a constant. We apply Formula (3.20) of Section 3.2 to the payoff function $G(S_T) = F(S_{t_1}, S_T)$ and derive that for $t_1 \leq t \leq T$

$$V_t = e^{-r(T-t)} \mathbb{E}\left(F(S_{t_1}, S_t e^{r(T-t)} e^{-\frac{\nu^2}{2}(T-t)+\nu(B_T-B_t)})\right)$$
$$= \frac{e^{-r(T-t)}}{\sqrt{2\pi\nu^2(T-t)}} \int\limits_{-\infty}^{\infty} F(S_{t_1}, S_t e^{r(T-t)} e^{-\frac{\nu^2}{2}(T-t)} \cdot e^z) e^{-\frac{z^2}{2\nu^2(T-t)}} dz$$

in particular for $t = t_1$ we get

$$(6.1) \quad V_{t_1} = \widetilde{F}(S_{t_1}) = \frac{e^{-r(T-t_1)}}{\sqrt{2\pi\nu^2(T-t_1)}} \int\limits_{-\infty}^{\infty} F(S_{t_1}, S_{t_1} e^{r(T-t_1)} e^{-\frac{\nu^2}{2}(T-t_1)} \cdot e^z) e^{-\frac{z^2}{2\nu^2(T-t_1)}} dz.$$

Now we apply for $0 \leq t \leq t_1$ the Black Scholes formula again, but this time for the payoff $\widetilde{F}(S_{t_1})$ and exercise date being t_1 and we derive that

$$V_t = \frac{e^{-r(t_1-t)}}{\sqrt{2\pi\nu^2(t_1-t)}} \int_{-\infty}^{\infty} \widetilde{F}(S_t e^{r(t_1-t)} e^{-\frac{\nu^2}{2}(t_1-t)} e^x) e^{-\frac{x^2}{2\nu^2(t_1-t)}} dx.$$

Replacing now in above integral the term

$$\widetilde{F}(S_t e^{r(t_1-t)} e^{-\frac{\nu^2}{2}(t_1-t)} e^x)$$

we obtain

$$\frac{e^{-r(T-t_1)}}{\sqrt{2\pi\nu^2(T-t_1)}} \int_{-\infty}^{\infty} F(S_t e^{r(t_1-t)} e^{-\frac{\nu^2}{2}(t_1-t)} e^x, S_t e^{r(t_1-t)} e^{-\frac{\nu^2}{2}(t_1-t)} e^{r(T-t_1)} e^{-\frac{\nu^2}{2}(T-t_1)} \cdot e^{x+z}) e^{-\frac{z^2}{2\nu^2(T-t_1)}} dz$$

wich is the claimed formula (b). $\qquad\qquad\qquad\qquad\qquad\qquad\square$

Remark: The formula in Proposition 6.1.1 might look unpleasant but it is not hard to implement it numerically. It also shows that the Black Scholes theory as developed in Chapter 3 provides a complete answer to price options depending only on finitely many predetermined trading times.

For options depending on infinitely many trading times, we might consider the following approach which, at least theoretically, leads to an approximative pricing formula.

We partition the time interval in sufficiently many intervals $[0, t_1], [t_1, t_2], \dots [t_{n-1}, T]$ and approximate the payoff function $F(S_{(.)})$ by a sequence of payoff functions $F_n(S_{t_1}, \dots S_{t_n})$. Under appropriate assumptions (which are satisfied by the functions F we usually considered) the value of the option $F_n(S_{t_1}, \dots S_{t_n})$ (which is computable as a multi dimensional integral) will converge to the value of the option $F(S_{(.)})$.

But there is a numerical problem: as the formula in Proposition 6.1.1 indicates, the value, at time 0, of an option with pay off $F(S_{t_1}, \dots S_{t_n})$ will be an n-dimensional integral. Now let us consider an option having an exercise period of three month (about 80 working days). It seems reasonable that we will need to partition this period into intervals not bigger than a day. Thus we need at least $n = 80$, which means that we have to compute an 80-dimensional integral. If we needed, say, 100 evaluations of a function in order to get a precise enough approximation for one dimensional integrals we would need about $100^{80} = 10^{160}$ evaluations for our 80-dimensional integral in order to get the same precision. With some more sophisticated methods (for example Monte Carlo methods) one might be able to reduce this number considerably. But nevertheless we will have to compute an integral for which the time of computation could be larger than the whole exercise period. Thus, this approach is not very suitable if we want to use it for "on time hedging".

In order to compute the value of path dependent options we will take an other, more direct approach.

First, we will have to compute the equivalent martingale measure $\mathbb{Q}$ within the Black Scholes model. As we will see this mainly consists in finding the distribution of the process B_t, which, under $\mathbb{P}$, is a Brownian motion. We will find out, that under the probability $\mathbb{Q}$, B_t is a "shifted Brownian motion". Secondly, we will have to compute the (one dimensional) distribution of the random variable $\omega \mapsto F(S_{(\cdot)}(\omega))$ Once we know its distribution (which is a probability on $\mathbb{R}$) and its density, say ρ, the value of our option will be a one dimensional integral.

6.2 The Distribution of Continuous Processes

We assume in this section that the stochastic process $(S_t)_{0 \le t \le T}$ describing the price of an underlying asset follows the Black-Scholes model. To keep it simple, we assume the drift μ and the volatility ν to be constant on the considered time interval $[0, T]$. Thus $(S_t)_{0 \le t \le T}$ satisfies the stochastic differential equation

$$(6.2) \qquad dS_t = \mu S_t dt + \nu S_t dB_t,$$

where $(B_t)_{0 \le t \le T}$ is a Brownian motion on our filtered probability space $(\Omega, \mathcal{F}, \mathbb{R}, (\mathcal{F}_t)_{0 \le t \le T})$. As shown in Section 2.4

$$(6.3) \qquad S_t = S_0 \cdot e^{(\mu - \frac{1}{2}\nu^2)t + \nu B_t}$$

is the solution to 6.2.

In this case we established two different approaches to price an option contingent to $(S_t)_{0 \le t \le T}$. Let us consider a European style option paying the amount of $f(S_t)$ at time $t \in [0, T]$ (i.e. we do not fix the exercise date to be T). In sections 3.1 and 3.2 we concluded that the value of such an option at time $u \in [0, t]$ must be

$$(6.4) \qquad f(S, t, u) = e^{-r(t-u)} \mathbb{E}_{\mathbb{P}}(f(Se^{(r - \frac{\nu^2}{2})(t-u) + \nu(B_t - B_u)}))$$

if S is the value of the underlying stock at time u.

Equation (6.4) can also be written as a conditional expectation:

$$(6.5) \qquad \mathbb{E}_{\mathbb{P}}(f(Se^{(r - \frac{\nu^2}{2})(t-u) + \nu(B_t - B_u)})) = \mathbb{E}_{\mathbb{P}}(f(Se^{(r - \frac{\nu^2}{2})(t-u) + \nu(B_t - B_u)}) | \mathcal{F}_u)$$
$$= \mathbb{E}_{\mathbb{P}}(f(S_u e^{(r - \frac{\nu^2}{2})(t-u) + \nu(B_t - B_u)}) | \mathcal{F}_u)(S_u = S),$$

where the notation

$$\mathbb{E}_{\mathbb{P}}(f(S_u e^{(r - \frac{\nu^2}{2})(t-u) + \nu(B_t - B_u)}) | \mathcal{F}_u)(S_u = S)$$

means the following: the $\mathcal{F}_u - measurable$ random variable

$$\mathbb{E}_{\mathbb{P}}(f(S_u e^{(r - \frac{\nu^2}{2})(t-u) + \nu(B_t - B_u)}) | \mathcal{F}_u),$$

which is, strictly speaking, a map of $w \in \Omega$ depends actually only on the value of $S_u(w)$.
Now, $\mathbb{E}_{\mathbb{P}}(f(S_u e^{(r-\frac{\nu^2}{2})(t-u)+\nu(B_t-B_u)})|\mathcal{F}_u)(S_u = S)$ is the value of that conditional expectation
evaluated at elements w for which $S_u(w) = S$.

On the other hand we discovered in Section 5.1 that the value of our option can be
represented as (Equation (5.3) in Section 5.1)

$$
(6.6) \qquad W(f,t,u) = e^{-r(t-u)}\mathbb{E}_{\mathbb{Q}}(f(S_t) \mid \mathcal{F}_u)
$$

$$
= e^{-r(t-u)}\mathbb{E}_{\mathbb{Q}}(f(S_u e^{(\mu-\frac{\nu^2}{2})(t-u)+\nu(B_t-B_u)}) \mid \mathcal{F}_u)
$$

where $\mathbb{Q}$ is a probability on $(\Omega, \mathcal{F})$ which is equivalent to $\mathbb{P}$ turning $\widehat{S}_t = e^{r(T-t)}S_t$ into a
martingale. Of course both approaches to evaluate the same option must lead to the same
value. In particular, the random variable $W(f,t,u)$ also depends only on the value of S_u
and we deduce that

$$
(6.7) \qquad \mathbb{E}_{\mathbb{P}}(f(S_u e^{(r-\frac{\nu^2}{2})(t-u)+\nu(B_t-B_u)})|\mathcal{F}_u)(S_u = S)
$$

$$
= \mathbb{E}_{\mathbb{Q}}(f(S_u e^{(\mu-\frac{\nu^2}{2})(t-u)+\nu(B_t-B_u)}) \mid \mathcal{F}_u)(S_u = S)
$$

Making a change of variables we deduce from Equation (6.7) the following observation:

Proposition 6.2.1 .   *We assume the Black Scholes model with constant drift μ and constant volatility ν, i.e. the price of the underlying asset is given by*

$$S_t = S_0 e^{(\mu - \frac{1}{2}\nu^2)t - \nu B_t},$$

where B_t is a Brownian motion on the filtered propbability space $(\Omega, \mathcal{F}, \mathbb{P}, (\mathcal{F}_t)_{0 \leq t \leq T})$. Let $\mathbb{Q}$ be an equivalent probability which turns the discounted process $\widehat{S}_t = e^{r(T-t)} S_t$ into a martingale.

Then it follows for any $t \in [0, T]$, any $u \leq t$ and any continuous and bounded $g: \mathbb{R} \to \mathbb{R}$ that

$$(6.8) \qquad \mathbb{E}_{\mathbb{Q}}(g(B_t - B_u) \mid \mathcal{F}_u) = \mathbb{E}_{\mathbb{P}}\left(g\left(\frac{r-\mu}{\nu}(t-u) + B_t - B_u\right) \mid \mathcal{F}_u\right)$$

or equivalently,

$$(6.9) \qquad \mathbb{E}_{\mathbb{P}}(g(B_t - B_u) \mid \mathcal{F}_u) = \mathbb{E}_{\mathbb{Q}}\left(g\left(\frac{\mu-r}{\nu}(t-u) + B_t - B_u\right) \mid \mathcal{F}_u\right).$$

Proof.   Assume that the value of the underlying asset at time $u \leq t$ is S. For a given bounded and continuous function $g : \mathbb{R} \to \mathbb{R}$ we define

$$f(y) = g\left[\frac{1}{\nu}\left(\log\left(\frac{y}{S}\right) - (\mu - \frac{1}{2}\nu^2)(t-u)\right)\right],$$

Note that if $y = S e^{(\mu - \frac{1}{2}\nu^2)(t-u) + \nu x}$ then $g(x) = f(y)$. We observe that

$$\mathbb{E}_{\mathbb{Q}}(g(B_t - B_u)|\mathcal{F}_u)(S_u = S) = \mathbb{E}_{\mathbb{Q}}(f(S_u e^{(\mu - \frac{1}{2}\nu^2)(t-u) + \nu(B_t - B_u)})|\mathcal{F}_u)(S_u = S)$$

$$= \mathbb{E}_{\mathbb{P}}(f(S_u e^{(r - \frac{1}{2}\nu^2)(t-u) + \nu(B_t - B_u)})|\mathcal{F}_u)(S_u = S)$$

$$[\text{By Equation } (6.7)]$$

$$= \mathbb{E}_{\mathbb{P}}\left(g(B_t - B_u + \frac{r-\mu}{\nu}(t-u))|\mathcal{F}_u\right)(S_u = S).$$

$$[\text{everything cancels nicely}]$$

$\square$

Proposition 6.2.1 says vaguely the following: The process B_t which was assumed to be a Brownian motion on the probability space $(\Omega, \mathcal{F}, \mathbb{P})$ "behaves like a shifted Brownian motion on $(\Omega, \mathcal{F}, \mathbb{Q})$". The rest of this section will be devoted to making this vague statement into a rigorous one.

We have to introduce the notion of *distributions of stochastic processes.*

Definition.   On $C([0, T])$ we consider the σ-algebra generated by the sets of the form

$$\{f \in C([0, T]) \mid f(t_1) \in A_1, f(t_2) \in A_2, \ldots, f(t_n) \in A_n\}$$

with any choice of $n \in \mathbb{N}$, $0 \leq t_1 < t_2 < \cdots < t_n \leq T$ and $A_1, A_2, \ldots, A_n \in \mathcal{B}_{\mathbb{R}}$. These sets are called *cylindrical sets.* We denote by $\mathcal{B}_C$ the σ-algebra on $C([0, T])$ generated by the cylindrical sets.

Remark.   The σ-algebra $\mathcal{B}_C$ is similarly defined as the σ-algebra $\mathcal{B}_{\mathbb{R}^n}$, with the difference that the finite index set $\{1, 2, \ldots, n\}$ is replaced by the uncountable set $[0, T]$. Note that $\mathbb{R}^n$ can be seen as the set of all functions $f \colon \{1, 2, 3, \ldots, n\} \to \mathbb{R}$.

Proposition 6.2.2 .   *Let $(X_t)_{0 \leq t \leq T}$ be a continuous process on $(\Omega, \mathcal{F}, \mathbb{P})$ then the map:*

$$X_{(\cdot)} \colon \ \Omega \ni \omega \mapsto X_{(\cdot)}(\omega) \in C([0, T])$$

is measurable, where $X_{(\cdot)}(\omega)$ is the path $[0, T] \ni t \mapsto X_t(\omega)$.

Proof.   For any choice of $n \in \mathbb{N}$, $0 \leq t_1 < t_2 < t_3 < \cdots < t_n \leq T$ and $A_1, \ldots, A_n \in \mathcal{B}_{\mathbb{R}}$

$$\{\omega | X_{(\cdot)}(\omega) \in \{f \in C([0, T]) | f(t_i) \in A_i, i = 1, \ldots, n\}\} = \bigcap_{i=1}^{n} \{\omega \mid X_{t_i}(\omega) \in A_i\} \in \mathcal{F}.$$

Since the cylindrical sets generate $\mathcal{B}_C$ the claim follows. $\square$

Definition.   Let $(X_t)_{0 \leq t \leq T}$ be a continuous process on $(\Omega, \mathcal{F}, \mathbb{P})$ we put for $A \in \mathcal{B}_C$:

$$\mathbb{P}_X(A) := \mathbb{P}(\{\omega \in \Omega \mid X_{(\cdot)}(\omega) \in A\})$$

is called *the distribution of* X. Note that $\mathbb{P}_X$ is a probability on $(C([0, T]), \mathcal{B}_C)$.

Definition. For $f \in C([0,T])$ we put

$$\|f\|_\infty = \sup_{0 \leq t \leq T} |f(t)|$$

and for $f, g \in C([0,T])$

$$\text{dist}(f,g) = \|f - g\|_\infty.$$

We call a function

$$F \colon C([0,T]) \to \mathbb{R}$$

continuous if:

$$\|f_n - f\|_\infty \to 0 \Rightarrow F(f_n) \xrightarrow[n \to \infty]{} F(f).$$

Remark. Functions F on $C([0,T])$ can (and will) be seen as "path dependent" or "exotic" options: $F(S_{(\cdot)}(\omega))$ is the pay-off if $\omega \in \Omega$ happens. The following Lemma is not hard but technical, the main ingredient is the fact that $C([0,T])$ *is separable* meaning that there is a countable set $D \subset C([0,T])$ (for example the polynomials with rational coefficients) which is *dense*, i.e. for any $f \in C([0,T])$, there is a sequence $f_n \in D$ with $\text{dist}(f_n, f) \xrightarrow[n \to \infty]{} 0$.

Lemma 6.2.3 . *A continuous function* $F \colon C([0,T]) \to \mathbb{R}$ *is measurable.*

The next theorem specifies some conditions which are equivalent to the statement $(X_t)_{0 \leq t \leq T}$ and $(\widetilde{X}_t)_{0 \leq t \leq T}$ have the same distribution, (and are easier to verify).

Theorem 6.2.4 .   *Assume $(X_t)_{0 \leq t \leq T}$ is a continuous process on the probability space $(\Omega, \mathcal{F}, \mathbb{P})$ and $(\widetilde{X}_t)_{0 \leq t \leq T}$ is a continuous on the probability space $(\widetilde{\Omega}, \widetilde{\mathcal{F}}, \widetilde{\mathbb{P}})$. Then the following are equivalent*

a) $\mathbb{P}_X = \widetilde{\mathbb{P}}_{\widetilde{X}}$.

b) *For all $n \in \mathbb{N}$ and $0 \leq t_1 < t_2 < \cdots < t_n \leq T$*

$$\mathbb{P}_{(X_{t_1}, X_{t_2}, \ldots, X_{t_n})} = \widetilde{\mathbb{P}}_{(\widetilde{X}_{t_1}, \ldots, \widetilde{X}_{t_n})}$$

$\mathbb{P}_{(X_{t_1}, X_{t_2}, \ldots, X_{t_n})}$ *denotes the joint distribution of the random vector $(X_{t_1}, X_{t_2}, \ldots, X_{T_n})$ (see Appendix B.2). The family $(\mathbb{P}_{(X_{t_1}, X_{t_2}, \ldots, X_{t_n})})_{0 \leq t_1 < t_2 < \cdots < t_n \leq T}$ is called the family of finite dimensional distribution of X.*

c) *For all $n \in \mathbb{N}$ and $0 \leq t_1 < t_2 < \cdots < t_n \leq T$*

$$\mathbb{P}_{(X_{t_1}, X_{t_2} - X_{t_1}, X_{t_3} - X_{t_2}, \ldots, X_{t_n} - X_{t_{n-1}})} = \widetilde{\mathbb{P}}_{(\widetilde{X}_{t_1}, \widetilde{X}_{t_2} - \widetilde{X}_{t_1}, \ldots, \widetilde{X}_{t_n} - \widetilde{X}_{t_{n-1}})}.$$

d) *For all $n \in \mathbb{N}$ and $0 \leq t_1 < t_2 < \cdots < t_n \leq T$ and continuous bounded functions $f_1, f_2, \ldots, f_n \colon \mathbb{R} \to \mathbb{R}$*

$$\mathbb{E}_{\mathbb{P}}(f_1(X_{t_1}) \cdot f_2(X_{t_2}) \cdot \ldots \cdot f_n(X_{t_n})) = \mathbb{E}_{\widetilde{\mathbb{P}}}(f_1(\widetilde{X}_{t_1}) \cdot f_2(\widetilde{X}_{t_2}) \cdot \ldots \cdot f_n(\widetilde{X}_{t_n})).$$

e) *For all $n \in \mathbb{N}$ and $0 \leq t_1 < t_2 < \cdots < t_n \leq T$ and continuous and bounded functions $f_1, f_2, \ldots, f_n \colon \mathbb{R} \to \mathbb{R}$*

$$\mathbb{E}_{\mathbb{P}}(f_1(X_{t_1}) f_2(X_{t_2} - X_{t_1}) \ldots f_n(X_{t_n} - X_{t_{n-1}})) =$$
$$\mathbb{E}_{\widetilde{\mathbb{P}}}(f_1(\widetilde{X}_{t_1}) f_2(\widetilde{X}_{t_2} - \widetilde{X}_{t_1}) \ldots f_n(\widetilde{X}_{t_n} - \widetilde{X}_{t_{n-1}})).$$

Remark. Theorem 6.2.4 says the the following:

Two distributions $\mathbb{P}_X$ and $\mathbb{P}_{\widetilde{X}}$ are, by definition, equal if $\mathbb{P}_X(A) = \mathbb{P}_{\widetilde{X}}(A)$ for all $A \in \mathcal{B}_C$. This is of course the same as saying that any measurable $F : C[0, T]\mathbb{R}$ is $\mathbb{P}_X$-integrable if and only it is $\mathbb{P}_{\tilde{X}}$-integrable, and that in that case

(6.10) $$\mathbb{E}_{\mathbb{P}_X}(F) = \mathbb{E}_{\mathbb{P}_{\tilde{X}}}(F)$$

Now Theorem 6.2.4 implies that in order to verify Equation (6.10) for all measurable functions $F : C[0,T] \to \mathbb{R}$ it is enough to verify it for functions of the form

$$F(\varphi) = f_1(\varphi(t_1))f_2(\varphi(t_2))\ldots f_n(\varphi(t_n)), \quad \varphi \in C[0,T],$$

where $n \in \mathbb{N}$ and $f_1, f_2, \ldots f_n : \mathbb{R} \to \mathbb{R}$ is bounded and continuous.

Proof. (Sketch)

$a \Rightarrow b$ is clear.

$b \Rightarrow a$ follows from the following general principle (compare Theorem B.2.5 in Appendix B.2): We are given two probabilities $\mathbb{P}_1$ and $\mathbb{P}_2$ on $(\Omega, \mathcal{F})$, and we assume that they coincide on a subset $\mathcal{D} \subset \mathcal{F}$ which has the following two properties: $\mathcal{D}$ generates $\mathcal{F}$, i.e. $\mathcal{F}$ is the smallest σ-algebra containing $\mathcal{D}$, and $\mathcal{D}$ is stable under taking intersections, i.e. $A, B \in \mathcal{D} \Rightarrow A \cap B \in \mathcal{D}$. Then $\mathbb{P}_1$ and and $\mathbb{P}_2$ coincide on all of $\mathcal{F}$. We apply this principle for $\mathcal{D}$ being the cylindrical sets on $C[0,T]$.

$(b) \Leftrightarrow (c) \Leftrightarrow (d) \Leftrightarrow (e)$ follows from the corresponding equivalences for finite dimensional distributions.

$\square$

Remark. As defined in Section 2.1 a Brownian motion is a process (B_t) which has the following three properties: $B_0 = 0$, (B_t) is continuous, and for all $0 \le t_1 < \cdots < t_n$ and all choices of $A_1, \ldots A_n \in \mathcal{B}_{mathbbR}$ it follows that

$$\mathbb{P}(B_{t_1} \in A_1, B_{t_2} - B_{t_1} \in A_2, \ldots, B_{t_n} - B_{t_{n-1}} \in A_n)$$
$$= N(0, t_1)(A_1) \cdot N(0, t_2 - t_1)(A_2) \cdot \ldots \cdot N(0, t_n - t_{n-1})(A_n).$$

The last conditions determines the finite dimensional distributions and thus by Theorem 6.2.4 $(c \Rightarrow a)$, it follows that any two Brownian motions have the same (infinite dimensional) distribution on $C[0,T]$.

The distribution of a Brownian motion is usually referred to as the *Wiener measure*.

After this short description of infinite dimensional distribution theory we go back to consider the process $S_t = S_0 e^{(\mu - \frac{1}{2}\nu^2)t + \nu B_t}$. We know, that B_t on the filtered space $(\Omega, \mathcal{F}, \mathbb{P}, (\mathcal{F}_t))$ is a Brownian motion. But this implies apriori nothing about the distribution of B_t seen as being defined on $(\Omega, \mathcal{F}, \mathbb{Q}, (\mathcal{F}_t))$. Let us illustrate that with an example for one dimensional distributions.

Example. Consider the standard normal distribution $N(0,1)$ on $\mathbb{R}$. Thus, the identity $X : \quad \mathbb{R} \to \mathbb{R}$, $x \mapsto x$, is normal distributed on $(\mathbb{R}, B_{\mathbb{R}}, N(0,1))$. Now consider any density function f on $\mathbb{R}$, and define $g = f \sqrt{2\pi} e^{x^2/2}$. For any $A \in \mathcal{B}_{\mathbb{R}}$ let

$$\mathbb{Q}(A) = \mathbb{E}_{N(0,1)}(1_A \cdot g)$$

$$[\text{i.e. } \mathbb{Q} \text{ has } g \text{ as Radon Nikodym derivative with respect to} N(0,1)]$$

$$= \frac{1}{\sqrt{2\pi}} \int_{-\infty}^{\infty} 1_A f(x) \sqrt{2\pi} \ e^{x^2/2} e^{-x^2/2} dx$$

$$= \int_{-\infty}^{\infty} 1_A f(x) dx.$$

Thus $\mathbb{Q}$ is a probability on $\mathbb{R}$ with density f. Now the same map $X : \mathbb{R} \ni x \mapsto x$ is $\mathbb{Q}$-distributed, with $\mathbb{Q}$ having the (arbitrarily chosen) density f.

Theorem 6.2.5 . $(B_t)_{0 \le t \le T}$, *as process on* $(\Omega, \mathcal{F}, \mathbb{Q})$, *is a "shifted Brownian motion" with shift being* $\frac{(r-\mu)}{\nu}t$, *i.e.* (B_t) *on* $(\Omega, \mathcal{F}, \mathbb{Q})$ *has the same distribution as the process* $(B_t + \frac{r-\mu}{\nu}t)_{0 \le t \le T}$ *on* $(\Omega, \mathcal{F}, \mathbb{P})$.

Proof.   By Theorem 6.2.4 $(e \Rightarrow a)$ we have to show that for any $n \in \mathbb{N}$, any choice $0 \le t_1 <$

$t_2 < \cdots < t_n \leq T$ and any choice of continuous bounded functions $g_1, g_2, \ldots, g_n \colon \mathbb{R} \to \mathbb{R}$

$$\mathbb{E}_{\mathbb{P}}\left(g_1\left(B_{t_1} + \frac{r-\mu}{\nu}t_1\right)g_2\left(B_{t_2} - B_{t_1} + \frac{r-\mu}{\nu}(t_2 - t_1)\right) \cdot \ldots \cdot \right.$$

$$\left. g_n\left(B_{t_n} - B_{t_{n-1}} + \frac{r-\mu}{\nu}(t_n - t_{n-1})\right)\right)$$

$$= \mathbb{E}_{\mathbb{Q}}(g_1(B_{t_1})g_2(B_{t_2} - B_{t_1}) \cdot \ldots \cdot g_n(B_{t_n} - B_{t_{n-1}})).$$

For that note that

$$\mathbb{E}_{\mathbb{Q}}(g_1(B_{t_1})g_2(B_{t_2} - B_{t_1}) \cdot \ldots \cdot g_n(B_{t_n} - B_{t_{n-1}}))$$

$$= \mathbb{E}_{\mathbb{Q}}(g_1(B_{t_1}) \cdot g_2(B_{t_2} - B_{t_1}) \cdot \ldots \cdot g_{n-1}(B_{t_{n-1}} - B_{t_{n-2}})\mathbb{E}_{\mathbb{Q}}(g_n(B_{t_n} - B_{t_{n-1}}) \mid \mathcal{F}_{t_{n-1}}))$$

$$= \mathbb{E}_{\mathbb{Q}}(g_1(B_{t_1}) \cdot \ldots \cdot g_{n-1}(B_{t_{n-1}} - B_{t_{n-2}})\mathbb{E}_{\mathbb{P}}(g_n(B_{t_n} - B_{t_{n-1}} + \frac{r-\mu}{\nu}(t_n - t_{n-1}) \mid \mathcal{F}_{t_{n-1}}))$$

[Proposition 6.2.1]

$$= \mathbb{E}_{\mathbb{P}}(g_n(B_{t_n} - B_{t_{n-1}} + \frac{r-\mu}{\nu}(t_n - t_{n-1}))) \cdot \mathbb{E}_{\mathbb{Q}}(g_1(B_{t_1}) \cdot \ldots \cdot g_{n-1}(B_{t_{n-1}} - B_{t_{n-2}}))$$

[Independence of $B_{t_n} - B_{t_{n-1}}$ and $\mathcal{F}_{t_{n-1}}$]

$$= \prod_{i=1}^{n} \mathbb{E}_{\mathbb{P}}\left(g_i(B_{t_i} - B_{t_{i-1}} + \frac{r-\mu}{\nu}(t_i - t_{i-1})\right) \qquad \text{[where } t_0 = 0, B_0 = 0\text{]}$$

[Repeat]

$$= \mathbb{E}_{\mathbb{P}}\left(g_1\left(B_{t_1} + \frac{r-\mu}{\nu}t_1\right)g_2\left(B_{t_2} - B_{t_1} + \frac{r-\mu}{\nu}(t_2 - t_1)\right) \cdot \ldots \cdot \right.$$

$$\left. g_n\left(B_{t_n} - B_{t_{n-1}} + \frac{r-\mu}{\nu}(t_n - t_{n-1})\right)\right)$$

[Independence]

$\square$

Let $F \colon C([0, T]) \to \mathbb{R}$ be measurable. We want to price the security which pays $F(S_{(\cdot)})$. By Equation (5.3) in Section 5.1, the value of such a security at time t equals to

$$V(F(S_{(\cdot)}), t) = e^{-r(T-t)}\mathbb{E}_{\mathbb{Q}}(F(S_{(\cdot)}) \mid \mathcal{F}_t).$$

We split the path of S_t into the two parts given by $S|_{[0,t]} = (S_u)_{u \in [0,t]}$ (this path is realized at time t) and the future path $S|_{[t,T]} = (S_u)_{u \in [t,T]}$.

We also use the following convention: for two continuous functions

$$f_1 \colon [0,t] \to \mathbb{R}, \quad f_2 \colon [t,T] \to \mathbb{R}$$

with $f_1(t) = f_2(t)$ we write (f_1, f_2) for the function on $[0,T]$ with

$$(f_1, f_2)(u) = \begin{cases} f_1(u) & \text{if } 0 \leq u \leq t \\ f_2(u) & \text{if } t \leq u \leq T. \end{cases}$$

We thirdly note that for $u \geq t$,

$$S_u = S_t \cdot e^{(\mu - \frac{1}{2}\nu^2)(u-t) + \nu(B_u - B_t)}.$$

Using these notations we are able to write

$$\mathbb{E}_{\mathbb{Q}}(F(S_{(\cdot)}) \mid \mathcal{F}_t) = \mathbb{E}_{\mathbb{Q}}(F(S|_{[0,t]}, S_t e^{(\mu - \frac{1}{2}\nu^2)((\cdot)-t) + \nu(B_{(\cdot)} - B_t)}) \mid \mathcal{F}_t).$$

Now we use Theorem 6.2.5 which allows us to "replace $\mathbb{Q}$ by $\mathbb{P}$" if we pass from (B_t) to a shifted version

$$\mathbb{E}_{\mathbb{Q}}\left(F(S|_{[0,t]}, S_t e^{(\mu - \frac{1}{2}\nu^2)((\cdot)-t) + \nu(B_{(\cdot)} - B_t)})\mid \mathcal{F}_t\right)$$
$$= \mathbb{E}_{\mathbb{P}}\left(F(S|_{[0,t]}, S_t e^{(r - \frac{1}{2}\nu^2)((\cdot)-t) + \nu(B_{(\cdot)} - B_t)}) \mid \mathcal{F}_t\right).$$

Finally, note that the process $(B_u - B_t)_{t \leq u \leq T}$ is independent to $\mathcal{F}_t$ and has the same distribution as $(B_{u-t})_{t \leq u \leq T}$. Thus we get

(6.11)
$$\mathbb{E}_{\mathbb{Q}}(F(S|_{[0,t]}, S_t e^{(\mu - \frac{1}{2}\nu^2)((\cdot)-t) + \nu(B_{(\cdot)} - B_t)}) \mid \mathcal{F}_t) = \mathbb{E}_{\mathbb{P}}(F(S|_{[0,t]}, S_t e^{(r - \frac{1}{2}\nu^2)((\cdot)-t) + \nu(B_{(\cdot)} - B_t)})).$$

In Equation (6.11) we think of $S|_{[0,t]}$ being realized. For the value of the option $F(S_{(\cdot)})$ we therefore derive the following value at time t.

(6.12) $$V(F(S_{(\cdot)}), t) = e^{-r(T-t)} \mathbb{E}_{\mathbb{P}}(F(S|_{[0,t]}, S_t e^{(r - \frac{1}{2}\nu^2)((\cdot)-t) + \nu(B_{(\cdot)} - B_t)})).$$

Thus, in order to price path dependent options we have to proceed as follows:

Given the path $S|_{[0,t]}$ find the (one dimensional distribution) of the random variable

$$F(S|_{[0,t]}, S_t e^{(r-\frac{1}{2}\nu^2)((\cdot)-t)+\nu(B_{(\cdot)}-B_t)}).$$

In particular, if $t = 0$, find the distribution of

$$F(S_0 e^{(r-\frac{1}{2}\nu^2)(\cdot)+\nu B_{(\cdot)}}).$$

Now the process $(\widetilde{B}_s)_{0 \leq s \leq T-t}$ defined by $\widetilde{B}_s = B_{s+t} - B_t$ is a Brownian motion on the filtered space $(\Omega, \mathcal{F}, \mathbb{P}, (\mathcal{F}_{t+s})_{0 \leq s \leq T-t})$ which, furthermore, is independent to $\mathcal{F}_t$.

Thus, we can state our end result as follows:

Theorem 6.2.6 . *Assume that $F : C[0,T] \to \mathbb{R}$ is measurable and bounded and assume that (S_t) satisfies the Black Scholes model with constant drift μ and constant volatility ν. Then the value of an option paying $F(S_{(\cdot)})$ at time T has at time $t \leq T$ the value*

(6.13) $$V(F(S_{(\cdot)}), t) = e^{-r(T-t)}\mathbb{E}_\mathbb{P}(F(S|_{[0,t]}, S_t e^{(r-\frac{1}{2}\nu^2)((\cdot)-t)+\nu \widetilde{B}_{(\cdot)}})).$$

6.3   Barrier Options

The goal of this section is to find the value of an option, which pays

$$f(\max_{0\leq t\leq T} S_t)$$

at time T assuming the price S_t of the underlying asset follows the Black Scholes model. As derived in the previous section this problem comes down to the problem of finding the value of

(6.14) $$e^{-r(T-t)}\mathbb{E}_{\mathbb{P}}(f(M_t \vee S_t \max_{0\leq s\leq T-t} e^{(r-\frac{1}{2}\nu^2)s+\nu\widetilde{B}_s})),$$

where $M_t = \max_{0\leq u\leq t} S_u$ ($\mathcal{F}_t$-measurable), and $(\widetilde{B}_s)_{0\leq s\leq T-t}$ is a Brownian motion independent to the σ-algebra $\mathcal{F}_t$. In order for the formula 6.14 to make sense we will assume tht f is integrable with respect to the distribution of $\omega \mapsto \max_{0\leq t\leq T} S_t(\omega)$. Later we will find out what this means concretely.

We will first compute the Radon Nikodym derivative of a probability $\mathbb{Q}$ on which a shifted Brownian motion turns into a Brownian motion without shift. This result can be used to find the Radon Nikodym derivatives for the equivalent martingale measures.

Theorem 6.3.1 *(Girsanov's Theorem).*

Let $(B_t)_{0 \leq t \leq T}$ be a Brownian motion and let c_t be an adapted process with right continuous paths having left limits on the filtered probability space $(\Omega, \mathcal{F}, \mathbb{P}, (\mathcal{F}_t)_{0 \leq t \leq T})$. Define:

$$X_t = \int_0^t c_u \, du + B_t$$

$$Y_t = e^{-\int_0^t c_u \, dB_u - \frac{1}{2} \int_0^t c_u^2 \, du}.$$

Then X_t is a Brownian motion on the space $(\Omega, \mathcal{F}, \mathbb{Q}, (\mathcal{F}_t)_{0 \leq t \leq T})$ where $\mathbb{Q}$ is defined by

$$\mathbb{Q}(A) = \mathbb{E}_\mathbb{P}(1_A \cdot Y_T),$$

i.e. $\mathbb{Q}$ is a probability whose Radon Nikodym derivative is Y_T with respect to $\mathbb{P}$.

Proof. We will only prove the claim in the case that c_t is constant, the only case we will need. Thus

$$X_t = ct + B_t \text{ and } Y_t = e^{-cB_t - \frac{1}{2}c^2 t}.$$

First note that Y_T is actually a Radon-Nikodym derivative. Indeed, from Proposition 2.2.3 in Section 2.2 it follows that $(Y_t)_{0 \leq t \leq T}$ is a $\mathbb{P}$-martingale, and thus $\mathbb{E}(Y_T) = \mathbb{E}(Y_0) = 1$. The process $(X_t)_{0 \leq t \leq T}$ is continuous and $X_0 = 0$. By Theorem 6.2.4 we need to show that for any choice of $n \in \mathbb{N}$, $0 \leq t_1 < t_2 < \cdots < t_n \leq T$ and continuous and bounded $f_1, \ldots, f_n \colon \mathbb{R} \to \mathbb{R}$ it follows that

$$\mathbb{E}_\mathbb{Q}\left(\prod_{i=1}^n f_i(X_{t_i} - X_{t_{i-1}})\right) = \mathbb{E}_\mathbb{P}\left(\prod_{i=1}^n f_i(B_{t_i} - B_{t_{i-1}})\right).$$

Assume, without loss of generality, that $t_1 = 0$, $t_n = T$, otherwise include $t_{n+1} = T$ and

$f_{n+1} \equiv 1$. Then

$$\mathbb{E}_{\mathbb{Q}} \left(\prod_{i=1}^{n} f_i(X_{t_i} - X_{t_{i-1}}) \right)$$

$$= \mathbb{E}_{\mathbb{P}} \left(\left[\prod_{i=1}^{n} f_i(B_{t_i} - B_{t_{i-1}} + c(t_i - t_{i-1})) \right] e^{-cB_T - \frac{1}{2}c^2 T} \right)$$

$$= \mathbb{E}_{\mathbb{P}} \left(\prod_{i=1}^{n} \left[f_i(B_{t_i} - B_{t_{i-1}} + c(t_i - t_{i-1})) \cdot e^{-c(B_{t_i} - B_{t_{i-1}}) - \frac{1}{2}c^2(t_i - t_{i-1})} \right] \right)$$

$$= \prod_{i=1}^{n} \mathbb{E}_{\mathbb{P}}(f_i(B_{t_i} - B_{t_{i-1}} + c(t_i - t_{i-1})) \cdot e^{-c(B_{t_i} - B_{t_{i-1}}) - \frac{1}{2}c^2(t_i - t_{i-1})})$$

[Independence]

Now note that for $s = t_{i-1}, t = t_i, f = f_i$

$$\mathbb{E}_{\mathbb{P}}(F(\underbrace{B_t - B_s + c(t - s)}_{N(c(t-s),t-s)-\text{distributed}}) \cdot e^{-c(B_t - B_s) - \frac{1}{2}c^2(t-s)})$$

$$= \frac{1}{\sqrt{2\pi(t - s)}} \int_{-\infty}^{\infty} F(x) \cdot e^{-c(x - c(t-s)) - \frac{1}{2}c^2(t-s)} \cdot e^{-\frac{(x - c(t-s))^2}{2(t-s)}} dx$$

$$= \frac{1}{\sqrt{2\pi(t - s)}} \int_{-\infty}^{\infty} F(x) e^{-\frac{x^2}{2(t-s)}} dx$$

$$= \mathbb{E}_{\mathbb{P}}(F(B_t - B_s)),$$

which implies the claim.   □

Remark.   Let $\mathbb{Q}$ be an equivalent martingale probability. We showed in the previous section that $(B_t)_{0 \le t \le T}$ (which is a Brownian motion on $(\Omega, \mathcal{F}, \mathbb{P})$) has on $(\Omega, \mathcal{F}, \mathbb{Q})$ the same distribution as the process $(B_t + \frac{r-\mu}{\nu}t)_{0 \le t \le T}$ on the space $(\Omega, \mathcal{F}, \mathbb{P})$.

Using Girsanov's formula we can compute ρ.

Note that for any continous and bounded $F : C[0, T] \to \mathbb{R}$.

(6.15) $\mathbb{E}_{\mathbb{P}}(F(B_{(\cdot)})\rho) = \mathbb{E}_{\mathbb{Q}}(F(B_{(\cdot)}))$

$$= \mathbb{E}_{\mathbb{P}}(F(B_{(\cdot)} + \frac{r - \mu}{\nu}t)).$$

Thus a possible choice for ρ is

(6.16) $$\rho = Y_T = e^{-\frac{r-\mu}{\nu}B_T - \frac{1}{2}\frac{(r-\mu)^2}{\nu^2}T}.$$

Let us explain why we say "a possible choice of ρ is Y_T" and why we do not claim that the only choice for ρ is Y_T. Our filtration $(\mathcal{F}_t)$ might not only be generated by (B_t) but also by other random variables (like for example the price of another stock). But if we denote by $(\mathcal{G}_t)$ the filtration only generated by (B_t) we conclude that for the Radon Nikodym derivative of any equivalent martingale probability $\mathbb{Q}$ we have

$$\mathbb{E}_{\mathbb{P}}(\rho|\mathcal{G}_T) = Y_T = e^{-\frac{r-\mu}{\nu}B_T - \frac{1}{2}\frac{(r-\mu)^2}{\nu^2}T}.$$

In the next theorem we compute the joint density of $\max_{0\le t\le T} B_t$ and B_T. This is exactly the distribution we will need in order to price a barrier style opyion.

Theorem 6.3.2   *(The joint distribution of $\max_{0\le t\le T} B_t$ and B_T).*
For $T \ge 0$ let $M_T = \sup_{0\le t\le T} B_t$. Then, the joint distribution of M_T and B_T has a density on $\mathbb{R}^2$, namely

$$f_{(M,B)}(m,b) = \begin{cases} 0 & \text{if } m < 0 \\ 0 & \text{if } 0 < m < b \\ \frac{2(2m-b)}{T\sqrt{2\pi T}}e^{-\frac{(2m-b)^2}{2T}} & \text{if } 0 < m, b < m. \end{cases}$$

The density of the distribution of M_T is

$$f_M(m) = \begin{cases} 0 & \text{if } m \le 0 \\ \frac{2}{\sqrt{2\pi T}}e^{-\frac{m^2}{2T}} & \text{if } m > 0 \end{cases}$$

Proof. The proof is divided in three steps.
Step 1: (Reflection principle) let τ be a stopping time, and $\tau \le T$. Then the random variable $B_T - B_\tau$ is *symmetric*, meaning that $\mathbb{P}(B_T - B_\tau > c) = \mathbb{P}(B_\tau - B_T > c)$ for $c \in \mathbb{R}$.

First assume that τ has finitely many values $0 \le t_1 < t_2 < \cdots < t_n \le T$. Then

$$\mathbb{P}(B_T - B_\tau > c) = \mathbb{E}\left(\sum_{i=1}^n 1_{\{\tau=t_i\}} 1_{[c,\infty)}(B_T - B_{t_i})\right)$$

$$= \mathbb{E}\left(\sum_{i=1}^n 1_{\{\tau=t_i\}} \mathbb{E}(1_{[c,\infty)}(B_T - B_{t_i}) \mid \mathcal{F}_{t_i})\right)$$

$$= \mathbb{E}\left(\sum_{i=1}^n 1_{\{\tau=t_i\}} \mathbb{E}(1_{[c,\infty)}(B_T - B_{t_i}))\right)$$

$$= \mathbb{E}\left(\sum_{i=1}^n 1_{\{\tau=t_i\}} \mathbb{E}(1_{[c,\infty)}(B_{t_i} - B_T))\right)$$

$$[B_T - B_{t_i} \text{ is symmetric}]$$

$$= \mathbb{P}(B_\tau - B_T > c)$$

[same computation backwards].

For a general stopping time $\tau \le T$ we first define a sequence of stopping times τ_n, all of the τ_n having finite range, with $\tau_n \to \tau$ a.s. for $n \to \infty$. For example we could define the following sequence of stopping times (τ_n) (compare Exercise ......)

$$\tau_n(\omega) := \sum_{i=1}^n t_i^{(n)} 1_{\{t_{i-1}^{(n)} \le \tau < t_i^{(n)}\}}(\omega) + T 1_{\{t_n=T\}}(\omega)$$

with $P_n = (t_0^{(n)}, \ldots, t_n^{(n)})$ being a partition of $[0,T]$ and and $\lim_{n\to\infty} ||P_n|| = 0$. Then note that

$$\mathbb{P}(B_T - B_\tau > c) = \lim_{n\to\infty} \mathbb{P}(B_T - B_{\tau_n} > c) = \lim_{n\to\infty} \mathbb{E}(B_{\tau_n} - B_T > c) = \mathbb{P}(B_\tau - B_T > c).$$

Step 2: We show for $b, m \in \mathbb{R}$

$$\mathbb{P}(M_T > m \,,\, B_T < b) = \begin{cases} \mathbb{P}(B_T < b) & \text{if } m < 0 \\ 2\mathbb{P}(m \le B_T) - \mathbb{P}(b < B_T) & \text{if } 0 \le m \le b \\ \mathbb{P}(B_T > 2m - b) & \text{if } 0 < m, b < m. \end{cases}$$

We start with the case $0 < m$ and $b < m$ and define the stopping time

$$\tau_m(\omega) = \begin{cases} T & \text{if } B_t < m \text{ for all } 0 \le t \le T \\ \inf\{t: \ B_t \ge m\} & \text{else} \end{cases}$$

for $\omega \in \Omega$.

Note that $B_{\tau_m} \equiv m$ on the set $\{\tau_m < T\}$. We observe the following equalities

$$\mathbb{P}(M_T > m, B_T < b) = \mathbb{P}(\tau_m < T, B_T < b)$$
$$= \mathbb{P}(\tau_m < T, B_T - B_{\tau_m} < b - m)$$
$$= \mathbb{P}(B_T - B_{\tau_m} < b - m)$$
$$[\text{For } \omega \in \{\tau_m = T\} \quad B_T - B_{\tau_m} = B_T - B_T = 0 > b - m]$$
$$= \mathbb{P}(B_{\tau_m} - B_T < b - m)$$
$$[\text{symmetry}]$$
$$= \mathbb{P}(\tau_m < T, B_{\tau_m} - B_T < b - m)$$
$$[\text{on } \{\tau_m = T\} \quad B_{\tau_m} - B_T = 0 > b - m]$$
$$= \mathbb{P}(\tau_m < T, -B_T < b - 2m)$$
$$= \mathbb{P}(-B_T < b - 2m)$$
$$[\text{on } \{\tau_m = T\} \quad B_T \le m, \text{ thus } -B_T \ge -m > b - 2m, \text{ since } b < m]$$
$$= \mathbb{P}(B_T > 2m - b).$$

If $0 \le m \le b$ we proceed in the following way

$$\mathbb{P}(M_T > m, \quad B_T < b) = \mathbb{P}(M_T > m, \quad m \le B_T < b) + \mathbb{P}(M_T > m, \quad B_T < m)$$
$$= \mathbb{P}(m \le B_T < b) + \lim_{\varepsilon \downarrow 0} \mathbb{P}(M_T > m, B_T < m - \varepsilon)$$
$$= \mathbb{P}(m \le B_T < b) + \lim_{\varepsilon \downarrow 0} \mathbb{P}(B_T > m + \varepsilon)$$
$$[\text{first case with } b = m - \varepsilon]$$
$$= 2\mathbb{P}(m \le B_T) - \mathbb{P}(b < B_T).$$

The last case that $m < 0$ is easy. Indeed, $M_T \ge M_0 = 0$. Thus we deduce in this case that

$$\mathbb{P}(M_T > m, \quad B_T < b) = \mathbb{P}(B_T < b).$$

This finishes the proof of claim 2.

Step 3: Now let $f_{(M,B)}(\cdot,\cdot)$ be the density of the joint distribution of M and B. Then

$$\int\limits_{m}^{\infty}\int\limits_{-\infty}^{b} f_{(M,B)}(x,y)dxdy = \mathbb{P}(M_T > m\,,\,B_T < b).$$

Thus

$$
\begin{aligned}
f_{(M,B)}(m,b) &= -\frac{\partial}{\partial m}\frac{\partial}{\partial b}\int\limits_{m}^{\infty}\int\limits_{-\infty}^{b} f_{(M,B)}(x,y)dxdy \\[2mm]
&= -\frac{\partial}{\partial m}\frac{\partial}{\partial b}\mathbb{P}(M_T > m, B_T < b) \\[2mm]
&= -\frac{\partial}{\partial m}\frac{\partial}{\partial b}
\begin{cases}
\mathbb{P}(B_T < b) & \text{if } m < 0 \\[1mm]
2\mathbb{P}(m \le B_T) - \mathbb{P}(b < B_T) & \text{if } 0 \le m \le b \\[1mm]
\mathbb{P}(B_T > 2m - b) & \text{if } 0 < m, b < m.
\end{cases} \\[3mm]
&=
\begin{cases}
0 & \text{if } m < 0 \\[1mm]
0 & \text{if } 0 < m < b \\[1mm]
-\frac{\partial}{\partial m}\frac{\partial}{\partial b}\mathbb{P}(B_T > 2m - b) & \text{if } 0 < m, b < m
\end{cases}
\end{aligned}
$$

And for $0 < m$ and $b < m$

$$
\begin{aligned}
-\frac{\partial^2}{\partial m\partial b}\mathbb{P}(B_T > 2m - b) &= -\frac{\partial^2}{\partial m\partial b}\left(\frac{1}{\sqrt{2\pi T}}\int\limits_{2m-b}^{\infty} e^{-\frac{x^2}{2T}}dx\right) \\[2mm]
&= -\frac{\partial}{\partial m}\frac{1}{\sqrt{2\pi T}}e^{-\frac{(2m-b)^2}{2T}} \\[2mm]
&= \frac{2(2m-b)}{T\sqrt{2\pi T}}e^{-\frac{(2m-b)^2}{2T}}
\end{aligned}
$$

which proves the formula for the density of the joint distribution of M_T and B_T.

The formula for the density of M_T can be obtained by integrating $f_{(M,B)}(m,b)$ with respect to b over $(-\infty,\infty)$. But there is a faster argument: For $0 \le m$

$$
\begin{aligned}
\mathbb{P}(M_T > m) &= \mathbb{P}(M_T > m\,,\,B_T < \infty) \\
&= 2\mathbb{P}(B_T > m) \quad \text{[Step 2]}
\end{aligned}
$$

since $\frac{1}{\sqrt{2\pi T}}e^{-\frac{x^2}{2T}}$ is the density of B_T, the claim follows. □

We now are in the position to price the value of a security which pays

$$F(\max_{0\leq t\leq T} S_t)$$

at time T.

Let $0 \leq t \leq T$ be the time we want to evaluate this security, and $M_t = \max_{0\leq u\leq t} S_u$ be the maximal value up to time t (M_t is known at time t and thus considered fixed). Then, by Equation (6.12) in Section 6.2

$$W(f(\max_{0\leq u\leq T} S_u), t) = e^{-r(T-t)}\mathbb{E}_{\mathbb{P}}(f(M_t \vee \max_{t\leq u\leq T} S_t \cdot e^{(r-\frac{1}{2}\nu^2)(u-t)+\nu(B_u-B_t)}))$$

$$= e^{-r(T-t)}\mathbb{E}_{\mathbb{P}}(f(M_t \vee S_t \cdot e^{\nu \max_{t\leq u\leq T}[(\frac{2r-\nu^2}{2\nu})(u-t)+B_u-B_t]}))$$

$$= e^{-r(T-t)}\mathbb{E}_{\mathbb{P}}(G_t(\max_{0\leq s\leq T-t} cs + \widetilde{B}_s)),$$

where $G_t(x) = f(M_t \vee S_t e^{\nu x})$, $c = \frac{2r-\nu^2}{2\nu}$, and $\widetilde{B}_s = B_{t+s} - B_t$, note that $(\widetilde{B}_s)_{0\leq s}$ is also a Brownian motion, which is independent to $\mathcal{F}_t$ and adapted to $(\mathcal{F}_{t+s})_{s\geq 0}$.

Now, we deduce that

$$\mathbb{E}_{\mathbb{P}}(G_t(\max_{0\leq s\leq T-t} cs + \widetilde{B}_s)) = \mathbb{E}_{\mathbb{P}}(G_t(\max_{0\leq s\leq T-t} cs + \widetilde{B}_s)e^{c\widetilde{B}_{T-t}+\frac{1}{2}c^2(T-t)}e^{-c\widetilde{B}_{T-t}-\frac{1}{2}c^2(T-t)})$$

$$= \mathbb{E}_{\mathbb{Q}}(G_t(\max_{0\leq s\leq T-t} cs + \widetilde{B}_s)e^{c[c(T-t)+\widetilde{B}_{T-t}]-\frac{1}{2}c^2(T-t)})$$

[where $\mathbb{Q}$ be the probability having the Radon Nikodym derivative $e^{-c\widetilde{B}_{T-t}-\frac{1}{2}c^2(T-t)}$]

$$= \mathbb{E}_{\mathbb{P}}(G_t(\max_{0\leq s\leq T-t} \widetilde{B}_s) \cdot e^{c\widetilde{B}_{T-t}-\frac{1}{2}c^2(T-t)})$$

[Girsanov's Theorem]

$$= e^{-\frac{1}{2}c^2(T-t)}\mathbb{E}_{\mathbb{P}}(G_t(\max_{0\leq s\leq T-t} \widetilde{B}_s)e^{c\widetilde{B}_{T-t}}).$$

Now we are in the situation, in which we need the joint distribution of $\max_{0\leq s\leq T-t} \widetilde{B}_s$ and $\widetilde{B}_{T-t}$ which is given by Theorem 6.3.2. Thus, we can continue

$$= e^{-\frac{1}{2}c^2(T-t)} \int_0^\infty \int_{-\infty}^m \frac{2(2m-b)}{(T-t)\sqrt{2\pi(T-t)}}e^{-\frac{(2m-b)^2}{2(T-t)}}G_t(m)e^{cb}\, db\, dm.$$

Finally, replacing G and c by their definitions, we end up with

$$W(f(\max_{0 \le u \le T} S_u, t))$$

$$= e^{-(r+\frac{1}{2}(\frac{2r-\nu^2}{2\nu})^2)(T-t)} \cdot \int_0^\infty \int_{-\infty}^m \frac{2(2m-b)}{(T-t)\sqrt{2\pi(T-t)}} e^{-\frac{(2m-b)^2}{2(T-t)}} e^{\frac{2r-\nu^2}{2\nu}b} f(M_t \vee S_t e^{\nu m}) db\, dm$$

□

6.4   Asian Style Options

We are now considering a path dependent option whose pay off at time T is of the form

$$(6.17) \qquad F(S_{(.)}) = G\left(S_T, \int_0^T g(S_u, u)du\right),$$

where G is a continuous function on $[0, \infty) \times \mathbb{R}$ and g a continuous function on $(0, \infty) \times [0, T]$.

Example. The *average strike call option*

$$F(S_{(.)}) = \left(S_T - \frac{1}{T}\int_0^T S_u du\right)^+.$$

In order to find the value of that option at a given time $t \in [0, T]$ we will proceed similar as in Section 3.1, where we derived the values of European style options. We will assume that the price S_t of the underlying asset follows the Black Scholes model with constant drift μ and constant volatility ν, i.e.

$$(6.18) \qquad dS_t = \mu S_t dt + \nu S_t dB_t, \text{ or } S_t = S_0 e^{(\mu - \frac{1}{2}\nu^2)t + \nu B_t},$$

where (B_t) is a Brownian motion on the filtered probability space $(\Omega, \mathcal{F}, \mathbb{P}, (\mathcal{F}_t))$. We start with the following "apriori assumption" which will be justified afterwards:

The value of the option having a pay off as in (6.17) depends only on t, S_t, and a third term namely

$$I_t = \int_0^t g(S_u, u)du.$$

We secondly assume that this dependence is twice differentiable in S_t and once differentiable in t as well as in I_t.

Thus, we can write the value of our option at time t as

$$V_t = f(t, S_t, I_t),$$

where $f : (0, T) \times (0, \infty) \times \mathbb{R} \to \mathbb{R}$ is differentiable in the first and third variable and twice differentiable in the second variable.

Note that $(I_t)_{t \in [0,T]}$ is an adapted stochastic process on $(\Omega, \mathcal{F}, \mathbb{P}, (\mathcal{F}_t))$ and can be written in differential form as

$$dI_t = g(t, S_t)dt.$$

In particular, we deduce that dI_t does not have an additional dB_t term and it follows that (in the notations introduced at the end of section 13) $(dI_t)^2 = 0$.

As in Section 3.1, we now assume that an investor can purchase any amount of bonds (with the coninuously compounded interest rate r) and shares of the underlying asset. His/her portfolio at time t is a pair (a_t, b_t), where a_t denotes the number of shares of the underlying asset and b_t denotes the number of bonds he/she owns at time t. $(a_t)_{0 \leq t \leq T}$ and $(b_t)_{0 \leq t \leq T}$ are processes on $(\Omega, \mathcal{F}, \mathbb{P})$ which are adapted to the filtration $(\mathcal{F}_t)_{0 \leq t \leq T}$.

Secondly, we assume (in order to be able to apply stochastic calculus) that $(a_t)_{0 \leq t \leq T}$ and $(b_t)_{0 \leq t \leq T}$ integrable with respect to dS_t and $d\beta_t$, respectively. $\beta_t = \beta_0 e^{rt}$ denotes the bond price.

We therefore deduce that

$$\int_s^t a_u \, dS_u, \quad \text{and} \int_s^t b_u \, d\beta_u$$

are the gains/losses between s and t caused by the holdings of the stock and bonds respectively.

Finally, assume that there is a self financing strategy (a_t, b_t) which replicates one unit of our option.

As in Section 3.1 we conclude that

$$(6.19) \qquad\qquad dV_t = a_t \, dS_t + b_t d\beta_t$$
$$= a_t \mu S_t \, dt + a_t \nu S_t \, dB_t + b_t r \beta_t \, dt$$
$$= a_t \nu S_t \, dB_t + [a_t \mu S_t + r b_t \beta_t] dt.$$

On the other hand we apply Ito's formula to $V_t = f(t, S_t, I_t)$ and obtain that

$$(6.20) \quad dV_t = \frac{\partial}{\partial t} f(t, S_t, I_t) dt + \frac{\partial}{\partial S} f(t, S_t, I_t) dS_t$$

$$+ \frac{\partial}{\partial I} f(t, S_t, I_t) dI_t + \frac{1}{2} \frac{\partial^2}{\partial S^2} f(t, S_t, I_t) d^2 S_t$$

$$[d^2 I_t = 0]$$

$$= \left[\frac{\partial}{\partial t} f(t, S_t, I_t) + g(t, S_t) \frac{\partial}{\partial I} f(t, S_t, I_t) + S_t \mu \frac{\partial}{\partial S} f(t, S_t, I_t) \right.$$

$$\left. + \frac{1}{2} S_t^2 \nu^2 \frac{\partial^2}{\partial S^2} f(t, S_t, I_t) \right] dt$$

$$+ S_t \nu \frac{\partial}{\partial S} f(t, S_t, I_t) dB_t$$

Comparing the "dB_t-term" of equation (3) and (4) we derive that

$$(6.21) \quad a_t = \frac{\partial}{\partial S} f(t, S_t, I_t).$$

Since the strategy (a_t, b_t) is replicating one unit of the considered derivative we obtain that

$$(6.22) \quad b_t = \frac{1}{\beta_t} \left[f(t, S_t, I_t) - a_t S_t \right]$$

$$= \frac{1}{\beta_t} \left[f(t, S_t, I_t) - S_t \frac{\partial}{\partial S} f(t, S_t, I_t) \right].$$

Inserting (6.21) and (6.22) into (6.19) and then comparing the "dt-term" of (6.19) with the "dt-term" of (6.20) we obtain the equation

$$(6.23)$$
$$\frac{\partial}{\partial t} f(t, S_t, I_t) + g(t, S_t) \frac{\partial}{\partial I} f(t, S_t, I_t) + \frac{1}{2} S_t^2 \nu^2 \frac{\partial^2}{\partial S^2} f(t, S_t, I_t) + r S_t \frac{\partial}{\partial S} f(t, S_t, I_t) - r f(t, S_t, I_t) = 0$$

Thus, we reduced the pricing of an Asian style option to solving the following partial differential equation.

This leads us to the following theorem :

Theorem 6.4.1 .   *Within the Black Scholes model the price at time $t \in [0, T]$ of an option paying at time T the amount of*

$$F(S_{(.)}) = G\left(S_T, \int_0^T g(S_u, u)du\right)$$

is given by

$$V_t = f(t, S_t, I_t),$$

where $I_t = \int_0^t g(S_u, u)du$ and where f is the solution of

(6.24)
$$\frac{\partial}{\partial t}f(t, S, I) + g(t, S)\frac{\partial}{\partial I}f(t, S, I) + \frac{1}{2}S^2\nu^2\frac{\partial^2}{\partial S^2}f(t, S, I) + rS\frac{\partial}{\partial S}f(t, S, I) - rf(t, S, I) = 0$$

with the terminal condition

$$f(T, S, I) = G(S, I).$$

In that case a hedging portfolio (a_t, b_t) is given by

(6.25) $$a_t = \frac{\partial}{\partial S}f(t, S_t, I_t), \text{ and}$$

(6.26) $$b_t = \frac{1}{\beta_t}\left[f(t, S_t, I_t) - S_t\frac{\partial}{\partial S}f(t, S_t, I_t)\right]$$

Remark. Note that the Equation (6.24) is a generalization of the Equation (BSE) we derived in Section 3.2 for European style options (take $g = 0$). Unfortunately, (6.24) is in general not solvable in closed form. In order to solve it, numerical methods have to be used to achieve approximate solutions.

Appendix A

Some Basic Notions and Results of Linear Analysis

A.1   Basics of Linear Algebra and Topology in $\mathbb{R}^n$

For $n = 1, 2, 3, \ldots$ we put $\mathbb{R}^n := \{(x_1, \ldots, x_n) \colon x_1, x_2, \ldots, x_n \in \mathbb{R}\}$, the canonical n-dimensional vector space over $\mathbb{R}$. For $x, y \in \mathbb{R}^n$, $x = (x_1, \ldots, x_n)$ and $y = (y_1, \ldots, y_n)$, the *scalar product of x and y* is defined by

$$x \cdot y = x_1 y_1 + x_2 y_2 + \cdots + x_n y_n = \sum_{i=1}^{n} x_i y_i.$$

The *euklidean length of x* is

$$\|x\| = \sqrt{x \cdot x} = \left(\sum_{i=1}^{n} x_i^2 \right)^{1/2}.$$

The following properties of the scalar products and lengths of vectors in $\mathbb{R}^n$ can be easily obtained from the definitions.

Proposition A.1.1 .   *Let $x, y, z \in \mathbb{R}^n$ and $a \in \mathbb{R}$.*

1) $x \cdot y = y \cdot x,$

2) $x \cdot (ay) = (ax) \cdot y = a(x \cdot y),$

3) $x \cdot (y + z) = x \cdot y + x \cdot z,$

4) $||x \pm y||^2 = ||x||^2 + ||y||^2 \pm 2x \cdot y$

5) $||x + y||^2 + ||x - y||^2 = 2||x||^2 + 2||y||^2$ *(Parallelogramm identity)*

6) $||x + y|| \leq ||x|| + ||y||$ *(Triangle inequality)*

7) $|x \cdot y| \leq ||x|| \cdot ||y||$ *(Inequality of Cauchy and Schwartz)*

For $x \in \mathbb{R}^n$ and $A \subset \mathbb{R}^n$, $\mathrm{dist}(x, A) = \inf_{y \in A} ||y - x||$ is the *distance between x and A*. For $x \in \mathbb{R}^n$ and $\varepsilon > 0$ the set $\mathcal{U}_\varepsilon(x) = \{y \in \mathbb{R}^n \mid ||x - y|| < \varepsilon\}$ is called the *ε-neighborhood of x*. A set $A \subset \mathbb{R}^n$ is called *open* if for each $x \in A$ there is an $\varepsilon > 0$ (depends on x) so that $\mathcal{U}_\varepsilon(x) \subset A$. A complement of an open set is called *closed*. Note that if $B \subset \mathbb{R}^n$ is closed and $x \notin B$, then $\mathrm{dist}(x, B) > 0$. Indeed, since x lies in the open set $\mathbb{R}^n \setminus B$ there is an $\varepsilon > 0$ so that $\mathcal{U}_\varepsilon(x) \subset \mathbb{R}^n \setminus B$. Thus $\mathcal{U}_\varepsilon(x) \cap B = \emptyset$ which means that for all $y \in B$ $||x - y|| \geq \varepsilon > 0$.

A sequence $(x^{(k)}) \subset \mathbb{R}^n$ is called *convergent to $x \in \mathbb{R}^n$* if $||x^{(k)} - x|| \to 0$, for $n \to \infty$. If $x^{(k)}$ lies in a closed set B and converges to an $x \in \mathbb{R}^n$ then also $x \in \mathbb{R}^n$. Indeed, if we had $x \notin B$ there would be an $\varepsilon > 0$ so that $\mathcal{U}_\varepsilon(x) \cap B = \emptyset$, but then it would follow that $\mathrm{dist}(x, \{x^{(k)} | k \in \mathbb{N}\}) \geq \mathrm{dist}(x, B) \geq \varepsilon$ which contradicts the convergence of the sequence to x. From the defintion of $|| \cdot ||$ it follows that a sequence $(x^{(k)}) \subset \mathbb{R}^n$ converges to some $x \in \mathbb{R}^n$ if and only if the coordinates of $x^{(k)}$ converge to the corresponding coordinates of x, i.e. if $x_j^{(k)} \to x_j$, $n \to \infty$, for all $j = 1, 2, \ldots, n$. Therefore we can conclude that every bounded sequence $(x^{(k)}) \subset \mathbb{R}^n$ (meaning $\sup_{\in \mathbb{N}} ||x^{(k)}|| < \infty$) has a convergent subsequence.

From these observations we can easily deduce the following Proposition which will be of use in the next section.

Proposition A.1.2 . *If $B \subset \mathbb{R}^n$ is closed and $a \in \mathbb{R}^n \setminus B$, then there exists a $b \in B$ with minimal distance to a, i.e.*

$$||a - b|| = \text{dist}(a, B) > 0.$$

Let $L \subset \mathbb{R}^n$ be a subspace of $\mathbb{R}^n$, i.e. a subset for which $\alpha x + \beta y \in L$, whenever $x, y \in L$ and $a, b \in \mathbb{R}$. The *orthogonal complement of L in $\mathbb{R}^n$* is the set

$$L^\perp = \{y \in \mathbb{R}^n | \forall x \in L : x \cdot y = 0\}.$$

It is easy to observe that $L^\perp$ is also a subspace of $\mathbb{R}^n$. If L is generated by the vectors $a^{(1)}, a^{(2)}, \dots a^{(r)}$, i.e. if

$$L = \{\sum_{i=1}^r \alpha_i a^{(i)} | \alpha_1, \alpha_2, \dots \alpha_r \in \mathbb{R}\}$$

we deduce that

$$L^\perp = \{y \in \mathbb{R}^n | \forall i = 1, \dots r : a^{(i)} \cdot y = 0\}.$$

Now let $c^{(1)}, c^{(2)}, \dots, c^{(d)}$ be a basis of L (every element of L can be written in a unique way as linear combination of $c^{(1)}, c^{(2)}, \dots, c^{(d)}$). Using the Gram-Schmidt method we turn $c^{(1)}, c^{(2)}, \dots, c^{(d)}$ into an orthonormal basis $a^{(1)}, a^{(2)}, \dots, a^{(d)}$ ($||a^{(i)}|| = 1$ and $a^{(i)} \cdot a^{(j)} = 0$ if $i \neq j$): Choose

$a^{(1)} = c^{(1)}/||c^{(1)}||$, and

$\tilde{a}^{(2)} = c^{(2)} - a^{(1)}(c^{(2)} \cdot a^{(1)})$ (Note that $\tilde{a}^{(2)} \cdot a^{(1)} = 0$) and then define $a^{(2)} = \tilde{a}^{(2)}/||\tilde{a}^{(2)}||$

More generally: If $a^{(1)}, a^{(2)}, \dots, a^{(i)}$ have been defined, then

$$\tilde{a}^{(i+1)} = c^{(i+1)} - \sum_{j=1}^i a^{(i)}(c^{(i+1)} \cdot a^{(i)}) \text{ and then define} a^{(i+1)} = \tilde{a}^{(i+1)}/||\tilde{a}^{(i+1)}||.$$

We can extend $a^{(1)}, a^{(2)}, \dots, a^{(d)}$ to a basis $a^{(1)}, a^{(2)}, \dots, a^{(n)}$ of $\mathbb{R}^n$ which, using the procedure of Gram and Schmidt again, can be assumed to be orthonormal. We observe that $a^{(d+1)}, a^{(2)}, \dots, a^{(r)}$ must be a basis of $L^\perp$. Indeed, since $a^{(d+1)}, a^{(d+2)}, \dots, a^{(n)}$ are orthogonal to a basis of L these vector lie in $L^\perp$. Secondly every vector y in $L^\perp$ is $(a^{(1)}, a^{(2)}, \ldots, a^{(n)}$ is a basis of $\mathbb{R}^n$) of the form

$$y = \sum_{i=1}^{n} \alpha_i a^{(i)},$$

it follows for $i = 1, \ldots d$ that $\alpha_i = y \cdot a^{(i)} = 0$ since $y \in L^\perp$. Thus y is actually a linear combination of $a^{(d+1)}, \ldots a^{(n)}$ and we deduce that $a^{(d+1)}, \ldots a^{(n)}$ is a basis for $L^\perp$. From these observations we deduce the following Proposition.

Proposition A.1.3 .   *If L is a subspace of $\mathbb{R}^n$. Then for each $x \in \mathbb{R}^n$ there are unique elements $x_1 \in L$ and $x_2 \in L^\perp$ so that $x = x_1 + x_2$.*

Secondly, the orthogonal complement of $L^\perp$ is L,i.e. $(L^\perp)^\perp = L$.

Proof. Let $a^{(1)}, a^{(2)}, \ldots, a^{(n)}$ be an orthogonal basis of $\mathbb{R}^n$ so that $a^{(1)}, a^{(2)}, \ldots, a^{(d)}$ is a basis of L and $a^{(d+1)}, a^{(d+2)}, \ldots, a^{(n)}$ is a basis of $L^\perp$. Such a basis exists as shown above. Thus, every $x \in \mathbb{R}^n$ can be represented in exactly one way as

$$(1) \qquad\qquad x = \sum_{i=1}^{n} \alpha_i a^{(i)}, \text{ with } \alpha_1, \ldots \alpha_n \in \mathbb{R}.$$

Thus $x_1 = \sum_{i=1}^{d} \alpha_i a^{(i)} \in L$, $x_2 = \sum_{i=d+1}^{n} \alpha_i a^{(i)} \in L^\perp$, and $x = x_1 + x_2$. This representation is unique since the representation of x in (1) is unique. Secondly, since $a^{(d+1)}, a^{(2)}, \ldots, a^{(n)}$ is a basis of $L^\perp$ it follows as observed above that $a^{(1)}, a^{(2)}, \ldots, a^{(d)}$ must be a basis of $(L^\perp)^\perp$, and thus it follows that $(L^\perp)^\perp = L$.   □

Now let $a^{(1)}, a^{(2)}, \ldots, a^{(r)} \in \mathbb{R}^n$ be any finite sequence which generates the subspace L. We define A to be the n by r matrix whose columns consist of $a^{(1)}, a^{(2)}, \ldots, a^{(r)}$. Then L is the *range* of A, denoted by $\mathcal{R}(A)$ i.e.

$$L = \{\sum_{i=1}^{r} x_i a^{(i)} : x_1, x_2, \ldots x_r \in \mathbb{R}\} = \{A \circ x | x \in \mathbb{R}^r\}.$$

The transpose A^t of A is the r by n matrix whose i-th row is the i-th column of A. We deduce that $L^\perp$ is the null space of A^t, denoted by $\mathcal{N}(A^t)$, i.e.

$$L^\perp = \{x \in \mathbb{R}^n : \forall i = 1, \ldots r : a^{(i)} \cdot x = 0\} = \{x | A^t \circ x = 0\} = \mathcal{N}(A^t).$$

From this observation and Proposition A.1.3 one can deduce the following principle, sometimes called the Fundamental Theorem of Linear Algebra.

Theorem A.1.4 . *Let A be an n by m matrix. Then $\mathcal{N}(A^t)$ is the orthogonal complement of $\mathcal{R}(A)$.*

A.2   The Theorem of Farkas and Consequences

In this section we want to present the results necessary to prove the existence of state price vectors in an arbitrage free Arrow-Debreu model (compare Section 1.1). These results are part of the theory of linear prgramming. We will not try to attempt to present an introduction to this area, neither will we present its important impact and use in Economics. The reader can be referred to a wide ranging literature (cf. [Gale],......). In order to order to keep this exposition as self-contained as possible we merely want to present one important result, the Theorem of Farkas, and derive some consequences which are important to us.

   The following Theorem is Tucker's version of Farkas' Theorem (for Farkas' original Theorem see Exercise....).

Theorem A.2.1 *(Tucker's version of Farkas' Theorem).*
Let A be an n by m matrix and $b \in \mathbb{R}^m$. Then one and only one of the following two statements is true.

   1) There exists an $x \in \mathbb{R}^n_+$ so that $A^t \circ x = b$.

   2) There exists a $y \in \mathbb{R}^m$ so that $A \circ y \in \mathbb{R}^n_+$ and $b \cdot y < 0$.

Proof. First we show that the statements are exclusive. Indeed if $x \in \mathbb{R}^n_+$ satsified (1) and $y \in \mathbb{R}^m$ satisfied (2) we would conclude on the one hand that $y \cdot (A^t \circ x) = (A \circ y) \cdot x \geq 0$ since x and $A \circ y$ have both non negative coordinates. On the other hand we would observe that $y \cdot (A^t \circ x) = y \cdot b < 0$ and derive a contradiction.

   Secondly we assume that (1) does not apply and have to show (2). We let $C = \{A^t \circ z : z \in \mathbb{R}^n_+\}$. Note that C is a cone in $\mathbb{R}^m$ which means that C is closed under addition and multiplication by non negative scalars. We can think of C being the set of all non negative combinations of the rows of A which we denote by $A_{(1,\cdot)}, A_{(2,\cdot)}, \ldots, A_{(n,\cdot)}$. Since (1) does not apply we deduce that $b \notin C$ and since C is a closed set it follows that $\mathrm{dist}(b, C) > 0$ and we can choose by Proposition A.1.2 a $y^{(0)} \in C$ having minimal distance to b. We now want to show that $y = y^{(0)} - b$ satisfies the conditions in (2).

First we claim that for all $z \in C$ it follows that $z \cdot y \geq 0$. Indeed, for $\varepsilon > 0$ it follows that $y^{(0)} + \varepsilon z \in C$ and thus that

$$||y^{(0)} - b||^2 \leq ||y^{(0)} + \varepsilon z - b||^2 \quad (\text{since} ||y^{(0)} - b|| = \text{dist}(b, C)).$$

By cancellation it follows that

$$0 \leq 2\varepsilon(y^{(0)} - b)z + \varepsilon^2 ||z||^2.$$

If it where true that $(y^{(0)} - b) \cdot z < 0$ we could choose $\varepsilon > 0$ small enough that this inequality reverses which would lead to a contradiction.

Since the rows of A lie in C we first deduce that $A_{(i,\cdot)} \cdot y \geq 0$ which implies that the coordinates of $A \circ y$ are non negative.

In order to verify the second condition of (2) we observe that in the proof of above claim we actually only used that $y^{(0)} + \varepsilon z \in C$. Since for $0 < \varepsilon < 1$, it follows that $y^{(0)} + \varepsilon y^{(0)}$ and $y^{(0)} - \varepsilon y^{(0)}$ lie in C we deduce from the proof of the claim that $y^{(0)} \cdot y = 0$ and, thus, we deduce that that $y \cdot b = y \cdot (b - y^{(0)}) = -||y||^2 = -\text{dist}^2(b, C) < 0$ which is the second condition in (2). □

From Farkas' Theorem we now can dedudce the following Corallaries.

Corollary A.2.2 . *Let A be an n by m matrix. Then one and only one of the following statements is true.*

1) *There an $x \in \mathbb{R}^n_+ \setminus \{0\}$ such that $A^t \circ x = 0$.*

2) *There is a $y \in \mathbb{R}^m$ such that $A \circ y \in \mathbb{R}^n_{++}$.*

Proof. The two statements are exclusive. Indeed, if x satisfied (1) and y satisfied (2) then on the one hand we would deduce by (1) that $y \cdot (A^t \circ y) = 0$. But on the other hand we would deduce from (2) that $y \cdot (A^t \circ x) = (A \circ y) \cdot x > 0$, since the coordinates of $(A \circ y)$ are strictly positive and since the coordinates of x are non negative and at least one of them is not equal to zero.

Secondly, we define

$$\widetilde{A} = \begin{bmatrix} 1 & A_{(1,1)} & A_{(1,2)} & \cdots & A_{(1,m)} \\ 1 & A_{(2,1)} & A_{(2,2)} & \cdots & A_{(2,m)} \\ \vdots & \vdots & & & \vdots \\ 1 & A_{(n,1)} & A_{(n,2)} & \cdots & A_{(n,m)} \end{bmatrix} = \begin{bmatrix} 1 \\ \vdots & & A \\ 1 \end{bmatrix}$$

and thus

$$\widetilde{A^t} = \begin{bmatrix} 1 & 1 & \cdots & 1 \\ A_{(1,1)} & A_{(2,1)} & \cdots & A_{(n,m)} \\ \vdots & \vdots & & \vdots \\ A_{(1,m)} & A_{(2,m)} & \vdots & A_{(n,m)} \end{bmatrix} = \begin{bmatrix} 1 & 1 & \cdots & 1 \\ & & A^t & \end{bmatrix}.$$

Put also

$$\widetilde{b} = \begin{bmatrix} 1 \\ 0 \\ \vdots \\ 0 \end{bmatrix}.$$

If now (1) of A.2.2 does not hold there cannot be an $x \in \mathbb{R}^n_+$ so that $\widetilde{A^t} \circ x = \widetilde{b}$. From A.2.1 it follows therefore that there is a $\widetilde{y} \in \mathbb{R}^{m+1}$ so that $\widetilde{b} \cdot \widetilde{y} = \widetilde{y}_1 < 0$ and $\widetilde{A} \circ \widetilde{y} \in \mathbb{R}^n_+$, thus

$$\widetilde{A} \circ \widetilde{y} = \widetilde{y}_1 \begin{bmatrix} 1 \\ 1 \\ \vdots \\ 1 \end{bmatrix} + A \circ \begin{bmatrix} \widetilde{y}_2 \\ \widetilde{y}_3 \\ \vdots \\ \widetilde{y}_{m+1} \end{bmatrix} \in \mathbb{R}^n_+.$$

Putting now $y = (\widetilde{y}_2, \widetilde{y}_3, \ldots, \widetilde{y}_{m+1})$, it follows that for each $i = 1, \ldots n$,

$$A_{(i,\cdot)} \cdot y = \widetilde{A} \circ \widetilde{y} - \widetilde{y}_1 \geq -\widetilde{y}_1 > 0,$$

which implies (2) of A.2.2, and finishes the proof. $\square$

If $L \subset \mathbb{R}^n$ is a subspace which is generated by the vectors $a^{(1)}, a^{(2)}, \ldots a^{(m)}$, and if A is the n by m matrix whose columns are these vectors, we observed in A.1 that L is the range of A and $L^\perp$ is the null space of A^t. Thus Corollary A.2.2 can be translated into the following result.

Corollary A.2.3 . *If $L \subset \mathbb{R}^n$ is a subspace of $\mathbb{R}^n$, and if $L^\perp$ is its orthogonal complement one and only one of the following statements can be true.*

1) $L^\perp \cap \mathbb{R}^n_+$ contains a non zero element.

2) L contains a vector with strictly positive coordinates.

The roles of L and $L^\perp$ in Corollary A.2.3 can be interchanged. If A is an n by m matrix we choose $L = \mathcal{N}(A^t)$ and $L^\perp = \mathcal{R}(A)$ and Corollary A.2.3 can be translated into a statement about A again.

Corollary A.2.4 . *Let A be an n by m matrix. Then one and only one of the following statements is true.*

1) There is an $x \in \mathbb{R}^n_{++}$ for which $A^t \circ x = 0$.

2) There is a $y \in \mathbb{R}^m$ for which $A \circ y \in \mathbb{R}^n_+ \setminus \{0\}$.

Appendix B

Basic Notions of Probability Theory, Conditional Expectations

In this part we want to recall the basic notions of probability theory. In particular we will introduce the concept of *conditional expectations*. This notion gives the theoretical frame for stating and solving questions of the following form:

– Assuming the Dow Jones index was 7'900 on April 17, what is it expected value on April 18?

– Assuming the Federal Bank increases the prime rate by .5%, what is the expected change of the IBM stock?

We will proceed as follows: First we discuss the theory using a single easy example (Section B.1) and discuss the log–binomial model of the Sections 1.3 and 1.4 in more detail. Using this model we will introduce the concepts of measurability, expected values and conditional expected values. We then deal with the more general case (sections B.2 and B.3). These two sections should by no means be seen as an exposition or even an introduction to the theory of probability. It merely mentions the most basic notations and recalls some theorems important to us.

For the reader who is for the moment only interested in the discrete theory as developped in Chapter 1 Section B.1 alone provides a sufficient back ground in probability theory for the understanding of discrete probability space as needed in Chapter 1.

B.1 An example: The Binomial and Log–Binomial Process

As in Section 1.3 we consider a stock whose price changes after each trading time either by the factor U or D, with $0 < D < U$. We consider n such moves and assume that the i-th movement of the price is *independent* from the previous one, a concept we will have to define precisely later. We can simulate this stock price by tossing a coin n times. Each time we obtain heads the stock price will be multiplied by U, if tails appears it will be multiplied by D.

The set of all possible outcomes is

$$\Omega = \{H, T\}^n = \big\{\omega = (\omega_1, \omega_2, \ldots \omega_n)|\ \omega_i \in \{H, T\} \text{ for } i = 1, 2, \ldots n\big\}.$$

We denote the probability that head appears by p (not necessarily equal to $\frac{1}{2}$) and the probability that tails comes up is denoted by $q = 1 - p$. Now, if $\omega = (\omega_1, \ldots, \omega_n) \in \Omega$, the probability that ω happens is given by

(1) $$\mathbb{P}(\{\omega\}) = p^{\#\ \text{Heads in } \omega} \cdot q^{\#\ \text{Tails in } \omega}.$$

For example

$$\mathbb{P}(\{\underbrace{H, H, \ldots H}_{k\text{-times}}, \underbrace{T, T, \ldots, T}_{n-k\text{-times}}\}) = p^k q^{n-k}.$$

For any *event*, i.e. any set $A \subset \Omega$, we let

$$\mathbb{P}(A) = \sum_{\omega \in A} \mathbb{P}(\{\omega\}).$$

Thus $\mathbb{P}$ is a map on all events having the following properties (Kolmogorov's axioms)

1) For any event A: $0 \le \mathbb{P}(A) \le 1$,

2) $\mathbb{P}(\emptyset) = 0$, and $\mathbb{P}(\Omega) = 1$,

3) if $A_1, A_2, A_3, \ldots$ are mutually disjoint (meaning $A_i \cap A_j = \emptyset$ if $i \ne j$) then

$$\mathbb{P}\left(\bigcup_{k=1}^{\infty} A_k\right) = \sum_{k=1}^{\infty} \mathbb{P}(A_k).$$

Remark. In (1) we tacitely assumed the outcomes of tossing the coin to be *indepen-dent*. This means the following. For $i = 1, \ldots n$ let $E_i(\omega_i)$ be the event that in the i-th tossing of the coin ω_i appears. For example if $n = 3$, $i = 2$, and $\omega_i = H$, then $E_2(H) = \{HHH, THH, HHT, THT\}$.

We have $\{\omega\} = \bigcap_{i=1}^{n} E_i(\omega_i)$ and $\mathbb{P}(E_i(\omega_i))$ is either p (if $\omega_i = H$) or q (if $\omega_i = T$). Independence of the tosses means now that the probability of the intersections of the $E_i(\omega_i)$)'s equals to the product of their probability, i.e.

$$(2) \qquad \mathbb{P}(\{\omega\}) = \mathbb{P}(\bigcap_{i=1}^{n} E_i(\omega_i)) = \prod_{i=1}^{n} \mathbb{P}(E_i(\omega_i)).$$

More generally if $1 \le i_1 < i_2 < \ldots < i_r \le n$, then

$$(3) \qquad \mathbb{P}(\bigcap_{j=1}^{r} E_{i_j}(\omega_{i_j})) = \prod_{j=1}^{r} \mathbb{P}(E_{i_j}(\omega_{i_j})).$$

We now define the prices of the stock at the times $0, 1 \ldots, n$ as *random variables* on Ω. In our case a random variable is simply a map $X : \Omega \to \mathbb{R}$. We let for $i = 0, 1, 2 \ldots n$ and $\omega \in \Omega$

$$(4) \qquad \varepsilon_i = \varepsilon_i(\omega) = \begin{cases} 1 & \text{if } \omega_i = H \\ 0 & \text{if } \omega_i = T \end{cases}$$

and

$$(5) \qquad H_i = H_i(\omega) = \sum_{j=1}^{i} \varepsilon_j \quad \text{(number of heads up to time } i\text{)}$$

$$T_i = T_i(\omega) = \sum_{j=1}^{i} 1 - \varepsilon_j = i - H_i \quad \text{(number of tails up to time } i\text{)}$$

$(H_0 = T_0 = 0)$

Note that with this notations we can write

$$(6) \qquad \mathbb{P}(\{\omega\}) = p^{H_n(\omega)} q^{T_n(\omega)}, \text{ for } \omega \in \Omega$$

And finally we define the stock price at time $i = 0, 1, \ldots n$ to be

$$S_i = S_0 U^{H_i} D^{T_i}. \tag{7}$$

Thus, S_i satisfies the following recursive formula for $i = 1, \ldots, n$

$$S_i = S_{i-1} U^{\varepsilon_i} D^{1-\varepsilon_i}. \tag{8}$$

The *expected value* of a random varibale $X : \Omega \to \mathbb{R}$ is defined to be

$$\mathbb{E}_{\mathbb{P}}(X) = \sum_{\omega \in \Omega} X(\omega)\mathbb{P}(\{\omega\}) = \sum_{\omega \in \Omega} X(\omega)p^{H_n(\omega)}q^{T_n(\omega)}. \tag{9}$$

Proposition B.1.1 .   *Taking expected values is a linear operation, i.e. X and Y are random variables on Ω and $\alpha, \beta \in \mathbb{R}$, then*

$$\mathbb{E}_{\mathbb{P}}(\alpha X + \beta Y) = \alpha \mathbb{E}_{\mathbb{P}}(X) + \beta \mathbb{E}_{\mathbb{P}}(Y) \tag{10}$$

If $A \subset \Omega$ is an event we denote by $1_A : \Omega \to \mathbb{R}$ the *indicator function of A*, the function assigning to each $\omega \in \Omega$ the value 1 if $\omega \in A$, and assigning to each $\omega \in \Omega \setminus A$ the value 0.Thus we have $\mathbb{E}_{\mathbb{P}}(1_A) = \mathbb{P}(A)$.

If X is a random variable on Ω with the values $x_1, x_2, \ldots x_r$, and if we let $A_i = X^{-1}(\{x_i\}) = \{\omega \in \Omega | X(\omega) = x_i\}$, we can write X as $X = \sum_{i=1}^{r} x_i 1_{A_i}$ and

$$\mathbb{E}_{\mathbb{P}}(X) = \sum_{i=1}^{r} \mathbb{P}(A_i)x_i. \tag{11}$$

For $i = 0, 1, \ldots n$ S_i can achieve the values $S_0 U^j D^{n-i}$ with $j = 0, 1, \ldots, i$ (stock moved by the factor U j times and moved by the factor D $i - j$ times) and we compute for the expected value of S_i

$$(12) \quad \mathbb{E}_{\mathbb{P}}(S_i) = S_0 \sum_{j=0}^{i} \mathbb{P}(S_i = S_0 U^j D^{i-j}) U^j D^{i-j}$$

$$= S_0 \sum_{j=0}^{i} \mathbb{P}(H_i = j) U^j D^{i-j} = S_0 \sum_{j=0}^{i} \binom{i}{j} U^j D^{i-j} p^j q^{i-j} \quad = S_0 (pU + qD)^i,$$

with $\binom{i}{j} = \dfrac{i!}{j!(i-j)!}$ $(0! = 1)$. The last equality in (12) uses the binomial formula while second to the last equality uses the following combinatorical principle:

Proposition B.1.2 .   *There are $\binom{i}{j}$ words one can form out of j H's and $i - j$ T's.*

Definition. A finite sequence of random variables $X_0, X_1, \ldots X_n$ on Ω is called a *Binomial process* of length n, with starting point X_0, step sizes u and d, and success probability p if X_0 is constant and

$$X_i = X_0 + \sum_{j=1}^{i} \varepsilon_j u + \sum_{j=1}^{i} (1 - \varepsilon_j) d = X_0 + H_i u + T_i d,$$

where ε_j, H_j and T_j were defined in (4) and (5).

In this case we call $Y_i = e^{X_i}$, $i = 0, 1 \ldots n$ the corresponding log–binomial process.

Remark.   Note that $S_0, S_1, \ldots, S_n$ is a log–binomial process, and $(\log S_i)$ is a binomial process with starting point $\log S_0$, step sizes $u = \log U$, and $d = \log D$, and success probability p.

We consider now a random variable $X : \Omega \to \mathbb{R}$ (for example $X = S_n$) and assume the time is i, $i \in \{1, 2, \ldots n\}$. At this time we know already the outcomes of the first i tosses, say they are $\nu_1, \nu_2, \ldots, \nu_i \in \{HT\}$. If the value $X(\omega)$ only depends on the first i outcomes (for example if $X = S_i$) then X *is realized*, meaning by the time i the value of X is determined. Otherwise, we can ask ourselves, what is the expected value of X, given that the first i outcomes were $\nu_1, \nu_2, \ldots, \nu_i$?

In our simple case the question can be answered easily, no theory is needed. Indeed we only have to change our random variable and the underlying probability space. Our new set of possible outcomes is

$$\widetilde{\Omega}^{(i)} = \{(\omega_1, \omega_2, \ldots, \omega_{n-i}) | \omega_j \in \{H, T\} \text{ for } j = 1, \ldots n - i\}.$$

Our new probability is given by

$$\widetilde{\mathbb{P}}^{(i)}(\{\tilde{\omega}\}) = p^{\# \text{ Heads in } \tilde{\omega}} \cdot q^{\# \text{ Tails in } \tilde{\omega}}, \text{ for } \tilde{\omega} \in \widetilde{\Omega}^{(i)},$$

and the new random variable we have to consider is

$$X_{(\nu_1, \ldots \nu_i)} : \widetilde{\Omega}^{(i)} \to \mathbb{R}, \qquad (\tilde{\omega}_1, \ldots, \tilde{\omega}_{n-i}) \mapsto X(\nu_1, \ldots, \nu_i, \tilde{\omega}_1, \ldots \tilde{\omega}_{n-i}).$$

The *conditional expectation of* X, given that the first i outcomes were $\nu_1, \ldots, \nu_i$, should then be defined to be

(13)
$$\mathbb{E}_{\widetilde{\mathbb{P}}^{(i)}}(X_{(\nu_1, \ldots \nu_i)}).$$

We denote this value for the moment by $\mathbb{E}_{\mathbb{P}}(X | \nu_1, \ldots \nu_i)$ and note that it can be seen as a map on all i-tuples $\nu \in \{H, T\}^i$.

For $\tilde{\omega} \in \widetilde{\Omega}^{(i)}$, we let $\widetilde{H}(\tilde{\omega})$ and $\widetilde{T}(\tilde{\omega})$ be the number of heads respectively tails in $\tilde{\omega}$. Then we deduce as in (9)

(14)
$$\mathbb{E}_{\mathbb{P}}(X | \nu_1, \ldots \nu_i) = \sum_{\tilde{\omega} \in \Omega} X(\nu_1, \ldots \nu_i, \tilde{\omega}_1, \ldots, \tilde{\omega}_{n-i}) \widetilde{\mathbb{P}}^{(i)}(\{\tilde{\omega}\})$$

$$= \sum_{\tilde{\omega} \in \Omega} X(\nu_1, \ldots \nu_i, \tilde{\omega}_1, \ldots, \tilde{\omega}_{n-i}) p^{\widetilde{H}(\tilde{\omega})} q^{\widetilde{T}(\tilde{\omega})}$$

For $X = S_n$ the computation of the conditional expectation is easy because we can write

$$S_n = S_0 U^{H_n} D^{T_n} = \underbrace{S_0 U^{H_i} D^{T_i}}_{\text{depends on } \omega_1 \ldots \omega_i} \cdot \underbrace{U^{H_n - H_i} D^{T_n - T_i}}_{\text{depends on } \omega_{i+1} \ldots \omega_n} = S_i U^{H_n - H_i} D^{T_n - T_i},$$

Therefore the same computations as in (12) lead to

$$E_{\mathbb{P}}(S_n|\nu_1,\ldots\nu_i) = S_i \sum_{j=0}^{n-i} \binom{n-i}{j} U^j D^{n-i-j} p^j q^{n-i-j}$$

(replace S_0 by S_i and n by $n-i$).

We want to pass to a more theoretical point of view. For $i = 0, 1, \ldots, n$ we let $\mathcal{F}_i$ be "all the events for which we know whether or not they will be realized by the time i". This has to made more precise as follows.

For $\nu_1, \ldots \nu_i \in \{H, T\}$ we let

$$A(\nu_1,\ldots\nu_i) = \{(\nu_1,\ldots\nu_i)\} \times \widetilde{\Omega}^{(i)} = \{\tilde{\omega} \in \Omega | \tilde{\omega}_1 = \nu_1, \ldots, \tilde{\omega}_i = \nu_i\} = \bigcap_{j=1}^{i} E_j(\nu_j),$$

i.e. $A(\nu)$ is the set of all possible extensions of $\nu \in \{H,T\}^i$ to an element in Ω. It follows that $\mathbb{P}(A(\nu)) = p^{H_i(\nu)} q^{T_i(\nu)}$. Note that by time i we know whether or not $A(\nu)$ occured.

Formally H_i is a map on $\{H,T\}^n$ but since $H_i(\omega)$ only depends on the first i entries the notation $H_i(\nu)$ for $\nu \in \{H,T\}^i$ is well defined. Since secondly it follows for $\omega = (\omega_1, \ldots \omega_n)$ that $H_n(\omega) = H_i(\omega_1, \ldots \omega_i) + \widetilde{H}_{n-i}(\omega_{i+1}, \ldots \omega_n)$ we note that from (14) it follows that for $\nu \in \{H,T\}^i$

$$
\begin{aligned}
(15) \qquad \mathbb{E}_{\mathbb{P}}(X|\nu_1,\ldots\nu_i) &= \sum_{\tilde{\omega}\in\Omega} X(\nu_1,\ldots\nu_i,\tilde{\omega}_1,\ldots,\tilde{\omega}_{n-i}) p^{\widetilde{H}(\tilde{\omega})} q^{\widetilde{T}(\tilde{\omega})} \\
&= p^{-H_i(\nu)} q^{-T_i(\nu)} \sum_{\tilde{\omega}\in\Omega} X(\nu_1,\ldots\nu_i,\tilde{\omega}_1,\ldots,\tilde{\omega}_{n-i}) p^{H(\nu,\tilde{\omega})} q^{T(\nu,\tilde{\omega})} \\
&= p^{-H_i(\nu)} q^{-T_i(\nu)} \sum_{\omega\in A(\nu)} X(\omega)\mathbb{P}(\{\omega\}) \\
&= \frac{\mathbb{E}_{\mathbb{P}}(1_{A(\nu)} X)}{\mathbb{P}(A(\nu))},
\end{aligned}
$$

We put $\mathcal{F}_i$ to be the set of all events consisting of $\emptyset$, Ω, and all possible unions of sets of the form $A(\nu_1, \ldots \nu_i)$. Note that $(A(\nu))_{\nu\in\{H,T\}^i}$ is a *partition* of Ω, meaning that these sets are pairwise disjoint and their union is all of Ω. Therefore there exists for each $A \in \mathcal{F}_i$ a unique set $I \subset \{H,T\}^i$ so that

$$A = \bigcup_{\nu \in I} A(\nu), \qquad (\bigcup_{\nu \in \emptyset} A(\nu) = \emptyset)$$

and each set which has such a representation is in $\mathcal{F}_i$. For example $\mathcal{F}_0 = \{\emptyset, \Omega\}$ (already before tossing the coin we know that Ω will happen and $\emptyset$ will not happen), and $\mathcal{F}_1 = \{\emptyset, \Omega, A(H), A(T)\}$.

For $i = 0, 1 \ldots, n$ the sets of events $\mathcal{F}_i$ are σ-algebras, meaning that:

Definition. A σ-algebra on Ω is a set $\mathcal{F}$, consisting of subsets of Ω, having the following three properties:

1) $\emptyset$ and Ω are in $\mathcal{F}$,

2) if $A \in \mathcal{F}$ then also $A^c = \Omega \setminus A \in \mathcal{F}$, and

3) if $A_1, A_2, \ldots \in \mathcal{F}$ (countably many) then also $\cup_{i=1}^{\infty} A_i = A_1 \cup A_2 \cup \ldots \in \mathcal{F}$.

A random varibale $X : \Omega \to \mathbb{R}$ is called $\mathcal{F}$-*measurable* if for all $a \in \mathbb{R}$

$$X^{-1}((-\infty, a]) = \{\omega \in \Omega | X(\omega) \leq a\} \in \mathcal{F}.$$

In our simple example $\mathcal{F}_i$-measurability can be described as follows.

Proposition B.1.3 . *For a random variable $X : \Omega \to \mathbb{R}$, and $i = 0, 1, \ldots n$, the following are equivalent*

1) X is $\mathcal{F}_i$-measurable,

2) X is constant on the sets $A_{(\nu_1, \ldots \nu_i)}$ for $\nu_1, \ldots, \nu_i \in \{H,T\}$, i.e. X can be written as

$$X = \sum_{\nu \in \{H,T\}^i} x_\nu 1_{A(\nu)},$$

where $x_\nu \in \mathbb{R}$ for $\nu \in \{H,T\}^i$.

Remark. Proposition B.1.3 says in particular that a random variable $X : \Omega \to \mathbb{R}$ is $\mathcal{F}_i$-measurable if and only if the value $X(\omega)$ only depends on the first i coordinates of ω. We therefore will often write $X(\omega_1, \ldots, \omega_i)$ instead of $X(\omega_1, \ldots, \omega_n)$.

Proof of B.1.3. Let $X : \Omega \to \mathbb{R}$ and let $x_1 < x_2 < \ldots x_r$ the possible values of X in increasing order.

If X is $\mathcal{F}_i$-measurable we find sets $I_1 \subset I_2 \subset \ldots I_r = \{H, T\}^i$, so that

$$X^{-1}((-\infty, x_j]) = \bigcup_{\nu \in I_j} A(\nu), \text{ for } j = 1, \ldots i.$$

This implies that

$$X^{-1}(\{x_j\}) = \bigcup_{\nu \in I_j \setminus I_{j-1}} A(\nu), \text{ for } j = 1, \ldots i, \qquad (I_0 = \emptyset),$$

which shows is constant on the sets $A(\nu)$, $\nu \in \{H, T\}^i$.

Conversely, if X is constant on the sets $A(\nu)$, $\nu \in \{H, T\}^i$, we are able to write X as

$$X = \sum_{\nu \in \{H,T\}^i} x_\nu 1_{A(\nu)}, \text{ for some choices of } x_\nu \in \mathbb{R}, \nu \in \{H, T\}^i.$$

We conclude that for $a \in \mathbb{R}$,

$$X^{-1}((-\infty, a]) = \bigcup_{\substack{\nu \in \{H,T\}^i \\ \text{with } x_\nu \leq a}} mA(\nu)$$

which imples that X is $\mathcal{F}_i$-measurable. $\square$

The following observation follows easily from Proposition B.1.3.

Proposition B.1.4 .   *For random variables $X, Y : \Omega \to \mathbb{R}$, which are $\mathcal{F}_i$-measurable, $i = 0, 1, \ldots n$, and for $\alpha, \beta \in \mathbb{R}$ the random variables $\alpha X + \beta Y$ and XY are also $\mathcal{F}_i$-measurable.*

Note that S_i is $\mathcal{F}_i$ measurable since $S_i(\omega)$ only depends on $\omega_1, \ldots \omega_i$.

For a random variable X we define now *the conditional expectation with respect to $\mathcal{F}_i$* to be the map on Ω denoted by $\mathbb{E}_{\mathbb{P}}(X|\mathcal{F}_i)$:

$$\mathbb{E}_{\mathbb{P}}(X|\mathcal{F}_i) : \Omega \to \mathbb{R}, \qquad \omega \mapsto \mathbb{E}_{\mathbb{P}}(X|\omega_1, \omega_2, ...\omega_i) \qquad [\text{see } (13)].$$

Using (15) we can write

$$(16) \qquad \mathbb{E}_{\mathbb{P}}(X|\mathcal{F}_i) = \sum_{\nu \in \{H,T\}^i} \frac{\mathbb{E}_{\mathbb{P}}(1_{A_\nu} X)}{\mathbb{P}(A(\nu))} 1_{A(\nu)}.$$

This means that for an $\omega = (\omega_1, \omega_2, \ldots, \omega_n) \in \Omega$

$$(17) \qquad \mathbb{E}_{\mathbb{P}}(X|\mathcal{F}_i)(\omega) = E_{\mathbb{P}}(X|\mathcal{F}_i)(\omega_1, \ldots, \omega_i) = \frac{\mathbb{E}_{\mathbb{P}}(1_{A(\omega_1,...,\omega_i)} X)}{\mathbb{P}(A(\omega_1, \ldots, \omega_i))}.$$

We note that the conditional expectation of a random variable X on Ω with respect to $\mathcal{F}_i$ is $\mathcal{F}_i$-measurable. Actualy more can be said. The following Proposition gives a characterization of conditional expectations and will lead to the general definition of this concept in Section B.3.

Proposition B.1.5 .   *If X is a random variable on Ω and $i = 0, 1, \ldots n$. Then $\mathbb{E}_{\mathbb{P}}(X|\mathcal{F}_i)$ is the only random variable Y on Ω which has the following two properties.*

1) Y is $\mathcal{F}_i$-measurable, and

2) for any $A \in \mathcal{F}_i$ it follows that

$$\mathbb{E}_{\mathbb{P}}(1_A X) = \mathbb{E}_{\mathbb{P}}(1_A Y).$$

Proof.   It follows from Proposition B.1.3 and from (16) that $\mathbb{E}_{\mathbb{P}}(X|\mathcal{F}_i)$ is $\mathcal{F}_i$ measurable.

For $A = \bigcup_{\nu \in I} A(\nu) \in \mathcal{F}_i$, $I \subset \{H, T\}^i$, we deduce that

$$
\begin{aligned}
\mathbb{E}_{\mathbb{P}}\left(1_A \mathbb{E}_{\mathbb{P}}(X|\mathcal{F}_i)\right) &= \mathbb{E}_{\mathbb{P}}\left(1_A \sum_{\nu \in \{H,T\}^i} \frac{\mathbb{E}_{\mathbb{P}}(1_{A_\nu} X)}{\mathbb{P}(A(\nu))} 1_{A(\nu)}\right) \\
&= \mathbb{E}_{\mathbb{P}}\left(\sum_{\nu \in I} \frac{\mathbb{E}_{\mathbb{P}}(1_{A_\nu} X)}{\mathbb{P}(A(\nu))} 1_{A(\nu)}\right) \\
&= \sum_{\nu \in I} \mathbb{E}_{\mathbb{P}}(X 1_{A(\nu)}) \\
&= \mathbb{E}_{\mathbb{P}}(X 1_A),
\end{aligned}
$$

which verifies (2). If the random variables Y and Z satisfy (1) and (2), and if $\nu \in \{H, T\}^i$, then by (1) they must be constant on $A(\nu)$. Say, they achieve on that set the values y_ν and z_ν respectively. Thus

$$
\begin{aligned}
y_\nu \mathbb{P}(A(\nu)) &= \mathbb{E}_{\mathbb{P}}(Y 1_{A_\nu}) \\
&= \mathbb{E}_{\mathbb{P}}(X 1_{A_\nu}) \quad \text{(By (2))} \\
&= \mathbb{E}_{\mathbb{P}}(Z 1_{A_\nu}) \quad \text{(By (2))} \\
&= z_\nu \mathbb{P}(A(\nu)),
\end{aligned}
$$

thus $y_\nu = z_\nu$ and thus $Y = Z$, which shows the uniqeness of a random variable satisfying (1) and (2). $\qquad \square$

Here some easy properties of conditional expectations:

Proposition B.1.6 . *Assume $X, Y : \Omega \to \mathbb{R}$, $\alpha, \beta \in \mathbb{R}$, and $i, j = 0, 1, \ldots n$.*

1) For $\mathbb{E}_{\mathbb{P}}(\cdot | \mathcal{F}_i)$ is linear, i.e.

$$\mathbb{E}_{\mathbb{P}}(\alpha X + \beta Y | \mathcal{F}_i) = \alpha \mathbb{E}_{\mathbb{P}}(X | \mathcal{F}_i) + \beta \mathbb{E}_{\mathbb{P}}(Y | \mathcal{F}_i).$$

2) If Y is $\mathcal{F}_i$-measurable then

$$\mathbb{E}_{\mathbb{P}}(Y X | \mathcal{F}_i) = Y \mathbb{E}_{\mathbb{P}}(X | \mathcal{F}_i).$$

3) (Tower property). If $i < j$. Then

$$\mathbb{E}_{\mathbb{P}}(X | \mathcal{F}_i) = \mathbb{E}_{\mathbb{P}}(\mathbb{E}_{\mathbb{P}}(X | \mathcal{F}_j) | \mathcal{F}_i).$$

Sketch of a proof. We have to verify that the left sides of the equation satisfy (1) and (2) of Theorem B.1.5. This can be done easily.   □

Finally we want to extend the notion of independence to random variables.

Definition. We call the random variables $X_1, X_2, \ldots, X_r$ *independent* if for any choice of $a_1 \leq b_1$, $a_2 \leq b_2$,..., $a_r \leq b_r$ it follows that

(18) $\qquad$. $\mathbb{P}(\bigcap_{j=1}^{r} \{X_j \in [a_j, b_j]\}) = \prod_{j=1}^{r} \mathbb{P}(\{X_j \in [a_j, b_j]\}).$

If $\mathcal{F}$ is a σ-algebra of subsets of Ω and X is a random variable we say that X is independent of $\mathcal{F}$ if for any $A \in \mathcal{F}$ it follows that X and 1_A are independent, i.e. if for $a \leq b$, $\mathbb{P}(\{a \leq X \leq b\} \cap A) = \mathbb{P}(\{a \leq X \leq b\})\mathbb{P}(A)$.

If X and Y are independent, write X and Y as $X = \sum_{i=1}^{m} 1_{A_i} x_i$ and $Y = \sum_{i=1}^{\ell} 1_{B_i} y_i$, with $x_1 < x_2 < \ldots, x_k$ and $y_1 < y_2 < \ldots < y_\ell$ being the possible values of X and Y respectively and $A_i = \{\omega | X(\omega) = x_i\}$ and $B_i = \{\omega | Y(\omega) = y_i\}$ then we deduce that

$$\mathbb{E}_{\mathbb{P}}(XY) = \mathbb{E}_{\mathbb{P}} = \sum_{i=1}^{k}\sum_{j=1}^{\ell} x_i y_j \mathbb{P}(A_i B_j) = \sum_{i=1}^{k}\sum_{j=1}^{\ell} x_i y_j \mathbb{P}(A_i)\mathbb{P}(B_j)$$

$$[\mathbb{P}(A_i \cap B_j) = \mathbb{P}(\{X \in [x_j, x_j]\} \cap \{Y \in [y_j, y_j]\})) \text{ and use } (18)]$$

$$= \sum_{i=1}^{k} x_i \mathbb{P}(A_i) \sum_{j=1}^{\ell} y_j \mathbb{P}(B_j) = \mathbb{E}_{\mathbb{P}}(X)\mathbb{E}_{\mathbb{P}}(Y).$$

More generally, we can prove in the same way the following Proposition.

Proposition B.1.7 . *If $X_1, X_2, \dots X_r$ are independent random variables on Ω it follows that*

$$\mathbb{E}_{\mathbb{P}}(\prod_{i=1}^{r} X_i) = \prod_{i=1}^{r} \mathbb{E}_{\mathbb{P}}(X_i)$$

Proposition B.1.8 . *If X is a random variable which is independent of $\mathcal{F}_i$ then*

$$\mathbb{E}_{\mathbb{P}}(X | \mathcal{F}_i) = \mathbb{E}_{\mathbb{P}}(X)$$

Sketch of a proof. We have to show that the constant variable $Y = \mathbb{E}_{\mathbb{P}}(X)$ satisfies (1) and (2) of Theorem B.1.5. (1) is clear while (2) follows from the definition of independence. $\square$

Proposition B.1.8 can be interpreted as follows. If the random X is independent to $\mathcal{F}_i$, then the knowledge of whether or not an event $A \in \mathcal{F}_i$ happened, does not give us any further information on what we expect X to be.

B.2 Some Basic Notions from Probability Theory

Assume Ω is the set of all possible outcomes of a stochastic experiment. A probability, is then a function which assigns to "certain subsets" A of Ω a value between 0 and 1, which we call the probability of A and denote by $\mathbb{P}(A)$. Probabilities will be defined on "σ-algebras on Ω".

Definition: A σ-*algebra* on Ω is a set $\mathcal{F}$ consisting of subsets of Ω with the following properties

a) For the empty set $\emptyset$: $\emptyset \in \mathcal{F}$

b) If $A \in \mathcal{F}$ then $\Omega \backslash A \in \mathcal{F}$ ($\Omega \backslash A = \{x \in \Omega | x \notin A\}$, the complement of A).

c) If $A_n \in \mathcal{F}$, $n \in \mathbb{N}$ then $\bigcup_{i=1}^{\infty} A_i = \{x \in \Omega | \exists i \in \mathbb{N} \quad x \in A_i\} \in \mathcal{F}$.

If $\mathcal{F}$ is a σ-algebra on Ω we call the pair $(\Omega, \mathcal{F})$ *measurable space*.

Examples. The following sets $\mathcal{F}$ of subsets of Ω are σ-algebras.

a) $\mathcal{F} = \{\emptyset, \Omega\}$,

b) for $A \subsetneq \Omega$, then $\mathcal{F} = \{\emptyset, A, \Omega \backslash A, \Omega\}$,

c) $\mathcal{F} =$ all subsets of Ω.

Often σ-algebras are "generated by a given set of subsets of Ω".

Proposition B.2.1 . *Let $\mathcal{E}$ be a set consisting of subsets of Ω. Then the intersection of all σ-algebras on Ω containing $\mathcal{E}$, i.e.*

$$\bigcap \{\mathcal{F} : \mathcal{F} \text{ is } \sigma\text{-algebra and } \mathcal{E} \subset \mathcal{F}\},$$

is again a σ-algebra which will be called the σ-algebra generated by $\mathcal{E}$ and denoted by $\sigma(\mathcal{F})$.

Examples.

a) If $\Omega = \mathbb{R}$, the *Borel σ-algebra on* $\mathbb{R}$ is the σ-algebra generated by all intervals. We
denote it by $\mathcal{B}_{\mathbb{R}}$. If $A \subset \mathbb{R}$, $\mathcal{B}_A$ denotes the *restriction of $\mathcal{B}_{\mathbb{R}}$ to A*, namely

$$\mathcal{B}_A = \{A \cap B : B \in \mathcal{B}_{\mathbb{R}}\}.$$

It is easy to see that $\mathcal{B}_A$ is still a σ-algebra.

b) If $\mathcal{F}_i$ is a σ-algebra on the set Ω_i, $i = 1, 2 \ldots n$, then the *product σ-algebra* is the σ-
algebra on $\Omega_1 \times \Omega_2 \ldots \Omega_n$ generated by the *rectangles* $A_1 \times A_2 \times A_n$, with $A_i \in \mathcal{F}_i$, for
$i = 1, 2, \ldots n$. We denote it by $\otimes_{i=1}^n \mathcal{F}_i$. In the case that $\Omega_i = \mathbb{R}$, $i = 1, \ldots n$ we put
$\mathcal{B}_{\mathbb{R}^n} = \mathcal{B}_{\mathbb{R}} \otimes \mathcal{B}_{\mathbb{R}} \ldots \mathcal{B}_{\mathbb{R}}$.

Proposition B.2.2 .   *If $\mathcal{F}$ is a σ-algebra on Ω, then*

a) $\Omega \in \mathcal{F}$

b) *If A, B then $A \cap B$, $A \backslash B = \{x \colon\ x \in A \quad x \notin B\}$, and $A \triangle B = (A \backslash B) \cup (B \backslash A) \in \mathcal{F}$.*

c) *If $A_1, A_2, A_3, \ldots \in \mathcal{F}$ then also $\bigcap_{i=1}^{\infty} A_i = \{x \in \Omega \colon\ \forall i \in \mathbb{N}\ x \in A_i\} \in \mathcal{F}$.*

Proposition B.2.2 can be easily shown using properties a), b) and c) of the definition of
a σ-algebra.

Now, as in the previous section, a probability can be defined to be a map defined on a
σ-algebra.

Definition: Assume $\mathcal{F}$ is a σ-algebra on the set Ω, a *measure* on $\mathcal{F}$ is a map

$$\mu : \mathcal{F} \to \mathbb{R} \cup \{\infty\}$$

with the following properties.

a) $\mu(\emptyset) = 0$

b) $0 \le \mu(A)$ for all $A \in \mathcal{F}$

c) If $A_1, A_2, A_3, \ldots$ are pairwise disjoint (meaning $A_i \cap A_j = \emptyset$ if $i \neq j$) then

$$\mu\left(\bigcup_{i=1}^{\infty} A_i\right) = \sum_{i=1}^{\infty} \mu(A_i)$$

A measure is called *finite* if $\mu(\Omega) < \infty$ (and thus $\mu(A) < \infty$ for all $A \in \mathcal{F}$). It is called σ-finite if there is a sequence $(A_n) \subset \mathcal{F}$, with $\mu(A_n) < \infty$ and $\bigcup_{n=1}^{\infty} A_n = \Omega$.

A *probability on* $\mathcal{F}$ is a measure $\mathbb{P}$ on $\mathcal{F}$ for which $\mathbb{P}(\Omega) = 1$. If $\mathbb{P}$ is a probability on $\mathcal{F}$ which is a σ-algebra on Ω then the triple $(\Omega, \mathcal{F}, \mathbb{P})$ is called *probability space*.

The above introduced condition (c) is called σ-*additivity*, it implies the following continuity properties.

Proposition B.2.3 *(Continuity from above and below).*

Let μ be a measure on a measurable space $(\Omega, \mathcal{F})$.

1) If $A_1 \subset A_2 \subset A_3 \subset \ldots$, $A_i \in \mathcal{F}$, $i = 1, 2, \ldots$, then

$$\lim_{n \to \infty} \mathbb{P}(A_i) = \mathbb{P}\left(\bigcup_{i=1}^{\infty} A_i\right).$$

2) If $A_1 \supset A_2 \supset A_3 \supset \ldots$, $A_i \in \mathcal{F}$, $i = 1, 2, \ldots$, and $\mu(A_i) < \infty$ then

$$\lim_{n \to \infty} \mathbb{P}(A_i) = \mathbb{P}\left(\bigcap_{i=1}^{\infty} A_i\right).$$

Often one has a non negative map defined on a certain subset $\mathcal{E}$ of all subsets of Ω and asks whether this map can be extended to a measure on $\sigma(\mathcal{E})$. The Extension Theorem of Caratheodory gives a satisfying answer to this question. Instead of recalling this Theorem let us only state the two important situation which are of interest to us.

Proposition B.2.4 .

1) *There is a unique measure λ on $\mathcal{B}_{\mathbb{R}}$ so that $\lambda([a, b]) = b-a$, for all intervals $[a, b] \subset \mathbb{R}$.*
   This measure is called the Lebesgues *measure on $\mathbb{R}$.*

2) *For $i = 1, 2 \ldots n$ let μ_i be a σ-finite measure (respectively probability) on $\mathcal{F}_i$, where $\mathcal{F}_i$*
   is a σ-algebra on a set Ω_i. Then there is a unique measure μ (respectively probability)
   on $\otimes_{i=1}^{n} \mathcal{F}_i$ so that for all choices of $A_1 \in \mathcal{F}_1$, $A_2 \in \mathcal{F}_2 \ldots A_n \in \mathcal{F}_n$

$$\mu(A_1 \times A_2 \ldots A_n) = \prod_{i=1}^{n} \mu_i(A_i), \qquad [\text{with } \infty \cdot 0 = 0].$$

   This measure is called the product of (μ_i) and denoted by $\otimes_{i=1}^{n} \mu_i$.

If one is interested in showing that two measures on $(\Omega, \mathcal{F})$ are equal the following general principle gives an answer. It implies the statements on the uniqueness in above Proposition B.2.4.

Theorem B.2.5 .   *Assume μ and ν are two σ-finite measures on $(\Omega, \mathcal{F})$, $\mathcal{F}$ being a σ-algebra on the set Ω. Assume That $\mathcal{D} \subset \mathcal{F}$ generates $\mathcal{F}$ and is stable taking intersections $(A, B \in \mathcal{D} \Rightarrow A \cap B \in \mathcal{D})$ then*

$$\mu = \nu \iff \mu(A) = \nu(A) \text{ for all } A \in \mathcal{D}.$$

Mostly we are not interested in the outcome $\omega \in \Omega$ itself but in some number assigned to it.

Definition: Let $(\Omega, \mathcal{F}, \mathbb{P})$ be a probability space a map

$$X: \ \Omega \to \mathbb{R}, \quad \omega \mapsto X(\omega)$$

is called a *random variable* if it is *measurable*, meaning that the preimage $X^{-1}(A) = \{\omega \in \Omega \mid X(\omega) \in A\} \in \mathcal{F}$ of any set $A \in \mathcal{B}(\mathbb{R})$ lies in $\mathcal{F}$.

More generally, if $F : \Omega \to \tilde{\Omega}$ is a map and $\mathcal{F}$ and $\tilde{\mathcal{F}}$ are σ-algebras on Ω respectively on $\tilde{\Omega}$, then F is called $(\mathcal{F}, \tilde{\mathcal{F}})$-*measurable* if $F^{-1}(A) \in \mathcal{F}$ whenever $A \in \tilde{\mathcal{F}}$.

Remark. If $F : \Omega \to \tilde{\Omega}$ and $\tilde{\mathcal{E}} \subset \tilde{\mathcal{F}}$ generates $\mathcal{F}$, it is enough to require that $F^{-1}(\tilde{E}) \in \mathcal{F}$ for all $\tilde{E} \in \tilde{\mathcal{E}}$ to deduce that F is measurable. Indeed, we only need to observe that the system $\{A \subset \tilde{\Omega} : F^{-1}(A) \in \mathcal{F}\}$ is a σ-algebra on Ω which contains $\tilde{\mathcal{E}}$, and thus must contain $\sigma(\tilde{\mathcal{E}})$.

This shows for example that $X : \Omega \to \mathbb{R}$ is a random variable if and only if $\{X \leq a\} = \{\omega \in \Omega : X(\omega) \leq a\}$ is in $\mathcal{F}$ for all $a \in \mathbb{R}$.

Proposition B.2.6 .   *If X and Y are random variables, $g : \mathbb{R} \to \mathbb{R}$ is measurable and if $a \in \mathbb{R}$, then $X + Y, aX, XY, g \circ X$ are also random variables.*

Assume $(X_n)_{n \in \mathbb{N}}$ is a sequence of random variables for which $X(\omega) = \lim_{n \to \infty} X_n(\omega)$ whenever $\omega \in \Omega$. Then X is also a random variable.

Given a probability $\mathbb{P}$ on $(\Omega, \mathcal{F})$ and a random variable X, we define the *distribution of X* to be a probability on $\mathbb{R}$: For $A \in \mathcal{B}(\mathbb{R})$

$$(19) \qquad\qquad \mathbb{P}_X(A) = \mathbb{P}(X^{-1}(A)).$$

For example: $\mathbb{P}_X([a,b]) = \mathbb{P}(X^{-1}([a,b])) = \mathbb{P}(a \leq X \leq b)$.

There are two important special cases.

Example. (The finite case). Assume the random variable $X \colon \Omega \to \mathbb{R}$ only assumes the values $\alpha_1, \alpha_2, \ldots, \alpha_n$ (distinct). If we let for $i = 1, 2, \ldots, n$

$$A_i = X^{-1}(\{\alpha_i\}) = \{\omega \in \Omega \mid X(\omega) = \alpha_i\}.$$

Note that the A_i's are disjoint and $A_1 \cup A_2 \cup \ldots A_n = \Omega$. We can write $X(\omega) = \sum_{i=1}^{n} \alpha_i 1_{A_i}(\omega)$. Recall that 1_A is the indicator function on $A \subset \Omega$ ($1_A(\omega) = 1$ if $\omega \in A$, and $1_A(\omega) = 0$ if $\omega \notin A$. In this case $\mathbb{P}_X$ can be seen as a probability on $\Omega_X = \{\alpha_1, \ldots, \alpha_n\}$ with $p_i = \mathbb{P}_X(\{\alpha_n\}) = \mathbb{P}(A_i)$ and for $E \subset \{\alpha_1, \ldots, \alpha_n\}$

$$\mathbb{P}_X(E) = \sum_{\alpha_i \in E} p_i.$$

Example. (Continuous case). Assume there is an integrable function $f \colon \mathbb{R} \to \mathbb{R}$ so that for any $A \in \mathcal{B}(\mathbb{R})$

$$\mathbb{P}_X(A) = \int_A f(x)dx.$$

In this case we f is *called the density of* $\mathbb{P}_X$.

Note: Since $\mathbb{P}_X$ is a probability a density f has the following two properties

1) $f \geq 0$, and

2) $\int\limits_{-\infty}^{\infty} f(x)dx = \mathbb{P}_X(\mathbb{R}) = 1$

Examples. (Of densities)

1) $f(x) = \frac{1}{b-a}1_{[a,b]}$ density of the *uniform distribution on the interval* $[a,b]$,

2) $f(x) = \frac{1}{\sqrt{2\pi}}e^{-x^2/2}$ density of the standard normal distribution.

   More generally, for $\mu \in \mathbb{R}$ and $\sigma > 0$

(20)
$$f_{(\mu,\sigma)} = \frac{1}{\sqrt{2\pi\sigma^2}}e^{-\frac{(x-\mu)^2}{2\sigma^2}}$$

   is the density of *the normal distributed random variable whith mean* μ *and variance* σ^2. We denote the normal distribution with mean μ and variance σ^2 by $N(\mu,\sigma^2)$, i.e.

(21)
$$N(\mu,\sigma^2)(A) = \frac{1}{\sqrt{2\pi\sigma^2}}\int_A e^{-\frac{(x-\mu)^2}{2\sigma^2}}\, dx \text{ whenever } A \in \mathcal{B}_{\mathbb{R}}$$

We now turn to a central notion : The expected value of a random variable.

Definition: (Expected value of random variables). Let X be a random variable on $(\Omega, \mathcal{F}, \mathbb{P})$

a) If X only assumes finitely many values, say $X = \sum_{i=1}^{n} \alpha_i 1_{A_i}$ then $\mathbb{E}_{\mathbb{P}}(X) = \sum_{i=1}^{n} \alpha_i \mathbb{P}(A_i)$.

Remark. In order to see that $\mathbb{E}_{\mathbb{P}}(X)$ is well defined for random variables which assume finitely many values we have to verify that if we write X in two different ways, say

(22)
$$X = \sum_{i=1}^{n} \alpha_i 1_{A_i} \quad \text{and} \quad X = \sum_{i=1}^{m} \beta_i 1_{B_i},$$

then

$$\sum_{i=1}^{n} \alpha_i \mathbb{P}(A_i) = \sum_{i=1}^{m} \beta_i \mathbb{P}(B_i).$$

b) If X is a positive random variable, then

(23) $\mathbb{E}_{\mathbb{P}}(X) = \sup\{\mathbb{E}_{\mathbb{P}}(Y) \mid Y \text{ has finitely many values and } 0 \le Y \le X\}.$

c) If X is arbitrary and $\mathbb{E}_{\mathbb{P}}(|X|) < \infty$ (we call X in that case *integrable*), let $X^+ = \max(0, X)$ and $X^- = \max(0, -X)$. Note that $X^+, X^- \ge 0$, and $X = X^+ - X^-$. In that case we define:

(24) $$\mathbb{E}_{\mathbb{P}}(X) = \mathbb{E}_{\mathbb{P}}(X^+) - \mathbb{E}_{\mathbb{P}}(X^-).$$

Remark. The above introduction of expected values for random variables on probability spaces, can be generalized to measures in exactly the same way. But in this case we speak of *the integral of a measurable function* $f : \Omega \to \mathbb{R}$ *with respect to the measure* μ and denote it by $\int_{\Omega} f(\omega) d\mu(\omega)$.

Definition: Assume that $\mathbb{E}(X^2) < \infty$, then *the variance of* X is defined by

$$\mathrm{Var}(X) = \mathbb{E}_{\mathbb{P}}((X - \mathbb{E}_{\mathbb{P}}(X))^2).$$

Proposition B.2.7   *(Linearity of $\mathbb{E}_{\mathbb{P}}(\cdot)$).*

For two integrable random variables X and Y the following identity holds.

$$\mathbb{E}_{\mathbb{P}}(\alpha X + \beta Y) = \alpha \mathbb{E}_{\mathbb{P}}(X) + \beta \mathbb{E}_{\mathbb{P}}(Y).$$

Proposition B.2.8   *(Monotonicity of $\mathbb{E}_{\mathbb{P}}(\cdot)$).*

For two integrable random variables X and Y, with $X \le Y$ it follows that

$$\mathbb{E}_{\mathbb{P}}(X) \le \mathbb{E}_{\mathbb{P}}(Y).$$

Proposition B.2.9 .   *Assume the distribution of the random variable X has density*
$f\colon \mathbb{R} \to \mathbb{R}$. *Then* $\mathbb{E}_{\mathbb{P}}(X) = \int\limits_{-\infty}^{\infty} x f(x) dx$ *as long as this integral exist (meaning that*
$\int\limits_{-\infty}^{\infty} |x| f(x) dx < \infty$).
More generally, if $g\colon \mathbb{R} \to \mathbb{R}$ is measurable, then $\mathbb{E}_{\mathbb{P}}(g \circ X) = \int g(x) f(x) dx$, if this integral
exists.

The next two theorems give an answer to the following question: if X_n is a sequence of random variables which converges to a random variable X. Under which condition does also the expected values of X_n converge to the expected value of X. In general (meaning without further conditions) $\mathbb{E}_{\mathbb{P}}(X_n)$ does not need to converge to $\mathbb{E}_{\mathbb{P}}(X)$ as the following easy example shows.

Take $\Omega = [0, 1]$ with the σ-algebra $\mathcal{B}_{[0,1]}$, and let $\mathbb{P}$ be the uniform distribution on $[0, 1]$. Then $X_n = n^2 1_{(0,1/n)}$ converges pointwise to 0 but $\mathbb{E}_{\mathbb{P}}(X_n) = n \to \infty$.

We say a sequence (X_n) of random variables on a probability space $(\Omega, \mathcal{F}, \mathbb{P})$ is *almost surely* increasing, decreasing, or convergent if there is a measurable $\widetilde{\Omega} \subset \Omega$ with $\mathbb{P}(\widetilde{\Omega}) = 1$ so that $(X_n(\omega))$ has this property for all $\omega \in \widetilde{\Omega}$.

Theorem B.2.10 *(Monotone Convergence Theorem).*
Assume that X_n is an almost surely increasing sequence of integrable random variables on
$(\Omega, \mathcal{F}, \mathbb{P})$. *Let $X(\omega) = \lim_{n \to \infty} X_n(\omega)$ for $\omega \in \Omega$ (might assume the value ∞).*
Then

$$\mathbb{E}_{\mathbb{P}}(X) = \lim_{n \to \infty} \mathbb{E}_{\mathbb{P}}(X_n).$$

Theorem B.2.11 *(Majorized Convergence Theorem).*
Assume that the sequence X_n of random variables on $(\Omega, \mathcal{F}, \mathbb{P})$ is almost surely converging to a random variable X. Furthermore assume that there is an integrable random variable Y so that $|X_n| \leq Y$ almost surely.
Then

$$\mathbb{E}_{\mathbb{P}}(X) = \lim_{n\to\infty} \mathbb{E}_{\mathbb{P}}(X_n).$$

Often it is not enough to know the distribution of a single random variable but one also needs to know how several random variables are "related to each other". For that we need the "joint distribution".

Definition: Assume $X_1, X_2, \ldots, X_n$ are random variables on $\left(\Omega, \mathcal{F}, \mathbb{P}\right)$. The *joint distribution* $\mathbb{P}_{X_1,\ldots,X_n}$ *of* $X_1, \ldots, X_n$ is a probability on $\mathcal{B}(\mathbb{R}^n)$ defined by

$$\mathbb{P}_{(X_1,\ldots,X_n)}(A) = \mathbb{P}(\{\omega \in \Omega \mid (X_1(\omega), X_2(\omega), \ldots, X_n(\omega)) \in A\}) \text{ for } A \in \mathcal{B}(\mathbb{R}^n).$$

We say that the joint distribution has a density f if $f\colon \mathbb{R}^n \to \mathbb{R}_0^+$ is measurable and

$$\mathbb{P}_{(X_1,\ldots,X_n)}(A) = \int \cdots \int_A f(x_1, x_2, \ldots, x_n) dx_1 dx_2 \ldots dx_n \text{ for all } A \in \mathcal{B}(\mathbb{R}^n).$$

Proposition B.2.12 . *If f is the density of the joint distribution of the random variables $X_1, X_2 \ldots, X_n$, then the distribution of each random variable has a density. Indeed, for $i = 1, 2, \ldots, n$, define f_i by*

$$f_i(x) = \underbrace{\int_{-\infty}^{\infty} \cdots \int_{-\infty}^{\infty}}_{n-1 \ times} f(x_1, x_2, \ldots, x_{i-1}, x, x_{i+1} \ldots x_n) dx_1 \ldots dx_{i-1} dx_{i+1}, \ldots, dx_n$$

(i.e. one integrates out all variables of $f(x_1, \ldots, x_n)$ but x_i) then f_i is the density of the distribution of X_i.

One of the most important concepts in probability theory is the notion of independence.

Definition. Let $(\Omega, \mathcal{F}, \mathbb{P})$ be a probability space and let $\mathcal{F}_1, \mathcal{F}_2, \ldots, \mathcal{F}_n$ be sub σ-algebras of $\mathcal{F}$. We say that $(\mathcal{F}_i)$ are *independent*, if for any choice of A_i, with $A_i \in \mathcal{F}_i$, for $i = 1, 2, \ldots n$, it follows that

$$(25) \qquad \mathbb{P}\left(\bigcap_{i=1}^n A_i\right) = \prod_{i=1}^n \mathbb{P}(A_i).$$

Assume $X_1, X_2, \ldots, X_n$ are random variables on $\left(\Omega, \mathcal{F}, \mathbb{P}\right)$. They are called *independent* if the σ-algebras $\mathcal{F}_i$, with $\mathcal{F}_i = \{X_i^{-1}(A) : A \in \mathcal{B}(\mathbb{R})\}$, for $i = 1, \ldots n$, are independent. This means that for any choice of $B_1, B_2, \ldots B_n \in \mathcal{B}_{\mathbb{R}}$ it follows that

$$(26) \qquad \mathbb{P}(\{X_1 \in B_1, X_2 \in B_2, \ldots X_n \in B_n\}) = \prod_{i=1}^n \mathbb{P}(\{X_n \in B_n\}).$$

Proposition B.2.13 .   *For random variables $X_1, X_2, \ldots, X_n$ on $(\Omega, \mathcal{F}, \mathbb{P})$, the following properties are equivalent*

a) *$X_1, \ldots, X_n$ are independent.*

b) *The joint distribution $\mathbb{P}_{X_1, \ldots, X_n}$ is the equal to the product (in the sense of probabilities) of the single distributions $\mathbb{P}_{X_1}, \mathbb{P}_{X_2}, \ldots \mathbb{P}_{X_n}$.*

c) *For any bounded measurable functions $g_1, g_2, \ldots, g_n \colon \mathbb{R} \to \mathbb{R}$*

$$\mathbb{E}_{\mathbb{P}}(g_1(X_1) \cdot g_2(X_2) \ldots g_n(X_n)) = \mathbb{E}_{\mathbb{P}}(g_1(X_1)) \cdot \mathbb{E}_{\mathbb{P}}(g_2(X_2)) \ldots \mathbb{E}_{\mathbb{P}}(g_n(X_n)).$$

Under the additional hypothesis that $\mathbb{P}_{X_1, \ldots, X_n}$ has a density (a)-(c) are equivalent to:

d) *The density of $\mathbb{P}_{X_1, \ldots, X_n}$ is the product of the densities of the $\mathbb{P}_{X_i}$'s.*

Proposition B.2.14 . *Assume X and Y are two square integrable random variables on $(\Omega, \mathcal{F}, \mathbb{P})$ (i.e. $\mathbb{E}_{\mathbb{P}}(X^2) < \infty$).*

Then XY is integrable and if X and Y are independent then $\mathbb{E}_{\mathbb{P}}(XY) = \mathbb{E}_{\mathbb{P}}(X)\mathbb{E}_{\mathbb{P}}(Y)$.

¿From this fact one can conclude that if $X_1, X_2, \ldots X_n$ are independent and square integrable then

$$\mathbb{V}ar\left(\sum_{i=1}^{n} X_i\right) = \sum_{i=1}^{n} \mathbb{V}ar(X_i).$$

Finally we want to state two crucial theorems, the first one formalizes the following well known fact:

If one repeats a stochastic experiment often enough independently, and takes the average of the outcomes (more precisely: of a measurement of the outcomes), then the average of the outcomes is close (the more trials, the closer) to the expected value.

Theorem B.2.15 *(The Law of Large Numbers).*

Assume that (X_i) is a sequence of independent integrable random variables all of them having the same distribution.

Then almost surely

$$\lim_{n \to \infty} \frac{1}{n} \sum_{i=1}^{n} X_i(\omega) = \mathbb{E}_{\mathbb{P}}(X_1).$$

The next theorem says how fast the convergence in the previous theorem is occurring. Secondly it formalizes the following principle:

If a random variable X is the sum of "a lot of" independent random variables all of which have expected value zero and all of which have a variance of the same magnitude. Then the distribution of X in close to a normal distribution.

Theorem B.2.16 *(Central Limit Theorem).*
Assume $X_1, X_2, \ldots$ are independent, $\mathbb{E}_\mathbb{P}(X_i) = 0$ for $i = 1, 2, \ldots$ and there are numbers $0 < r < R$ so that

$$r < \mathbb{V}ar(X_i) < R \quad all \quad i = 1, 2 \ldots$$

denote $\sigma_i^2 = \mathbb{V}ar(X_i)$.
Then

$$\lim_{n \to \infty} \mathbb{P} \left(\left\{ \frac{\sum\limits_{i=1}^{n} X_i}{\left(\sum\limits_{i=1}^{n} \sigma_i^2 \right)^{1/2}} \in [a, b] \right\} \right) = \frac{1}{\sqrt{2\pi}} \int_a^b e^{-x^2/2} \, dx = N(0,1)[a, b].$$

Finally a more quantitative version of the Central Limit Theorem due to Berry and Esseen.

Theorem B.2.17 *(Berry-Esseen).*
Assume $\in \mathbb{N}$ and $X_1, X_2, \ldots, X_n$ are independent square integrable random variables having mean 0. Let $\sigma_i^2 = \mathbb{V}ar(X_i)$, for $i = 1, \ldots, n$.
Then for all $a < b$

$$\left| \mathbb{P} \left(\sum_{i=1}^{n} X_i \in [a, b] \right) - N \left(0, \sum_{i=1}^{n} \sigma_i^2 \right) ([a, b]) \right| \leq \frac{12}{\left(\sum_{i=1}^{n} \sigma_i^2 \right)^3} \sum_{i=1}^{n} \mathbb{E}_\mathbb{P}(|X_i|^3).$$

B.3 Conditional Expectations

Definition: Assume that X is a random variable on a probability space $(\Omega, \mathcal{F}, \mathbb{P})$ with $\mathbb{E}_{\mathbb{P}}(|X|) < \infty$.

Now let $\widetilde{\mathcal{F}}$ be a sub-σ-algebra of $\mathcal{F}$, i.e. a σ-algebra which is contained in $\mathcal{F}$.

Then $\widetilde{X} \colon \Omega \to \mathbb{R}$ is called *conditional expectation of X with respect to* $\widetilde{\mathcal{F}}$ if

1) $\widetilde{X}$ is $\widetilde{\mathcal{F}}$-measurable, and $\mathbb{E}_{\mathbb{P}}(|\widetilde{X}|) < \infty$

2) For any $\tilde{A} \in \widetilde{\mathcal{F}}$

$$\mathbb{E}_{\mathbb{P}}(1_{\tilde{A}} \widetilde{X}) = \mathbb{E}_{\mathbb{P}}(1_{\tilde{A}} X).$$

Using a theorem of Real Analysis, the *Radon Nikodym Theorem*, we always can insure the existence of conditional expectations and show that it is unique up to almost sure equality.

Theorem B.3.1 *(The Radon Nikodym Theorem).*
Assume that μ and ν are two measures on $\mathcal{F}$, a σ-algebra on the set Ω and assume that ν is σ-finite.
The two following statements are equivalent:

1) For every $A \in \mathcal{F}$ it follows that:

$$\mu(A) = 0 \Rightarrow \nu(A) = 0$$

(we say that ν is absolute continuous with respect to μ*).*

2) There is an $\mathcal{F}$-measurable function $f : \Omega \to [0, \infty)$ so that:

$$\nu(A) = \int_A f(\omega) d\mu(\omega), \text{ for all } A \in \mathcal{F}$$

(we say that the Radon Nikodym *derivative of ν with respect to ν is f).*

Theorem B.3.2 *(Existence and uniqeness of conditional expectations).*
If X is a random variable on $(\Omega, \mathcal{F}, \mathbb{P})$, with $\mathbb{E}(|X|) < \infty$, and $\widetilde{\mathcal{F}} \subset \mathcal{F}$ is a sub-σ-algebra,
then there exists a $\widetilde{\mathcal{F}}$-measurable random variable $\widetilde{X}$ with

(27) $$\mathbb{E}_{\mathbb{P}}(1_A \widetilde{X}) = \mathbb{E}_{\mathbb{P}}(1_A X) \quad for \ all \quad A \in \widetilde{\mathcal{F}}.$$

This variable is unique up to almost sure equality, i.e. if $\tilde{X}_1$ and $\tilde{X}_2$ are $\widetilde{\mathcal{F}}$-measurable
random variables both satisfying equation (27) then $X_1 = X_2$.
We denote $\widetilde{X}$ by $\mathbb{E}_{\mathbb{P}}(X|\widetilde{\mathcal{F}})$.

Proof.

First assume that $X \geq 0$. Define $\nu(A) = \mathbb{E}_{\mathbb{P}}(1_A X)$, for $A \in \mathcal{F}$.

Now ν is a measure on $\mathcal{F}$ which is absolute continuous to $\mathbb{P}$. Also the restriction of
μ to the sub-σ-algebra $\widetilde{\mathcal{F}}$ is absolute continuous with respect to the restriction of $\mathbb{P}$ to $\widetilde{F}$.
Therefore we can apply the Theorem of Radon Nikodym to both restrictions and obtain an
$\widetilde{\mathcal{F}}$-measurable random variable $\widetilde{X} \geq 0$ so that for all $\tilde{A} \in \widetilde{\mathcal{F}}$:

$$\mathbb{E}_{\mathbb{P}}(1_{\tilde{A}} \widetilde{X}) = \nu(\tilde{A}) = \mathbb{E}_{\mathbb{P}}(1_{\tilde{A}} X).$$

Note that this implies that $\mathbb{E}_{\mathbb{P}}(\widetilde{X}) = \mathbb{E}_{\mathbb{P}}(X) < \infty$

In the general case we write $X = X^+ - X^-$, and obtain by above argument $\mathcal{F}$-measurable
and integrable random variables $\tilde{X}^+$ and $\tilde{X}^-$ so that for $\tilde{X} = \tilde{X}^+ - \tilde{X}^-$

$$\mathbb{E}_{\mathbb{P}}(1_{\tilde{A}} \widetilde{X}) = \mathbb{E}_{\mathbb{P}}(1_{\tilde{A}} \widetilde{X}^+) - \mathbb{E}_{\mathbb{P}}(1_{\tilde{A}} \widetilde{X}^-) = \mathbb{E}_{\mathbb{P}}(1_{\tilde{A}} X^+) - \mathbb{E}_{\mathbb{P}}(1_{\tilde{A}} X^-) = \mathbb{E}_{\mathbb{P}}(1_{\tilde{A}} X).$$

To show uniqueness of $\widetilde{X}$ assume that $\tilde{X}_1$ and $\tilde{X}_2$ are $\mathcal{F}$-measurable and satisfy (27). For
$\varepsilon > 0$ the set $A = \{\tilde{X}_1 \geq \tilde{X}_2 + \varepsilon\}$ is $\mathcal{F}$-measurable and it follows that

$$0 = \mathbb{E}_{\mathbb{P}}(1_A(\tilde{X}_1 - \tilde{X}_2)) \geq \varepsilon \mathbb{P}(A).$$

This implies that $\mathbb{P}(A) = 0$, and since $\varepsilon > 0$ can be chosen arbitrarily small we deduce from
Proposition B.2.3 that $\mathbb{P}(\tilde{X}_1 > \tilde{X}_2) = 0$. Exchanging the roles of $\tilde{X}_1$ and $\tilde{X}_2$ we also deduce
that $\mathbb{P}(\tilde{X}_2 > \tilde{X}_1) = 0$. $\square$.

We start with some general properties of conditional expectations.

Proposition B.3.3 . *Let X and Y be two random variables on $(\Omega, \mathcal{F}, \mathbb{P})$ with $\mathbb{E}_{\mathbb{P}}(|X|), \mathbb{E}_{\mathbb{P}}(|Y|) < \infty$. Let $\widetilde{\mathcal{F}} \subset \mathcal{F}$ be a sub-σ-algebra. Then*

1) For $a, b \in \mathbb{R}$: $\mathbb{E}_{\mathbb{P}}(aX + bY | \widetilde{\mathcal{F}}) = a\mathbb{E}_{\mathbb{P}}(X | \widetilde{\mathcal{F}}) + b\mathbb{E}_{\mathbb{P}}(Y | \widetilde{\mathcal{F}})$ a.s..

2) If furthermore $\mathbb{E}_{\mathbb{P}}(|XY|) < \infty$ and if Y is $\widetilde{\mathcal{F}}$-measurable then

$$\mathbb{E}_{\mathbb{P}}(YX | \widetilde{\mathcal{F}}) = Y\mathbb{E}_{\mathbb{P}}(X | \widetilde{\mathcal{F}}) \quad a.s.$$

3) If X and $\widetilde{\mathcal{F}}$ are independent then $\mathbb{E}_{\mathbb{P}}(X | \widetilde{\mathcal{F}}) = \mathbb{E}_{\mathbb{P}}(X)$ a.s..

4) If $X \leq Y$ almost surely then

$$\mathbb{E}_{\mathbb{P}}(X | \widetilde{\mathcal{F}}) \leq \mathbb{E}_{\mathbb{P}}(X | \widetilde{\mathcal{F}}).$$

Proof.

The first assertion (1) can be shown by simply verifying that $a\mathbb{E}_{\mathbb{P}}(X | \widetilde{\mathcal{F}}) + b\mathbb{E}_{\mathbb{P}}(Y | \widetilde{\mathcal{F}})$ satisfies equation (27) for the random variable $aX + bY$. Also if X and $\widetilde{\mathcal{F}}$ are independent one needs to verify that the constant random variable $\mathbb{E}_{\mathbb{P}}(X)$ satisfies equation (27). This shows claim (3)

In order show (2) we first assume that $Y = 1_B$ for some $\tilde{B} \in \widetilde{\mathcal{F}}$ and observe that for any $\tilde{A} \in \widetilde{\mathcal{F}}$

$$\mathbb{E}_{\mathbb{P}}\left(1_{\tilde{A}} 1_{\tilde{B}} \mathbb{E}_{\mathbb{P}}(X | \widetilde{\mathcal{F}})\right) = \mathbb{E}_{\mathbb{P}}\left(1_{\tilde{A} \cap \tilde{B}} \mathbb{E}_{\mathbb{P}}(X | \widetilde{\mathcal{F}})\right) = \mathbb{E}_{\mathbb{P}}(1_{\tilde{A} \cap \tilde{B}} X) = \mathbb{E}_{\mathbb{P}}(1_{\tilde{A}} 1_{\tilde{B}} X).$$

This proves the claim in that case and by assertion (1) the claim follows for all random variables of the form $Y = \sum_{i=1}^{m} \beta_i 1_{B_i}$, $B_i \in \mathcal{F}$ and $\beta_i \mathbb{R}$, for $n \in \mathbb{N}, i = 1, 2, \ldots n$.

For general Y we can find a sequence Y_n of $\tilde{F}$-measurable random variables so that each Y_n has only finitely many values, $|Y_n| \leq |Y|$, for $n \in \mathbb{N}$ and $\lim_{n \to \infty} Y_n = Y$ almost surely.

For $\tilde{A} \in \mathcal{F}$ it follows by the Majorized Convergence Theorem B.2.11 that

$$\mathbb{E}_{\mathbb{P}}\left(1_{\tilde{A}}Y\mathbb{E}_{\mathbb{P}}(X|\widetilde{\mathcal{F}})\right) = \lim_{n\to\infty} \mathbb{E}_{\mathbb{P}}\left(1_{\tilde{A}}Y_n\mathbb{E}_{\mathbb{P}}(X|\widetilde{\mathcal{F}})\right) = \lim_{n\to\infty} \mathbb{E}_{\mathbb{P}}(1_{\tilde{A}}Y_n X) = \mathbb{E}_{\mathbb{P}}(1_{\tilde{A}}YX)$$

which proves the claim (2).

In order to prove claim (4) assume that $X \leq Y$ almost surely and define

$$A = \{\omega \in \Omega : \mathbb{E}_{\mathbb{P}}(X|\widetilde{\mathcal{F}}) > \mathbb{E}_{\mathbb{P}}(Y|\widetilde{\mathcal{F}})\}.$$

A is $\widetilde{\mathcal{F}}$-measurable and

$$0 \leq \mathbb{E}_{\mathbb{P}}(1_A(Y - X)) = \mathbb{E}_{\mathbb{P}}\left(1_A[\mathbb{E}_{\mathbb{P}}(Y|\widetilde{\mathcal{F}}) - \mathbb{E}_{\mathbb{P}}(X|\widetilde{\mathcal{F}})]\right) \leq 0,$$

which implies $\mathbb{P}(A) = 0$ and finishes the proof of claim (3). $\square$

Unfortunately Theorem B.3.2 is one of those theorems asserting unique existence of a certain object without giving a hint how to find it. We will describe the computation of conditional expectation in two important situations.

Proposition B.3.4 .   *Assume that X is a random variable on $(\Omega, \mathcal{F}, \mathbb{P})$ with $\mathbb{E}_{\mathbb{P}}(|X|) < \infty$. Assume that the sub-$\sigma$ algebra $\widetilde{\mathcal{F}}$ is generated by the sets $A_1, A_2, \ldots A_n \in \mathcal{F}$, which are mutually disjoint and whose union is all of Ω. Furthermore we assume that all of the A_i's have strictly positive probability.*
Then

$$\mathbb{E}_{\mathbb{P}}(X|\widetilde{\mathcal{F}}) = \sum_{i=1}^{n} 1_{A_i} \frac{\mathbb{E}_{\mathbb{P}}(1_{A_i}X)}{\mathbb{P}(A_i)}.$$

We now turn to a case important for stochastic processes $\Omega = \mathbb{R}^n$, $\mathcal{F} = \mathcal{B}_{\mathbb{R}^n}$,

Let $\mathbb{P}$ be a probability on $\mathcal{B}_{\mathbb{R}^n}$.

We define the following sub-σ-algebras $\mathcal{F}_0, \mathcal{F}_1, \mathcal{F}_2, \ldots, \mathcal{F}_n$.

$\mathcal{F}_0 = \{\emptyset, \Omega\}$ [the "trivial σ-algebra"]

$\mathcal{F}_1 = $ all sets of the form $A \times \mathcal{B}_{\mathbb{R}^{n-1}}, A \in \mathcal{B}_R$

$\mathcal{F}_2 = $ all sets of the form $A \times \mathbb{R}^{n-2}$, with $A \in \mathcal{B}_{\mathbb{R}^2}$

in general:

$$\mathcal{F}_j = \text{all sets of the form } A \times \mathbb{R}^{n-j}, \text{ with } A \in \mathcal{B}_{\mathbb{R}^j}.$$

Proposition B.3.5 .   *Assume $F\colon \mathbb{R}^n \to \mathbb{R}$ is $\mathcal{F}_j$-measurable. Then F only depends on $(x_1, \ldots, x_j)$ (i.e. F is a function of $(x_1, \ldots, x_j)$).*

Proof.   For $j = 1$ (other cases similar). Assume F being $\mathcal{F}_1$-measurabel and define $g\colon \mathbb{R}^n \to \mathbb{R}$ by $g(x_1, \ldots, x_n) = g(x_1) = F(x_1, 0, \ldots, 0)$. We need that

$$\{(x_1, \ldots, x_n) \in \mathbb{R}^n \mid 0 \neq F(x_1, \ldots, x_n) - g(x_1)\} = \emptyset.$$

Since F and g are both $\mathcal{F}_1$-measurable also $F - g$ is $\mathcal{F}_1$-measurable, thus there is an $A \in \mathcal{B}_{\mathbb{R}}$ with

$$A \times \mathbb{R}^{n-1} = \{(x_1, \ldots, x_n) \in \mathbb{R}^n \mid 0 \neq F(x_1, \ldots, x_n) - g(x_1)\}.$$

Assume $A \neq \emptyset$ and pick $x_1 \in A$. For this x_1 it follows that $F(x_1, x_2, \ldots, x_n) \neq F(x_1, 0, \ldots, 0)$ for all $(x_2, \ldots, x_n) \in \mathbb{R}^{n-1}$ in particular for $x_2 = x_3 = x_4 = \cdots = x_n = 0$. Thus $F(x_1, 0, 0, \ldots, 0) \neq g(x_1)$, which is a contradiction. Now since $A = \emptyset$ also $A \times \mathbb{R}^{n-1} = \emptyset$. $\square$

Proposition B.3.6 .   *Assume $X\colon \mathbb{R}^n \to \mathbb{R}$ is a random variable and $\mathbb{P}$ is a probability with density $f\colon \mathbb{R}^n \to \mathbb{R}$.*
Then $\mathbb{E}_{\mathbb{P}}\big(X|\mathcal{F}_j\big)$ is a function in $x_1, \ldots, x_j$ (by Proposition B.3.5) and

$$\mathbb{E}_{\mathbb{P}}(X|\mathcal{F}_j)(x_1, \ldots, x_j)$$
$$= \frac{\int \cdots \int f(x_1, \ldots, x_j, z_{j+1}, \ldots, z_n) X(x_1, \ldots, x_j, z_{j+1}, \ldots, z_n) dz_{j+1} \ldots dz_n}{\int \cdots \int f(x_1, \ldots, x_j, z_{j+1}, \ldots, z_n) dz_{j+1} \ldots dz_n} \quad a.s.$$

[Note: the denominator could be equal to zero, but then the numerator must also vanish, in this case we define this fraction to be 0.]

Proof.   We will not prove that the function

$$\tilde{X}\colon (x_1,\ldots,x_j) \mapsto \frac{\int\cdots\int f(x_1,\ldots,x_j,z_{j+1},\ldots,z_n)X(x_1,\ldots,x_j,z_{j+1},\ldots,z_n)dz_{j+1}\ldots dz_n}{\int\cdots\int f(x_1,\ldots,x_j,z_{j+1},\ldots,z_n)dz_{j+1}\ldots z_n}$$

is almost surely well defined and $\mathcal{F}_j$-measurable. Let $A \times \mathbb{R}^{n-j} \in \mathcal{F}_j$, i.e. $A \in \mathcal{B}_{\mathbb{R}^j}$. We need to show that

$$\mathbb{E}_{\mathbb{P}}(1_{A\times\mathbb{R}^{n-j}}\tilde{X}) = \mathbb{E}(1_{A\times\mathbb{R}^{n-j}}X).$$

$$\mathbb{E}_{\mathbb{P}}(1_{A\times\mathbb{R}^{n-j}} \cdot X) = \int \cdots \int 1_A(x_1,\ldots,x_j)X(x_1,\ldots,x_n)f(x_1,\ldots,x_n)dx_1\ldots dx_n$$

[Note: $1_{A\times\mathbb{R}^{n-j}}(x_1,\ldots,x_n) = 1_A(x_1,\ldots,x_j)$]

$$= \underbrace{\int \cdots \int}_{j\text{-times}} 1_A(x_1,\ldots,x_j)$$

$$\cdot \left[\underbrace{\int \cdots \int}_{(n-j)\text{-times}} X(x_1,\ldots,x_n)f(x_1,\ldots,x_n)dx_{j+1}\ldots dx_n \right] dx_1 \ldots dx_j$$

$$= \int \cdots \int 1_A(x_1,\ldots,x_j)\frac{\left[\int\cdots\int X(x_1,\ldots,x_n)f(x_1,\ldots,x_n)dx_{j+1}\ldots dx_n\right]}{\int\cdots\int f(x_1,\ldots,x_n)dx_{j+1}\ldots dx_n}$$

$$\left[\int\cdots\int f(x_1,\ldots,x_n)dx_{j+1}\ldots dx_n\right]dx_1\ldots dx_j$$

$$= \int \cdots \int 1_A(x_1,\ldots,x_j)\tilde{X}(x_1,\ldots,x_j)$$

$$\left[\int\cdots\int f(x_1,\ldots,x_n)dx_{j+1}\ldots dx_n\right]dx_1\ldots dx_j$$

$$= \underbrace{\int \cdots \int}_{n\text{-times}} 1_A(x_1,\ldots,x_j)\tilde{X}(x_1,\ldots,x_j)f(x_1,x_2,\ldots,x_n)dx_1dx_2\ldots dx_n$$

change of order of integration

$$= \mathbb{E}_{\mathbb{P}}(1_{A\times\mathbb{R}^{n-j}}\tilde{X}(x_1,\ldots,x_j)).$$

Thus we showed

$$\mathbb{E}_{\mathbb{P}}\left(X|\mathcal{F}_j\right) = \tilde{X} \quad \text{a.s.} \qquad \square$$

The following result is a usefull inequality for conditional expectations.

Theorem B.3.7 *(Jensen's inequality).*

Let X be an integrable random variable on a probability space $(\Omega, \mathcal{F}, \mathbb{P})$ and let $\widetilde{\mathcal{F}} \subset \mathcal{F}$ be a sub σ-algebra. Secondly, let $\varphi \colon \mathbb{R} \to \mathbb{R}$ be a convex function for which $\varphi(X)$ is also $\mathbb{P}$-integrable. Then it follows that

$$(28) \qquad\qquad \mathbb{E}(\varphi(X)|\widetilde{\mathcal{F}}) \geq \varphi(\mathbb{E}(X|\widetilde{\mathcal{F}})).$$

Proof. Define for $x_0 \in \mathbb{R}$

$$D^{-}\varphi(x_0) = \lim_{h \searrow 0} \frac{\varphi(x_0) - \varphi(x_0 - h)}{h}$$

(if φ is differentiable in x_0 then $D^{-}\varphi(x_0)$ is simply the derivative). Now for $x_0 \in \mathbb{R}$ the straight line:

$$\frac{y - \varphi(x_0)}{x - x_0} = D^{-}\varphi(x_0), \quad \text{or}$$

$$y = x D^{-}\varphi(x_0) - x_0 D^{-}\varphi(x_0) + \varphi(x_0)$$

is a tangent to the graph of φ at $(x_0, \varphi(x_0))$. One of the equivalent conditions for convexity of φ is the condition that the graph of φ is above every tangent line.

Thus for any $x, x_0 \in \mathbb{R}$ it follows that $\varphi(x) \geq x D^{-}\varphi(x_0) - x_0 D^{-}\varphi(x_0) + \varphi(x_0)$.

Applying this inequality to the random variable X (replacing x) and the random variable $X_0 = \mathbb{E}(X|\widetilde{\mathcal{F}})$ (replacing x_0) it follows that

$$\varphi(X) \geq X D^{-}\varphi(X_0) - X_0 D^{-}\varphi(X_0) + \varphi(X_0).$$

Taking now $\mathbb{E}(\cdot|\widetilde{\mathcal{F}})$ on both sides we deduce

$$\mathbb{E}(\varphi(X) \mid \widetilde{\mathcal{F}}) \geq \mathbb{E}(X D^{-}\varphi(X_0) - X_0 D^{-}\varphi(X_0) + \varphi(X_0) \mid \widetilde{\mathcal{F}})$$

$$= \mathbb{E}(X|\widetilde{\mathcal{F}}) D^{-}\varphi(X_0) - X_0 D^{-}\varphi(X_0) + \varphi(X_0) = \varphi(\mathbb{E}(X|\widetilde{\mathcal{F}})).$$

□

B.4 Distances and Convergence of Random Variables

We already introduced one notion of convergence for a sequence of random variables. Recall that a sequence of random variables (X_n) on a probability space $(\Omega, \mathcal{F}, \mathbb{P})$ is converging to the random variable X almost surely if

$$\mathbb{P}(\{\omega \in \Omega : \lim_{n \to \infty} X_n(\omega) = X(\omega)\}) = 1.$$

In this section we will introduce two other notions of convergence. We call $L_0(\mathbb{P})$ the set of all measurable functions $\Omega \to \mathbb{R}$. We will identify two elements in $L_0(\mathbb{P})$ if they are almost surely equal. Note that $L_0(\mathbb{P})$ is a vectorspace.

Defintion. A sequence $(X_n) \subset L_0(\mathbb{P})$ is said to *converge in probability* to $X \in L_0(\mathbb{P})$ if

(29) $\qquad$ For all $\varepsilon > 0 \qquad \lim_{n \to \infty} \mathbb{P}(\{\omega \in \Omega : |X_n(\omega) - X(\omega)| > \varepsilon\}) = 0.$

The following two estimations relate $\mathbb{P}(|X| > a)$ to expected values.

Proposition B.4.1 . $\quad$ *Assume X is positive a random variables and $\phi : \mathbb{R}_0^+ \to \mathbb{R}_0^+$ a positive, increasing and measurable. For $a > 0$ it follows that*

$$a\mathbb{P}(\phi(X) \geq a) \leq \mathbb{E}_{\mathbb{P}}(\phi(X)).$$

Applying this inequality to $\phi(x) = x$ and to $\phi(x) = x^2$, and to the random variable $|X|$ implies that

1) *(Markov's inequality)* $\mathbb{P}(|X| \geq a) \leq \frac{1}{a}\mathbb{E}_{\mathbb{P}}(|X|).$

2) *(Tschebyscheff's inequality)* $\mathbb{P}(|X| \geq a) = \mathbb{P}(X^2 \geq a^2) \leq \frac{1}{a^2}\mathbb{E}_{\mathbb{P}}(|X|^2).$

Proof. $\quad$ Note that $a1_{\{\phi(X) \geq a\}} \leq \phi(X)$ and integrate both sides. $\qquad \square$

Proposition B.4.2 .   *For $X, Y \in L_0(\mathbb{P})$ define*

$$d_{L_0}(X, Y) = \mathbb{E}_{\mathbb{P}}\big(\min(1, |X - Y|)\big).$$

Then $d(\cdot, \cdot)$ is a metric on $L_0(\mathbb{P})$, which means that $d_{L_0}(\cdot, \cdot) \geq 0$ and

1) $d_{L_0}(X, Y) = 0 \iff X = Y$ almost surely, whenever $X, Y \in L_0(\mathbb{P})$

2) $d_{L_0}(X, Z) \leq d_{L_0}(X, Y) + d_{L_0}(Y, Z)$, whenever $X, Y, Z \in L_0(\mathbb{P})$.

Moreover $(X_n) \subset L_0(\mathbb{P})$ converges in probability to $X \in L_0(\mathbb{P})$ if and only if $\lim_{n \to \infty} d_L(X_n, X) = 0$.

Proof.   Note that for $X, Y \in L_0(\mathbb{P})$: $\mathbb{P}(X = Y) = 1 \iff \min(1, |X - Y|) = 0$ a.s. which implies (1). Secondly, it follows for numbers x, y and z that $\min(1, |x - z|) \leq \min(1, |x - y| + |y - z|) \leq \min(1, |x - y|) + \min(1, |y - z|)$ which implies claim (2).

Finally note that for $X, Y \in L_0(\mathbb{P})$ and $1 > \varepsilon > 0$ it follows from Proposition B.4.1 that

$$\mathbb{P}(|X - Y| > \varepsilon) = \mathbb{P}(\min(1, |X - Y|) > \varepsilon) \leq \frac{1}{\varepsilon} \mathbb{E}_{\mathbb{P}}(\min(1, |X - Y|)) \leq \frac{1}{\varepsilon} \mathbb{P}(|X - Y| > \varepsilon).$$

This implies that

$$\lim_{n \to \infty} \mathbb{P}(|X - X_n| > \varepsilon) = 0 \iff \lim_{n \to \infty} \mathbb{E}_{\mathbb{P}}(\min(1, |X - X_n|)) = 0,$$

which proves the last assertion.   □

To state the next result we will need the following notion: $(X_n) \subset L_0(\mathbb{P})$ is called a Cauchy sequence with respect to the convergence in probability if for all $\varepsilon > 0$ there is an $N \in \mathbb{N}$ so that $\mathbb{P}(|X_n - X_m| > \varepsilon) < \varepsilon$ whenever $n, m \geq N$. Equivalently this means that (X_n) is a Cauchy sequence with respect to $d_{L_0}(\cdot, \cdot)$: for all $\varepsilon > 0$ there is an $N \in \mathbb{N}$ so that $d_{L_0}(X_n, X_m) < \varepsilon$, whenever $n, m \geq N$.

It is clear that sequences which converge in probability are Cauchy. The following result states the inverse.

Proposition B.4.3 . *The space* $L_0(\mathbb{P})$ *is* complete *with respect to the concergence in probability. This means that every Cauchy sequence converges.*

Proof. Assume that (X_n) is Cauchy. It is enough to show that there is a subsequence (X_{n_k}) which converges to some $X \in L_0(\mathbb{P})$. Indeed, if (X_{n_k}) converges to X then for

$$d_{L_0}(X_n, X) \leq d_{L_0}(X_n, X_{n_k}) + d_{L_0}(X_{n_k}, X).$$

For given $\varepsilon > 0$ we can choose k_0, so that the second summand is smaller than ε for all $k \geq k_0$ and we can choose $N \in \mathbb{N}$, $N \geq n_{k_0}$ so that the first summand is smaller that ε for all $k \in \mathbb{N}$, with $n_k \geq N$, and all $n \geq N$.

By the assumption we can choose a subsequence (X_{n_k}) so that

$$\mathbb{P}(|X_{n_k} - X_m| > 2^{-k}) < 2^{-k}, \text{ for } m \geq n_k.$$

We observe that for any k_0

$$\mathbb{P}(\{\omega : X_{n_k}(\omega) \text{ does not converge}\}) = \mathbb{P}(\{\omega : \sum_{k=k_0}^{\infty} X_{n_{k+1}}(\omega) - X_{n_k}(\omega) \text{ does not converge}\})$$

$$\leq \mathbb{P}(\{\omega : \sum_{k=k_0}^{\infty} |X_{n_{k+1}}(\omega) - X_{n_k}(\omega)| = \infty\})$$

$$\leq \mathbb{P}(\bigcup_{k=k_0}^{\infty} \{|X_{n_{k+1}} - X_{n_k}| > 2^{-k}\})$$

$$\leq \sum_{k=k_0}^{\infty} 2^k = 2^{k_0+1}$$

Since k_0 can be chosen arbitrarily large we deduce that

$$\mathbb{P}(\{\omega : X_{n_k}(\omega) \text{ does not converge}\}) = 0$$

and define $X(\omega) = \lim_{k \to \infty} X_{n_k}(\omega)$ if $\omega \in \tilde{\Omega} = \{\omega : X_{n_k}(\omega) \text{ converges}\}$ and $X(\omega) = 0$ else. It follows that X_{n_k} converges almost surely to X and thus by the Majorized Convergence Theorem B.2.11 it follows that

$$d_{L_0}(X_{n_k}, X) = \mathbb{E}_{\mathbb{P}}(\min(1, |X_{n_k} - X|)) \to 0, \text{ for } k \to \infty,$$

which implies the claim by Proposition B.4.2.   □

To introduce the second notion of convergence we let $L_2(\mathbb{P})$ be the vector space of all square integrable random variables on (Ω, P), i.e. $X \in L_2(\mathbb{P}) \iff \mathbb{E}_{\mathbb{P}}(X^2) < \infty$.

Definition. For $X, Y \in L_2(\mathbb{P})$ define $< X, Y >= \mathbb{E}_{\mathbb{P}}(XY)$, the *scalarproduct of X and Y*.

Note: Since $|X| \cdot |Y| \leq \frac{1}{2}[X^2 + Y^2]$, it follows that XY is integrable as long as X and Y are square integrable.

$$\|X\|_{L_2} = < X, X >^{1/2} = \sqrt{\mathbb{E}_{\mathbb{P}}(X^2)}$$

is called the L_2-*norm of X*, and

If $(X_n)_{n=1}^{\infty} \subset L_2(\mathbb{P})$ is a sequence of random variables we say $X \in L_2(\mathbb{P})$ is the L_2-limit of (X_n) if

$$\lim_{n \to \infty} \|X_n, X\|_{L_2} = \lim_{n \to \infty} \sqrt{\mathbb{E}_{\mathbb{P}}((X_n - X)^2)} = 0$$

and we write

$$X = L_2 - \lim_{n \to \infty} X_n.$$

Theorem B.4.4 *(Cauchy-Schwartz inequalit). Assume X and Y are two random variables with finite L_2-norm. Then*

$$| < X, Y > | \leq \|X\|_{L_2} \|Y\|_{L_2}.$$

Proof. We first can assume that neither X nor Y are 0 almost surely, in that case both sides of the inequality vanish. Therefore $\|X\|_{L_2} > 0$ and $\|Y\|_{L_2} > 0$. Letting $\tilde{X} = X/\|X\|_{L_2}$ and $\tilde{Y} = Y/\|Y\|_{L_2}$ we deduce for $\omega \in \Omega$ from the binomial formula that $|\tilde{X}\tilde{Y}| \leq \frac{1}{2}(\tilde{X}^2 + \tilde{Y}^2)$ and integrating both sides we derive that

$$\mathbb{E}_{\mathbb{P}}(|\tilde{X}\tilde{Y}|) \leq \frac{1}{2}\mathbb{E}_{\mathbb{P}}(\tilde{X}^2 + \tilde{Y}^2) = 1.$$

Multiplying both sides by $\|X\|_{L_2}\|Y\|_{L_2}$ leads to the claim.   □

Theorem B.4.5 . $\|\cdot\|_{L_2}$ *is a* norm *on* $L_2(\mathbb{P})$, *meaning the following.*

1) *For* $X \in L_2(\mathbb{P})$: $\|X\|_{L_2} = 0 \iff X = 0$ *almost surely.*

2) *(Homogeneity) For* $X \in L_2(\mathbb{P})$ *and* $\alpha \in \mathbb{R}$: $\|\alpha X\|_{L_2} = \alpha \|X\|_{L_2}$.

3) *(Triangle inequality) For* $X, Y \in L_2(\mathbb{P})$: $\|X + Y\|_{L_2} \le \|X\|_{L_2} + \|Y\|_{L_2}$.

Proof. We will only show condition (3). Conditions (1) and (2) follow immediately.

For $X, Y \in L_2(\mathbb{P})$ apply the Cauchy-Schwartz inequality B.4.4 to $|X| \cdot |X + Y|$ and to $|Y| \cdot |X + Y|$ in order to deduce that

$$\mathbb{E}_{\mathbb{P}}(|X| \cdot |X + Y|) \le \|X\|_{L_2}\|X + Y\|_{L_2} \text{ and } \mathbb{E}_{\mathbb{P}}(|Y| \cdot |X + Y|) \le \|Y\|_{L_2}\|X + Y\|_{L_2}$$

Adding now both equation we deduce that

$$\|X + Y\|_{L_2}^2 = \mathbb{E}_{\mathbb{P}}((X + Y)^2) \le \mathbb{E}_{\mathbb{P}}((|X| + |Y|)|X + Y|) \le \left[\|X\|_{L_2} + \|Y\|_{L_2}\right]\|X + Y\|_{L_2}$$

which implies the assertion after cancellation. $\square$

The following implications on the different notions of convergence are true.

Proposition B.4.6 .

If $X_n \subset L_0$ *converges almost surely it converges in probability.*

If $X_n \subset L_0$ *converges in probability there is a subsequence which converges almost surely.*

If $X_n \subset L_2$ *converges in* L_2 *then it converges in probability.*

Proof. The first implication follows from the Majorized Convergence Theorem B.2.11 and Proposition B.4.2 as it was already observed in the last part of the proof of Proposition B.4.3. The second implication was also shown in the proof of B.4.2. The third implication follows from the Inequality of Tschebyscheff (see Proposition B.4.1). $\square$

Theorem B.4.7 .   *The space $L_2(\mathbb{P})$ is complete with respect to $\|\cdot\|_{L_2}$.*

Proof. Let (X_n) be a Cauchy sequence with respect to $\|\cdot\|_{L_2}$. Using the same arguments as in the proof of Proposition B.4.3 we only need to show that (X_n) has a convergent subsequence. By the Inequality of Tschebyscheff (Proposition B.4.1) the sequence is Cauchy with respect to the convergence in probability and thus convergent in probability to some $X \in L_0(\mathbb{P})$ by Proposition B.4.3. By Proposition B.4.6 we can first pass to a subsequence which almost surely converges to X and to a further subsequence (X_{n_k}) so that $\|X_{n_{k+1}} - X_{n_k}\|_{L_2} < 2^{-k}$ for all $k \in \mathbb{N}$. By the Monoton Convergence Theorem B.2.10

$$\mathbb{E}_{\mathbb{P}}(\sum_{k=1}^{\infty} |X_{n_{k+1}} - X_{n_k}|^2) = \lim_{K \to \infty} \mathbb{E}_{\mathbb{P}}(\sum_{k=1}^{K} |X_{n_{k+1}} - X_{n_k}|^2) < \infty.$$

Letting now $Y = |X_{n_1}| + \sum_{k=1}^{\infty} |X_{n_{k+1}} - X_{n_k}|$ it follows that $|X_{n_k}| \leq Y$ for all $k \in \mathbb{N}$. By the triangle inequality it also follows that

$$\|Y\|_{L_2} \leq \|X_{n_1}\|_{L_2} + \sum_{k=1}^{\infty} \|X_{n_{k+1}} - X_{n_k}\|_{L_2} < \infty.$$

Now it follows for $k \in \mathbb{N}$ from the Majorized Convergence Theorem B.2.11 that

$$\|X - X_{n_k}\|_{L_2} = \mathbb{E}_{\mathbb{P}}^{1/2}((X - X_{n_k})^2) = \lim_{m \to \infty} \mathbb{E}_{\mathbb{P}}^{1/2}((X_{n_m} - X_{n_k})^2) \leq 2^{-k+1},$$

which implies the claim $\qquad\qquad\square$

The following observation is an immediate consequence of Jensen's inequality (see Theorem B.3.7 in Appendix B.3).

Proposition B.4.8 .   *The conditional expectation with respect to a sub-σ-algebra $\tilde{\mathcal{F}}$ is a contraction on $L_2(\mathbb{P})$, i.e. for $X, Y \in L_2(\mathbb{P})$ it follows that*

$$\|\mathbb{E}_{\mathbb{P}}(X - Y | \tilde{\mathcal{F}})\|_{L_2} \leq \|X - Y\|_{L_2}.$$

In particular this implies that the conditional expectation is a continuous map on $L_2(\mathbb{P})$.

Bibliography

[AD]   Arrow, K. und Debreu, G. *Existence of an equilibrium for a competitive economy*

[ADEH] Artzner, P., Delbaen, F., Eber, J.-M. und Heath, D. *Coherent measures of Risk*, manuskript (1998)

[BP]   Back, K. und Pliska, S. *On the fundamental theorem of asset pricing with an infinite state space* J. Math. Econ. **20**, 1-18 (1991)

[BR]   Baxter, M. und Rennie, A. *Financial calculus - an introduction to derivative pricing* Cambridge: Cambridge University Press (1996)

[Be]   Beike, R. und K"ohler, A. *Risk-Management mit Zinsderiveten - Studienbuch mit Aufgaben*, Oldenbourg Verl., M"unchen-Wien (1997)

[Bi]   Biermann, B. *Die Mathematik der Zinsinstrumente*, Oldenbourg Verl., M"unchen-Wien (1999)

[BlS]   Black,F. und Scholes, M. *The pricing of options and corporate liabilities* J. Pol. Econ. **81**, 637-654 (1973)

[DMW] Dalang, R. C., Morton, A., and Willinger, W., *Equivalent martingale measures and no-arbitrage in stochastic securities market models.* Stochastics and stochastic Rep.,**29**(1989),189–202.

[D1]   Delbaen, F. (1992), *Representing martingale measures when asset prices are continuous and bounded.*, Math. Finance, **2**, 107–130.

[DS1] Delbaen, F. und Schachermayer, W. *Arbitrage and free lunch with bounded risk for unbounded continuous processes* (1993)

[DS2] Delbaen, F. und Schachermayer, W., *A general version of the fundamental theorem of asset pricing* Math. Ann. **300** 463-520 (1994)

[DS3] Delbaen, F. und Schachermayer, W., *The fundamental theorem of asset pricing for unbounded processes*, prepint.

[DS4] Delbaen, F. und Schachermayer, W., *The variance-optimal martingale measure for continuous processes*, Bernoulli, **2(1)**, 81–105.

[FL1] F"ollmer, H. und Leukert, P. *Quantile Hedging*

[FS]   F"ollmer,H. und Schweizer,M. *Hedging of contingent claims under incomplete information.* in: Davis, M.H.A., Elliott, R.J. (eds.) *applied stochastic analysis* (Stochastic Monogr., vol. 5, pp. 389-414) london, New York: Gordon and Breach

[HK]   Harrison, M. und Kreps, D. *Martingales and arbitrage in multiperiod security markets* J. Econ Theory **20** 381-408 (1979)

[HP]   Harrison, M. und Pliska, S. *Martingales and stochastic integrals in the theory of continuous trading* Stochastic Processes Appl. **11** 215-260 (1981)

[HKW] Howison, S.D., Kelly, F.P. und Wilmott, P. *Mathematical models in finance* Boca Raton: Chapman Hall (1995)

[Ir]   Irle, A. *Finanzmathematik. Die Bewertung von Derivaten* Teubner, Stuttgart (1998)

[K1]   Karatzas, I. *Lectures in mathematical finance* Providence, American Mathematical Society (1996)

[K2]   Karatzas, I. *Lectures in mathematics of finance* CRM Monograph Series Vol. 8, American Mathematical Society, Providence (1997)

[KS1] Karatzas,I. und Shreve, S.E. *Brownian motion and stochastic calculus* Berlin, Heidelberg, New York: Springer(1988)

[KS2] Karatzas, I. und Shreve, S.E. *Methods of mathematical finance* Berlin, Heidelberg, New York: Springer(1998)

[Kr] Kreps,D. *Arbitrage and equilibrium in economies with infinitely many commodities*, J. Math. Econ. **8**, 15-35 (1981)

[KK] Korn, R. und Korn, E. *Moderne Methoden der Finanzmathematik* Vieweg (1999)

[LL1] Lamberton, D. und Lapeyre, B. *Introduction to stachastic calculus applied to finance* Boca Raton: Chapman Hall (1996)

[Ma] Mandelbrot, B.B. *Fractals and Scaling in Finance* Springer, New York-Berlin (1997)

[Me] Merton, R. *Theory of rational option pricing* Bell Journal of Economics and Management Science **4** 141-183 (1973)

[MR] Musiela, M. und Rutkowski, M. *Martingale methods in mathematical finance* Springer, Berlin Heidelberg New York (1997)

[P1] Pliska, S.R. *Introduction to mathematical finance: Discrete Time Models* Blackwell, Oxford (1997).

[Ø] Øksendal, B. *Stochastic Differential equation - an introduction with applications* Graduate Texts in Mathematics, Springer, Berlin Heidelberg (1992).

[RT] Rogers, L.C.G. und Talay, D. (eds.) *Numerical Methods in Finance* Cambridge: Cambridge University Press (1997)

[Sch] Schweizer, M.,*Mean variance hedging for general claims*, Annals of Applied Probabilities, **2**,(19??) 171–179.

[Sp]   Spremann, K. *Wirtschaft, Investment und Finanzierung*, Oldenbourg Verl., M"unchen (1996).

[WHD] Wilmott, P., Howison, S. und Dewynne, J. *The mathematics of financial derivatives* Cambridge: Cambridge University Press (1995).